Chicago Rage

Ronald J Schulz

Tumbleweed Books
Tumble through the pages of our books

CHICAGO RAGE
RONALD J SCHULZ

Tumbleweed Books
Tumble through the pages of our books

Tumbleweed Books
HTTP://TUMBLEWEEDBOOKS.CA
An imprint of DAOwen Publications
Copyright © 2022 by Ronald J Schulz
All rights reserved

Chicago Rage / Ronald J Schulz

ISBN 978-1-928094-83-8
EISBN 978-1-928094-84-5

This is a memoir. Names, characters, places, and incidents are the product of the author's memory and recorded to the best of his ability to be actual persons, living or dead, businesses, companies, events, or locales recreated to the best of his ability.

Cover art by MMT Productions
Edited by Douglas Owen

10 9 8 7 6 5 4 3 2 1

With deep gratitude to my wild companions and racy loves: Rea Fichter, Lee Swanson, John Bell, Ruby, Bonnie, and most especially Karen Mucci. You made my life into a meaningful adventure and I hope we'll meet again on the far side.

And we walked off to look for America

—Simon & Garfunkel–America

Unleashed

The youthful crowd around us formed into ranks and began chanting slogans. Karen and I joined in, our voices piercing the night.

Ho, Ho, Ho Chi Minh! NLF is gonna win! Ho, Ho, Ho Chi Minh! Dare to struggle, dare to win!

It was Chicago, October 8, 1969, the first day of the *Weatherman Rage*, billed as the Second Battle of Chicago. The first Battle of Chicago had been at the 1968 Democratic Convention. I'd missed that hallowed event and wanted to make up for it.

A sudden command and we surged forward. Our slogans became war whoops as we burst out of Lincoln Park. We charged into the financial district, catching the police off guard. Our comrades, armed with sticks or bricks, found targets and went to work.

Ka-ka-ka-crashhhhh, the din of smashing windows blended with our screams like a million Fourth of July's rolled into one. The cacophony of sound echoed off the towering buildings that stood like canyon walls along our route. The vibrant chaos filled me with a wild ecstasy. Karen stared openmouthed at the exploding scene, squeezing my hand tight. Whether in terror or amazement, I couldn't tell. We'd come a long way together for this chance to fight back against the Establishment.

After dropping out of high school when I turned seventeen that spring, I'd hit the road to join the counterculture springing up all over America. I'd long known there was no place for me in conservative American society. The hippie culture was full of people who thought like me, and I lost the lonely isolation of my conservative neighborhood. The worthy cause of social revolution grabbed my heart and soul. I belonged, at long last, to something worth fighting for.

Six-foot-tall and lanky, my shoulder length hair bleached yellow by the sun, it embarrassed me that I was still almost beardless. Friends said I had piercing blue eyes, but it put off some chicks who thought I was too intense. Yeah, I suppose I was, but after leaving home, my pimples had vanished as my anxieties melted away. The boundless love and the freedom I found on the open road soothed my tormented soul.

Black-haired, brown-eyed Karen, who ran at my side, was a beauty several inches shorter than me. Her true age and last name were our guarded secret. She was a fifteen-year-old runaway. Her passport, hidden deep in her backpack, gave her birthplace as Korea, of all places, whereas I hailed from the nearby suburbs of Chicago.

We'd arrived in Chicago only that morning after a grueling odyssey across the country with drivers who were generous, drunken, or horny, a true spectrum of humanity. Although trying to be helpful, they'd taken us far off track along backcountry roads. Yet we'd made it to "Pig City" Chicago, as did hundreds of other idealists like us, to bring the Southeast Asia war home to roost in Middle America.

With youthful passion, we hurled ourselves at real and imagined symbols of the capitalist war machine in downtown Chicago. But some of our overeager comrades began smashing the windows of rundown Volkswagens parked on the street.

Karen shouted, "Those are people's cars, you idiots! Go after the Cadillacs, for Christ's sake."

Giddy as mischievous kids, they paid her no mind. Bank windows representing our corporate foes were proper targets. The collateral damage to the possessions of ordinary people seemed inappropriate, but almost inevitable to me. It was war.

Karen yanked my arm. "Look out behind you, Ron!"

I turned just in time to miss a police club that fanned my head by an inch.

Whack-whack-whack! Uniformed cops, wearing baby blue riot helmets, leaned out each of an unmarked police car's four windows, clubbing everyone within reach. With sickening thuds, they split slower, moving heads all around me as the car zigzagged through our charging crowd from behind. A few slowpokes bounced off the hood. The better prepared rioters wore padded clothing and football helmets or hats stuffed with rags to cushion the blows. Karen and I had no such protection.

Screeching to a halt at the next intersection, four leather jacketed troopers spilled out of the car to block our advance up the street. Spacing themselves ten feet apart, they half crouched, steadying their revolvers with both hands in a firing stance. The vehicle careened away to fetch reinforcements, the doors flapping shut as it sped back through our scattering ranks.

At the sight of the guns, comrades in front of us wheeled to either side, trotting back in retreat. Karen and I found ourselves among the few who remained to face the enemy. For armor, we had only our exalted spirit to confront their steady aim.

Our *sisters*, as we in the movement called our female comrades, who were more often our lovers, demanded the right to join us as equals. It was their battle as much as ours. Like the Amazons and Viking Shield Maidens of yore, they would not be denied their combat laurels. We men were supposed to *struggle* against our sexism, our male chauvinism, our instinct to protect the heretofore *weaker* sex, even if it ran against our ingrained sense of honor and duty.

Nonetheless, I feared for Karen. We'd grown tight over the past week's adventures. She embodied all that I craved in a woman, a woman I wanted to share my future with. Politically correct or not, I needed to protect her. Releasing her hand, I yelled, *Run back with the others*. Wide-eyed with unfeigned fear, she obliged without a mummer. But full of arrogant bravado, I held my ground, not wanting to give these pigs the satisfaction of seeing me run. It was a sobering yet exhilarating experience to stare down the business end of a gun for the first time in my short life. A sane person knew to run or *hit the deck*. But fired up on adrenaline, I wasn't sane or sober. The past few days functioning on raw nerves with little food or sleep left me feeling crazy drunk.

My eyes locked with that mercenary thug fifteen feet before me. The moment froze into eternity while my mind raced a million miles a minute. The pig's face, grimacing through the clear visor on his helmet, looked as scared as I should have been. He blinked, tense, his blood rushing through his brain and heart like mine. Pigs were only human, after all. I didn't hate him. He was only a cog in the machine, following the orders of his capitalist masters, whereas we rebels against the Establishment had a higher calling.

Ours was a continued struggle, picking up the red banner of oppressed people from previous generations, including the dispossessed Native Americans. The land grab continued into our era, to the Third World populations living under American bombs. For all our sakes, we assumed the struggle against our county's neocolonial tyranny.

Wild thoughts raced through my mind. All I had to counter the firepower of this armed enemy were the cosmic forces I insisted on believing in. Raising my eyes to the heavens, I tried to conjure the spirit power of the Lakota Indian Ghost Dancers, invoking their aid to right the wrongs of centuries. Would their power shield me from bullets? It hadn't worked in the last century when blue coated soldier's firepower cut through warriors wearing Ghost shirts at Wounded Knee. If my spirit power failed, I'd only be one more casualty, a mere statistic, dying to bring the Revolution home to America.

POP-POP-POP-POP! A ragged volley of shots blasted forth, echoing off the brick buildings to either side of us. Then another volley rang out. I was still standing. The magic worked. But of course, they'd fired above our heads. Okay, I'd made my point and needn't stick around.

With as much dignity as I could muster, I backed off, then turned to jog in retreat, hoping to find Karen safe with our impromptu affinity group, people we'd met only an hour before. The life or death seriousness of the situation jolted me back to reality. If the pigs killed me, some other guy would grab my Karen. She was gorgeous, smart, and sexy far beyond her mid-teen years, and I'd be a fool to lose her.

October 8, 1969, came to an end, but it was only the first of four days of demonstrations and street battles. The Weatherman faction of SDS called them the *Days of Rage* to *Bring the War Home* to America. Fuck non-violence, they said, and I agreed. We wanted justice.

Years of peaceful protests by the Civil Rights and Anti-war Movements had gotten few gains. The Vietnamese body count rose higher each day as the war dragged on with no good end in sight. Middle-class people couldn't empathize with faraway people they considered primitive and, therefore, less worthy. Weathermen wanted stronger methods. Let them feel an ounce of the pain our military was inflicting on other countries in their name. We felt duty bound to attack the war machine and encourage our brothers and sisters of conscience to join us. On the ashes of this imperialist nation, we'd build a society of bold, boundless love.

That's why I'd come back to *sweet home Chicago*. That I'd found Karen, who jumped at the chance to join me, amazed me even more. It felt like Providence, whatever that was, had blessed our rebel endeavor. We would change the world together.

Everything in my life had been pulling me to this showdown with the culture that raised me, a culture I'd come to reject as selfish and materialistic.

Earlier that day, an older, gray haired woman, a pacifist church volunteer, had pulled me aside, her face etched with maternal concern.

"You're so young," she clucked. "What inspires a nice suburban kid like you to become a wild-eyed revolutionary?"

Nice suburban kid? I'd felt that label since I was fifteen. My flip answer: *We have to fight for what's right*, didn't satisfy her. It would take me time to produce a thoughtful response.

Real people aren't cartoon characters or fit neat stereotypes. Many ingredients bubble up into the brew of who our whole generation of seekers had evolved into. To understand ourselves, we write histories, not only of spectacular events like the winning of battles, or the passage of laws that may or may not affect our lives, but the small, overlooked details. step back to June 1969 for the background of that impassioned time.

Part One
The Re-launch

Wood Dale Wasteland

"Hey, Ron!" Jennie waved me over. "Where ya been, man?"

Under the hot June sun, I'd been walking along busy Irving Park, the main arterial connection to Chicago. It was twenty miles east of Wood Dale, my once again hometown. Skinny Jake and Fat Jennie, my old greaser pals, stood outside Charlotte's juke joint, joshing with a guy I didn't recognize.

Jennie put her ample arms around me, then Jake thumped my back and said, "Let's grab a bite and catch up." It had been at least six months since I'd seen them, and their enthusiastic welcome soothed my troubled mind. I'd only gotten back to Wood Dale the night before. The other guy said nothing but stared at me. I wondered if I should recognize him.

As I followed them inside, it hit me - Chuck Lawford! With his wild blond mane shorn to stubble, he no longer looked ferocious, yet a wave of panic shot through me. Maybe I ought to scram while I could. Instead, I sucked in a lungful of air and put on a bold front. I'd never live it down if I ran; a guy's rep was everything.

Jake and Jennie took one side of a booth. Unsure if this public place constituted neutral ground, I slid in beside Chuck, playing dumb as if I still hadn't recognized him. The others chattered away while I watched Chuck out of the corner of my eye, my fists balled tight, ready if he launched a sudden attack. The others ordered burgers and shakes and rambled on about nothing. Chuck and I ordered coffee, but no food. The few coins in my pocket told me it was all I could afford. Neither of us said a word to each other.

Heavy moments ticked by as Chuck and I stirred our cups in silence. Then Chuck half turned to face me. His narrowed, hostile eyes bore into me. His voice, though quiet, was menacing. But I'd steeled myself for it.

"Remember that night at the Down Under?"

I returned his gaze without flinching. "Yeah, Chuck, I remember. I remember the whole fucking thing."

His eyes darted back to his coffee. My steady response spooked him.

Fuck yeah, I remembered. He'd been roaring drunk that night. I pulled his shrieking girlfriend, Nicky, out of the car and got between them so she could run off to safety with Heidi. It's not like she was his only girl. Christ, they all went ape over Chuck. But that night she'd had enough of him, and I did what I had to. A simple matter of chivalry, even if it meant turning on a pal, but Chuck took it as an unforgivable betrayal of our tight male bond.

After Nicky got away, Chuck charged at me, screaming vengeance. His berserker rage was legendary. I'd ducked his drunken punches that missed my face by an inch. Frustrated, he'd gone for a stationary target.

Wham-wham-wham. With three swift punches, he'd flattened an oversize metal mailbox. Jesus! I'd seen what he was capable of. That battered box could have been my face. Although he hadn't let on, and I didn't guess it, he'd broken five bones in his hand.

"You're a dead man, Ron!" He staggered around, still swinging his arms. "I swear to god I'll kill you for this." We'd gone from bosom buddies to enemies in a heartbeat.

4

Wearing a heavy cast, Chuck had patrolled the neighborhood for a week afterward, telling everyone that he'd kill me with it. I had no reason to doubt him, but somehow, he never ran into me or came to find me at my house. A couple of months later, I heard the Army drafted him. Soon after that, I left too, expecting never to return from the western communes. But there I was, back in town, flat broke and seeking a job.

Chuck and I had been tight once. Why should we remain enemies? I wanted to relax my guard, to ask him about the Army, but I didn't know how to bridge the divide. Maybe he didn't either.

Jennie giggled, oblivious to the tension across the table. "So, where ya been, Ron? We ain't seen ya in a hell of a long time."

"Yeah, I dropped out of school in April, split out west to Taos and Drop City. I joined a fantastic group marriage, groovy chicks, great guys, until the old man who called the shots ran me off."

Jake made a disgusted face. "I bet it's nothing but desert out there. Right, Ron? How'd you live?"

"We farmed, had to irrigate the land, a lot of hard work, but I was in love with two women."

Jennie shot me a curious look and snorted. "Love? If it was so great, why'd ya come back here?"

"I would have stuck around except for old Joe Sage. They called him the Mad Monk of Taos. He ruined it by screaming at us all the time until I had to talk back and try to settle him down. Our hippie commune had great potential. No, it wasn't all peace and love, but I dug it and will keep trying."

I didn't want to delve into the whole story. Fuck no; I was still processing how much of a pussy I'd been to let that son of a bitch, who owned our land and called himself a guru, run me off after my fumbled attempts to reason with him got me driven out. None of the others stood up for me; he'd even cowed beautiful Tike, the tanned, blond Earth Goddess who'd smothered me in hot kisses. Under Joe's glare, she sat staring at the floor, numb and defeated, while Joe lambasted me, calling me a snot-nosed punk, driving me to frustrated tears because my seventeen-year-old brain couldn't come up with a meaningful response to his accusations.

They needed me there. I was the hardest worker who never complained, but how could I stay after he'd shamed me like that? I'd stood, waiting for any of them to speak up for me, waiting for an apology from Joe. A simple, *I'm sorry*, would do it. It never came, and he slammed the door behind me. The scene still played out in my dreams, but I had to let it go. I'd find new friends who wanted to build a better society in this budding Age of Aquarius. Maybe we'd build our utopia right there in the Midwest.

Jennie bounced up and down in the booth with excitement. "So, what are you gonna do now, huh, Ron? Maybe stick around here for good?"

"Not for good, just long enough to earn some bread. I'm flat broke now."

Bread was the oh-so-necessary means of survival. Enough of it created power over others. That's why tyrants like the Mad Monk ruled us. Money talked, even in Taos. Already I missed the place that had begun to feel like home to me.

"The southwest is a groovy place to live, but..." I glanced at the ceiling, trying to come up with a reason for leaving that made sense, even to me. "It's like economically depressed there. Get it? Agricultural jobs don't pay more than beans."

Jennie and Jake bobbed their heads in agreement. They thought we lived in the best place in the world. Chuck stared into his coffee cup, morose. He had bigger things on his mind than me. I wasn't afraid of him anymore.

I shook my head. "Jobs should pay better here, but I'll be heading out again, looking for another commune or something as soon as I got some dough."

"Wow," Jake said, shaking his head back and forth. "Seems like everyone's leaving the neighborhood. Chuck is back here on leave for a few days before going to Vietnam." He grinned at Chuck, still deep in thought. "Tell him, Chuck, like you told me."

Jake chuckled, rubbed his hands together, and smacked his lips. "He's looking forward to killing some gooks! Maybe he'll mail me some ears, too. You heard about that, right? Cutting off VC ears for trophies, like WOW man, I can't wait to see them."

"Jake," I couldn't let his shit slide and jumped into a lecture. "The VC, Viet Cong, are fighting to free their homeland from foreign control. That means us, man. Their guerilla force had been our allies in World War Two, but we'd betrayed them, giving their country back to the French when the Japanese surrendered.

"When they finally kicked the French out, we'd taken over, keeping Diem's rapacious puppet state in power in the southern half of the country. Our land of liberty and democracy is betraying the ideals of our own revolution. Get it? Instead of being a beacon of democracy, we're fighting to prevent another country's independence."

Jennie clucked and shook her head. "Hopefully, that war will be over soon."

"Maybe, but I hope not," said Jake, his eyes almost popping out of his head with excitement. "In another year, I'm gonna sign up too."

"Oh, come on," Jennie said. "More and more of our classmates are getting sent over. Too many, like John Heaps, killed already. When will it be enough?"

I hated the word *gook* and was sick of only hearing about the danger to *our* precious boys. Asian lives didn't matter; I had to spell it out for them.

"What about the Vietnamese? If the body counts are even close, we're massacring the shit out of them, just like John Wayne did to the Indians in the movies. It's inhuman the way we treat those people, burning their *hooches*, shooting everyone the chopper gunners see in our free-fire zones, driving them into hamlets that are more like concentration camps, which is exactly what the Indian Reservations had been. We're fighting a war of conquest."

Jake scrunched his face. "Well, they're the fucking enemy. Aren't they? Atheist Communists who want to take over the world themselves. Goddamn it, the sooner we bomb that country back into the Stone Age, make it a fucking parking lot, the sooner our boys can come home winners."

Jake echoed the Hawkish line, pissing me off, but I struggled to remain tactful to convince him of the facts.

"Those people are fighting for their own country, Jake, like *we* did against the British. What are we really fighting for, anyway? Supporting the corrupt Saigon government that we helped the French put there."

"Jesus Christ, Ron." Jake made a theatrical grimace. "You sound like a goddamn Commie yourself. Ever hear of the domino theory? They're gobbling up the whole fucking world, bringing countries behind the Bamboo Curtain, like the goddamn Ruskies did with their Iron Curtain in Europe."

His face relaxed, and he winked at me. "Anyway, man, I wanna try out some of those Asian broads. Right, Chuck?"

"Jake!" Jennie frowned and smacked him on the shoulder. "What about Lilly? You have a girlfriend."

"What about her? I ain't ready for marriage just yet. A guy needs to sow his oats. Huh, Chuck?"

Chuck finally cracked a smile, and Jake went on. "It's not like I'd marry one of those slant eyes and bring her home to Ma. Jesus, this war might be my best chance for an adventure, to see the fucking world and get all the pussy I can before I come back a hero."

Jake grinned widely at all of us. "Just like my dad did in double-u-double-u-two. Now that was a real war. He brought home a luger and an Iron Cross from a dead Kraut. He told me plenty of wild stories, too." He emitted a high-pitched giggle. "But we're in mixed company now, so I can't tell 'em."

He winked again and gave Jennie a playful smack on her shoulder. "It's our generation's turn now. I just want my share of the glory—and pussy too—before it's all over."

Jake's thinking wasn't foreign to me; we had the same male biology running our engine. Sex has been interconnected with war since long before the first pages of the Iliad gloried in the kidnap and rape of foreign women. The Old Testament echoes that theme. Conquest and rape fill the branches of our human family tree. We are all descended from ancient, forced unions. I'd read enough to know the details.

Neither Jake nor Chuck questioned the morality of the current war, the way our nation treated people of different cultures, or the flawed strategy that destroyed a village to save it. Hardly anyone in the neighborhood questioned why we were fighting there. None of them knew much about history, geography, or read honest to god books as much as I did. Chuck, Jake, and I were on different trajectories. They didn't give a shit about the crucial issues of our times until it smacked them in the face. But I couldn't let this bullshit distract me from my mission.

Leaving the restaurant, I continued east along Irving Park, pondering how I was going to make some fast cash.

"Ron, over here!" I turned to see Bob Albertson's head sticking out of a car window. He pulled onto the shoulder across the road. As soon as I saw a break in the traffic, I ran across the busy two-lane highway and hopped into the passenger side.

"Ain't she a beauty? This is my car, bought with my own money. Not too old or banged up, like my last beater."

Bob had graduated that spring. After pumping me for details of my recent adventure, he told me he'd been working at Beeline Fashions.

"It's a huge clothing warehouse on the other side of Bensenville, Ron. They stock and ship all around the country."

"Think they'll hire me?"

"Well, your hair isn't *too* long yet." He chuckled. Local employers almost never hired longhairs. "I tell you what, I just got off work, but I'll take you back there if you want to apply."

"Great, Bob, appreciate it. Running into you was a stroke of luck. Remember the Green Tree Inn? It was you who broke me in on my first job, washing dishes and busing tables in my freshman year.

Remember how you spiked my iced tea with Tabasco sauce on my first break?"

"Ha-ha, right! Those were the good old days, huh, Ron? Good to have you back where you belong. Wood Dale ain't so bad. Not to me, anyway. I got a car and plenty of cash to go cruising. Sure, we gotta slave away eight hours of our day, but shit, we get money we can spend on chicks."

Bob was an all right guy and had a point. Wood Dale was no longer the semi-rural village of forest and field that my family had moved to in 1955 when I was three years old. My forest haunts were bulldozed and burned in great bonfires to be replaced with the sidewalks and trim lawns of housing developments and schools that sported Native American names, like Hiawatha and Black Hawk, which struck me as an awful irony. My changing hometown felt less and less welcoming to me.

It was a mix of Protestant and Catholic, Italian, and Eastern European, especially Polish and German white working-class families. The only Chinese family had moved out before I entered Junior high. Soon after, a bona fide black girl appeared in my class who insisted that she was white against all physical evidence. True, her parents were white. She had to have been adopted, but I gave up trying to convince her to support SNCC, the Student Non-Violent Coordinating Committee and the Black Power movements. She told me that as a *white* girl, she couldn't identify with them. Shit. A pretty and popular girl like her, buzzed around by the jocks, could talk crazy and get away with it. If I kept my mouth shut and didn't let myself get so irritated by the racist, pro-war attitudes of people around there, maybe I too could fit in for a few months. But I just had to speak up. I'd been silent too long.

At the Beeline office, I filled out the application form and answered standardized questions. Using Bob as my reference, they hired me on the spot to start the next day.

Things were moving fast. Only the night before, I'd gotten back in town and set up a deal with my folks. They'd let me live in my old room. Not as a kid, a dependent freeloader. Fuck no, I'd pay rent, asking only that they treat me as an adult. They seemed relieved and vindicated that I, their only son, the prodigal, had returned. Even if I wasn't going back to high school, I'd be employed. But I had to be straight with myself. How long could I stay in that town before I blew a gasket?

Nine to Five at Beeline Fashion

Like any proletariat slob, I rose early and breakfasted with Dad before my later rising mother and five sisters got up. Then I walked to the end of the driveway on Addison Road to meet Bob Albertson. He'd have already picked up his former classmate, Bob Klein, who lived only a couple of houses down from me. Klein and I gave him a couple of bucks for gas. We psyched ourselves up for the day's work as the radio blared the latest hits.

Good morning star-shine, the earth says hello ...

Oh, Sweet Pea, come on and dance with me, come on, come on, come on and dance with mee-eee...

Hot town, summer in the city, back of my neck getting dirty gritty...

The syrupy-sweet feel good tunes grew on me, becoming souvenir memories of that magic summer. At the end of each week, I'd have a paycheck of not quite a hundred bucks, a decent amount for an inexperienced new hire. My folks didn't gouge me for rent and food, so I saved most of it by frugal living.

Bob Albertson trained me. My work consisted of pulling a hand-pumped hydraulic stock cart, which I piled high with incoming and outgoing shipments. Reading a list of serial numbers which corresponded to aisles and sections of the huge warehouse, I pulled out the long boxes, stocking never-ending shelves that reached the ceiling twelve feet up or fed a busy loading dock. Our redheaded crew cut boss, always frantic, urged me on.

"Move faster, Schulz! You're still on probation. You'd better damn well hurry if you want to keep this job."

Always dressed in a short-sleeve white shirt and tie, as befitted his managerial position, Mr. Crew Cut seemed a stunted one-dimensional man. His face, framed by black horn-rimmed glasses, always had a peculiar expression, like he needed to take a shit and was just looking for a place to do it.

Older guys like Albertson drove the larger forklifts that brought down orders from higher up. "Be patient," Bob told me. "I'll let you train on my machine when we have a moment. You'll get promoted to drive one in a few months."

My life developed a certain manic rhythm as I threw myself into long sweating hours of working at full speed. I shut down my mind, took a vacation from the larger cares of the world and showed off for the bevy of girls who worked the easier sorting and packing jobs. Most of them were Fenton graduates. As I'd dropped out two years before graduation, I was younger than all of them. They had that attractive older woman allure but steady boyfriends too, and I didn't want to waste my time by tying myself to a woman who didn't share my high aspirations. Maybe I'd sold them short, but none of them seemed interested in widening their horizons. I resigned myself to being without a love life until I made my pile of dough and could escape back to the free, hippie world I belonged in.

After work on the hot afternoons, Bob Klein brought over his long black-haired sister, Sandy. Despite her being as rail thin as her brother with no tits to speak of, I developed a crush on Sandy. Her long black hair and languorous all-knowing gaze captivated me. Unfortunately, she, like every local girl I knew, wanted a much older guy.

Sandy even flirted with my father. He didn't try to dissuade her. They had long chats away from the rest of us. Although it unsettled me at first, Dad's relationship with Mom was far from satisfactory. The old man needed more than endless chores to fill his life. Good for him, I decided. Whether or not Sandy and he managed any illicit rendezvous, he became mellower, yelled at me less, and appeared more cheerful than usual. That was good for everyone, even Mom.

We'd cool off in our family's swimming pool. The pool was a plastic Doughboy model, eighteen feet in diameter, four feet deep. Nothing as grand as the big cement pool our wealthy neighbor across the backyard had. Dad and I had to break ours down every fall and put it back up in the spring. It was such a lot of work. I wondered how he'd manage when I was gone.

Joey Peters, like Bob and Sandy, a couple of years older than me, caroused in the pool with us. He brought his future bride, the blond bombshell, Diane. She was my age, and she'd been my almost girlfriend back in grade school, the first girl to rob me of my power of speech. All she'd had to do then was look at me with those big blue eyes and ask a simple question to tie my tongue. It took a long moment to force my speech mechanism to blurt out words. And they weren't always the ones I intended.

The first time that occurred, we were in the fifth grade. I'd come in her back door after a snowfall to play with her brother. She was on the phone with my sister.

"Just a minute," she said into the receiver and turned to me. "Ron, Dar wants to know if there's much snow outside."

I tried to say 'there's pretty much snow outside,' but only one word popped out, *pretty*.

"What?" Diane looked puzzled. I tried again. "Pretty." That one word was all I could produce. Nonplused, Diane got back on the phone.

"He said *pretty much*." She'd filled in the missing word for me, and I went to hang out with her brother like I was supposed to.

Along with her brothers and my year younger sister, many

childhood shenanigans followed. We were precocious kids, who figured things out for ourselves, the girls more willing than us boys were at that age, exploring what we knew to be dangerous territory as our bodies progressed into puberty. But we didn't go all the way across forbidden boundaries that beguiled and terrified us.

That golden age was long ago. We weren't kids anymore, and Diane had hooked up with Joey, a mellow, reliable kind of guy. He had good vibes, and I liked him. We staged chicken fights in the pool. The girls rode on our shoulders, trying to knock over and dunk the opposing team. It was a rush just to have a girl ride me in that contact sport, which allowed us guys to cop a feel once in a while. All in good, clean fun, of course.

A more enduring connection would have to wait until I got back out in the real world. I assured myself that I'd meet gutsy, adventurous women out there. Gals who were on my wavelength, like Tike and Joanne, back in Taos. None of these status conscious shopaholics around Wood Dale could compare with them.

As other employees took off for summer vacations, Crew Cut piled ever larger workloads on me. He expected me to pick up the slack. I ran my ass off to please him, convinced he'd fire me if I didn't.

A middle-aged guy with a laid-back attitude and a protruding paunch ran into the giant green box crushing machine. It sat in the far corner by the loading dock. He watched me sweating like a racehorse as I ran by and called me over.

"Look, kid, you're doing the work of three men. The harder you work, the more they put on you. They can hire fewer guys doing more for less! Get it?"

I got it, but standing up to Crew Cut was easier said than done. He rode my ass, berating me for not getting his tall orders done faster. The crusher man prepared to take off on his own vacation, and Crew Cut allowed him to train me to take his place. I'd run over to set up and crush a load of boxes between pulling orders. It was fun, a matter of lining the long rectangular boxes in a row of six on the elevator, lowering it and placing six more on them, repeating until the elevator hit bottom.

Then came the fun part, closing the steel door and running it up. It crushed the rows into nice compact layers that eventually made up a bale. We'd run plastic straps around and tie it up before we opened the heavy latches and had one of the forklift guys, usually Albertson, pick up the tightly packed bale and run it out onto the loading dock for pick up. Crew Cut expected me to keep pulling orders on the double in between crushing boxes. Even so, I snuck in moments when I could take a breather and recreate. I did so with art.

Painted in drab, prison like institutional green, I decided to color up the box crusher and give it my own distinctive touch, make it a shrine to my spiritual beliefs. Using markers of assorted colors in an attempt at an artistic script, I wrote on the side facing the wall.

Welcome to ancient Tibet. Give up hope all ye who enter here.

The latter was the motto over the gates of Hades, which I thought appropriate in my situation. Then I drew the relevant symbols of our Age of Aquarius, mixing the old with the new. The Tao circle, the Buddhist eight-spoked wheel, the hippie Peace symbol, which the paranoid Right-Wing John Birch society called the *broken cross*. Then I drew a hand forming the other Peace sign, two fingers upraised in a V.

Maintaining a meditative attitude was a challenge with Crew Cut on my back, but I tried to rise above my surroundings. Orthodox religion seemed stale and lifeless; however, Tantric Buddhism recognized the psychic power of combining sex with spiritual practices. That made practical sense to me, and I read all I could find on it. My interest in both sex and spirituality was the path to spiritual wholeness. Not, as my Christian pastors declared, a sign of depravity.

Sex was not dirty but transformative, an important expression of spirituality. Denying our sexuality made us unhealthy in so many ways. I faulted our Puritanical cultural norms by creating an off kilter anti-sexual bias that turned untold numbers of priests and holy men into hypocrites, living double lives by hiding their vital, life affirming sexuality while professing celibacy or monogamy. Our culture refused to acknowledge the ancient wisdom that found them compatible parts of an integrated whole. Yes, I was still confused, trying to understand, and come to terms with the intricate process, but I strove to work them together into the fabric of my life, whatever people said.

Proud of my artwork, I showed it to my co-workers as they came through on business and quick stolen moments. Their praise and wonderment helped me feel more at home in the rat race. Workaday life wasn't too bad, I decided. I did my jobs with as much dignity as I could, pulling orders and running my beloved crusher with a song in my heart. Little by little, I was becoming content with my humble niche in life. Maybe I'd stay at it longer, through the New Year at least.

A week went by, and then Crew Cut himself stopped by, looking pissed-off, as usual. "What the hell do you think this is?" He screamed as I lined up boxes in the crusher.

I turned to face him. "What do ya mean?"

"This crap!" He pointed to my artwork. "This damn hippie shit has to go!"

"It's only a little decoration. Makes me happy while I work, and it's in the back. No one can see it unless they come all the way back here."

"This is a goddamn workplace, not some hippie pad!" He handed me a rag. "Wipe it off fast and get back to work. New orders are piling up!"

Why was a little color in our life such a threat? Did our work life have to be so sterile, so isolated from our sliver of so-called personal life that we had to slay all beauty, everything that made our lives meaningful, all for a goddamn paycheck?

The crusher-man came back a few days later, but only to say goodbye. Crew Cut had fired him.

"I didn't mean to take your job, man," I told him.

"Aw, shit, kid, it ain't your fault. I just won't kiss ass like they want." After a spate of nasty words with Crew Cut, he'd gotten fired. He gave me a wide smile, exposing jagged teeth that needed fixing.

"There are plenty of other jobs around. Time for me to move on." He grabbed my hand in his meaty paw. "It's your baby now. You'll have to look out for yourself, kid. Remember what I told ya? Don't take no guff from these assholes. Good luck!"

With a rough shake of my hand, he was gone. It hurt to lose such a good working-class comrade. Albertson insisted I shouldn't fret about it.

"That guy was always looking for trouble. It was only a matter of time before they'd shit-can him whether you were here or not."

That didn't sit well with me. We workers needed to organize and support each other. Along with my interest in sex and spirituality, I considered myself a Marxist after reading *The Communist Manifesto*. *Tears* came to my eyes and wading through part of *Das Kapital* reinforced my understanding of it. If there was a Union to organize the employees at Beeline, I never heard about it.

Escaping Earth's Gravity

O n Sunday, July 20, 1969, my uncles, aunts and cousins on Dad's side came over to watch the first ever moon landing in our large rec room. We had a color TV and space for a crowd. I hadn't seen any of them since I was about nine years old, even though we all lived within Du Page County, only a short drive away. Normal families got together regularly, even traveling cross-country to visit their relatives. Why our extended family allowed so many years to go by without seeing each other was a mystery to me.

"Our families just aren't close," Mom told me with a shrug when I asked her. "And you know how busy your father is."

True, Dad was always tinkering with endless *do-it-yourself* projects. It was rare for him to socialize more than a few minutes before he slipped down into the basement or out to the garage, where he lost himself in never ending tasks. He'd often be out there into the late night. I counted myself lucky if he didn't pull me out with him on some grueling project, because he'd forget about time until Mom came running out.

"Jimmy, it's well past midnight. Ronnie has school in the morning."

Mom lay the blame on Dad for all her problems; however, it wasn't all his fault. Neither of them socialized with adult friends. Compared to the parents of my friends, they seemed socially isolated.

A series of long submerged childhood memories resurfaced. When I was little, we'd often gone to Dad's twin brother's house. My sisters and I frolicked in their yard with our cousins one warm summer's day. Dad went inside with my aunt and uncle, but Mom stayed out in the car. Dad finally came back out to shout through the open window.

"Honey, come on! Don't be this way. You're embarrassing me."

"Jimmy, I told you NO. I'm fine out here and not going in. You go on and have your fun with those people."

"Those people? *They* are my family."

"I don't even want to see that woman your brother married. She's *so* special, is she?"

"Joyce, get over it. You're too sensitive. At least come in for a cup of coffee and a piece of cake, for god's sake. Just a few minutes, then we'll leave, I promise. Come on, Honey..."

Dad finally ran back in to say goodbye. "Come on, kids," he called to us with resignation. "Your mother wants to go home already."

"Oh, not yet," one of my sisters whined. "We barely just got here, and I'm still *It*." We kids had to break off our game of tag before she could tag one of us to become *It*, and it didn't make sense that we all had to load back in the car so soon. My aunt and uncle, faces taut, waved farewell from the porch. They seemed to tamp down the emotion they must have felt. After a few more visits ended this same way, our families stopped seeing each other altogether.

Mom had her issues, and steady drinking was only part of it. As the only child of my grandparents, Dad accused her of being a spoiled brat when he dumped a whole bottle of her whiskey down the sink. He only did that once because it was expensive, and she'd just go out and buy more, anyway. I thought she was just too sensitive to the imagined snubs from her sister-in-law. She'd asked Aunt Lorraine how she managed to keep her home so clean. There was never even a speck of dust on her shelf after shelf of Hummel figurines.

"Oh, I haven't gotten around to dusting in weeks," Lorraine said, downplaying all the hours of housework she *had* to have put in to keep her place looking like a showcase for *Home and Garden* magazine.

Mom took offence at her pretended nonchalance. Out in the car on our way home that day, she screamed at Dad. "That bitch! She's nothing but a big fat liar!"

Mom had a point. She and Lorraine both had the same number of kids underfoot, but Mom could never meet Lorraine's impossible standards. Maybe it triggered a sense of her being a failure as a homemaker, the ideal of womanhood for her generation. Early on, I recognized that the adults around me were just big children, some more so than others.

By itself, that wasn't a bad thing. Having fun and playing around for fun's sake was underrated in our society, all due to our sober work obsessed Puritan heritage. That's how I saw it. It was all the more reason for me to reject that bankrupt system for the all-embracing, joyful love of communal living. That theory, too, as I'd discovered in Taos, needed work, but I had faith that if we kept at it, we'd make a society that was better than the mess we inherited from our elders.

After all, a woman, even if a middle-aged mother, is only a girl who'd grown up to find herself controlled by a man. Whether she still loved him or not, her husband became her head of the household, curtailing her free expression, especially if she was overwhelmed by the birth of one child after another, like my mom was.

She might also have to endure the emotional distance of a burned-out husband the workaday rat race had crushed into dust whose own dreams. Dad's foray into fatherhood was no more rewarding than his experience as a boy who could never measure up to his father's demands. His twin brother was the favored son. Dad's father, my strict, opinionated grandfather, called my uncle Ed the smart one.

Dummkopf was what Grandpa Schulz yelled at Dad as a boy. True, he wasn't as quick to figure out his math assignments as his brother, who excelled and went on to ROTC and enlisted as an officer in the Army during World War Two. Dad got drafted at the ordinary enlisted rank into the Navy with less fanfare. After the war, he worked hard but never achieved the promotions that went to *those damn college boys*, as he called them. Dad was socially challenged. His words came out slow, to be lost in conversation, so even new hires that he had trained were promoted above him.

Not all of us can succeed in our money-obsessed competitive culture. Not every job was given the aura of importance. Most of us were doomed to become losers in the unending rat race. Even if we win a few perks, we may see ourselves as failures in society. The ridicule of a man's wife, who defined his own worth, only exaggerates his problems.

Dad sought peace and quiet from his wife and kids in his after-work projects. I saw it as escapism and took his painful existence as an abject lesson. Work, for work's sake, repelled me. There had to be more to life than that because our time is short. Death grabs us at a time of its choosing, whether we've finished what we set out to do or not.

This putting a man on the moon thing was a big occasion. America was in competition with the godless Russians for the glory of conquering infinite space. Our nation was optimistic about winning the Space Race, even though Bonny, the last monkey they'd sent up, died only twelve hours after coming back to earth. Death was something you had to risk if you wanted to push the Last Frontier out into the vastness of the galaxy, where no man nor monkey had gone before.

Maybe Astronauts were true heroes, but I was sick of hearing about how great America was. We were still bombing the shit out of Southeast Asia. Claiming dibs on the Moon while ignoring the problems we were causing back on Earth. The Moon was only one more trophy in our upward climb of Manifest Destiny. Our planet was a mess, and we needed to focus on the environment and the political oppression that our nation, as much as any, was responsible for.

My family knew my views on the subject and rolled their eyes when I opened my mouth. But there was no sense wasting my breath to convince them. I'd stopped yakking about everything that really mattered to me and longed to be back among people who understood.

After a few excited comments about space, which I pretended interest in, the rec room conversation turned somber as another middle-aged couple arrived.

"Ronnie," my mother called me over to meet them. "You remember your cousin Carolyn, don't you?"

"I guess so." I said, trying to be polite, but it had been too long.

"This is your uncle Frank and Aunt Rosemary, Carolyn's parents."

Frank gripped my hand tight as a vise and held on, crushing it. Rosemary was red-eyed, her makeup smeared as if she'd been crying, but she put on a brave smile for me. My mother put her hand over her eyes. Maybe she'd been crying too.

"Carolyn," Mom said and paused to begin again. "Your cousin Carolyn passed away on Friday."

Aunt Rosemary put her hand on mine, which was still in Uncle Frank's grip. "She was only thirteen, you know. Too young, way too young." She turned away and headed for the bathroom.

Thirteen? No wonder I couldn't remember her. She'd been far too young for me to play with all those years ago. Looking at the faces around the room, I wasn't sure who was who. I'd never gotten our relationships straight. None of that matters when you're just a kid more interested in running around the yard, climbing trees, and jumping on the slide and swing set Dad had set up on our huge park like property. In my dim memory, none of my cousin's yards were as big as ours.

Uncle Frank and Aunt Rosemary didn't stay long. The rest of us, like patrons in a theater, ensconced ourselves on couches, beanbags, or the bright red carpet, to watch the otherworldly televised event. Astronaut Armstrong's words carried in from deep space via technical magic to our television set and into our ears.

"Houston, Tranquility Base here. The Eagle has landed."

Carolyn's mortal remains lay stiff in her coffin, surrounded by perfume and sweet-smelling flowers at the funeral. That's my only memory of her, my pretty, too young, deceased cousin. Uncle Frank and Aunt Rosemary blur even more in my mind. After the funeral, we remained strangers. If I ran into them, I wouldn't recognize them. No matter, I'd come to realize that all of us humans and even animals were relatives. Whether we recognize our common bond or not, we arise from a common source. We all share the same planet and journey through the same tribulations, confusion, and pain. The earth nourishes while the sky rains down blessings upon us, literally and figuratively. We ought to be happy, despite all the ups and downs of life. So whether we win or lose, true joy doesn't come from such transient things, but despite them. We all have the potential to fill the hole in each other's heart and create happiness right here on Terra firma.

Carolyn had gotten her diagnosis of heart cancer only a day or two before it claimed her, but we all carry a Death Sentence whether we are aware of it or not. Young or old, it comes to each of us, often without warning. Buddhism asserts that the awareness of our inevitable death makes our life more meaningful. We must prioritize doing what is most meaningful, as tomorrow may be too late.

Seeking the Great Beyond

My heart was less and less in my job. I didn't belong there, wasting my precious youth working for the *Man*, groveling before self-important egotists to exchange my humanity for a paycheck. There was more important work to do. The Revolution screamed for my attention. I had to accept the challenge to help build a more humane political system while at the same time expanding my consciousness. The hippie culture and the New Left were parts of the same revolution. We needed to achieve a synthesis of the spiritual, political, and practical parts of life.

I needed a girlfriend and wanted a mature woman, one with a lust for adventure and her eyes open to what was happening in the world. It had been three months–too damn long–since my brief sexual romp with Joanne back in Taos. With a few hundred bucks saved up, I was ready to hit the road again, explore the country and find my niche on a commune, a better one than Joe Sage's place in New Mexico. Before I could tell my parents, they had a bombshell of their own.

Mom sang as she stirred a pot on the stove. That joyful image was a rare sight. As I came in from work, she dropped the ladle, gave me a hug, and shouted her good news.

"Dad and I are leaving for Hawaii!"

Mom, normally morose and sarcastic, was as excited as a schoolgirl. Ever since getting shore leave there during World War Two, Dad talked of going back to live in that tropical paradise. Mom, who'd never traveled beyond the Midwest, wanted that too. Hawaii would be their retirement destination, but with a house full of half-grown kids, that magic moment was a long way off.

"We're going on an all expense paid tour," she gushed. "We'll look at property with a group of investors and buy a lot, so Dad can build our dream house. We need you to look after your sisters while we're away, Ronnie, but we'll be back before they start school."

"Maybe we can all go over and see the lot on our next family vacation," she said.

I couldn't spoil it for her, so I tried to fake enthusiasm. "Gee, that sounds great."

My sisters ranged in age from seven to sixteen and could pretty much fend for themselves. Our parents deserved this outing. I'd wait until they got back to spill my own plans and amass more savings in the meantime.

My parents returned on schedule, rejuvenated from their adventure. They'd bought an overgrown jungle lot to build their retirement home on. Every worker lives for the dream of getting off the tyranny of the clock to do what their spirit craves. I sympathized with them and held my tongue, waiting for the right moment to break in and tell them my own plans. I knew it would upset them, but I had to get on with my own life. When they paused for breath, I jumped in.

"Mom, Dad, I'm leaving town."

"What!" Dad was incredulous, and Mom was too stunned to speak. "For god's sake, Ronnie, you've got a job now!" He said it as if that were the keys to the kingdom.

"I gave my notice. Yesterday was my last day." To avoid a

shouting match, I said no more and grabbed my dilapidated, ready-packed satchel. Before I stepped out, I pulled Mom aside and handed her a packet.

"Mom, could you hold on to a few hundred bucks for me, just in case?"

In a few weeks of working for Beeline, I'd earned nine hundred fifty dollars but didn't want to take the whole wad with me. Two hundred bucks should keep me going for a while, so I let Mom bank some in an account she controlled and hide the rest in the back closet, where it would be handy if I needed it.

Kissing Mom on the cheek, I promised to stop in from time to time and then ran out the door before I lost my momentum. My initial destination was the West End Tree Fort in Fischer's Woods. Before I dived into Chicago, I'd meditate a few days to clear my head of all the anxiety working at Beeline dumped on me. Being an earnest advocate of mystic meditation, based on books I'd found at the Occult Bookstore on State Street in Chicago, I'd been trying to break on through to the other side of reality.

My well-worn copy of *Tibetan Yoga and Secret Doctrines* by Evans-Wentz, was my principal guided into the mystic arts, like astral projection and the inner psychic *heat* called Tummo that adepts used to survive the bitter cold in the mountains. The book claimed I couldn't open my chakras to the spiritual flow of kundalini without a guru's secret, ear-whispered teachings. Lacking that, I'd call upon the divine beings to light my way and find a guru on the astral plane, as the great Tilopa had done.

I'd been putting my heart into it and had supreme faith. The blissful sensations I aroused during meditation, and auspicious dreams of flying and facing down enemies, meant I was close to seeing results. Only a little more effort, a few days in retreat, should yield a breakthrough on the Diamond Path of Tantra.

The Familiar Temptress

After a pleasant three-mile cross-country trek on that sunny afternoon, through golf courses and forest preserves, I veered east off Route 83 into the West End neighborhood where I had friends, and almost one hundred acres of Fischer's Woods extended unspoiled on the far side. The first corner, Oakdale Road and Oak Lane, was appropriately named as a giant oak tree stood guard there.

Under its broad canopy sat a gaggle of kids. They burst out laughing as I reached them, and I could smell the marijuana. Seated amongst them was Rea Fichter, she of the wavy brown hair. Parted down the middle, it cascaded over her shoulders to the middle of her back. With a shake of her head, she seized my full attention.

Over the past year, Rea had changed from being just another girl, a sister of my friends Mike and Bubba, someone I only glimpsed briefly as she came and went, to manifest as a regal beauty. Her brothers seemed unaware that I'd become smitten, and all my attempts to talk with her fell flat. Oblivious to me, Rea would sail on by without acknowledging my earnest *hello*.

One night, her brother Mike and I had sat alone before a bonfire in the woods, drinking beer we'd swiped from a trucker's garage, who in turn had pilfered it from his shipping company, or so we told ourselves to assuage our conscience. After a long swig and a belch, Mike became morose and launched into a tale I'd not heard before.

"When Dad married Mom, his parents called her gypsy trash. They made him keep her in a shack out back like she was a dog or something." He spat into the fire for emphasis. "That's where she stayed, pregnant with my older brother, until Dad finally got our house built here in the West End."

"Are you shitting me? Your mother doesn't look anything like a gypsy." The few Romany gypsies I'd met in downtown Chicago were dark complexioned with black eyes. Mrs. Fichter had light hazel eyes and was whiter than me.

"Well, that's what Mom told me." He stirred the fire with a long stick as he ruminated, then tossed it in. "Maybe she's not pure gypsy. How the hell should I know? I heard about white gypsies called Tinkers and Travelers, Irish or something. Anyway, Dad never brings her when we go to see my grandparents."

We called Mr. Fichter *Baron Von Vince*, the Copper King. He was a gruff building contractor and too much like my dad for comfort. Prone to fits of temper when he didn't get his way. The boys ran and hid when he pulled into the driveway until they divined his mood. He collected scrap copper in his basement and paid kids a small fee for it, no questions asked about where it came from. The boys harvested most of it from unguarded building sites at night. The Baron expected the price of copper to rise through the roof someday, and he'd make a huge profit.

Mrs. Fichter was more approachable. Mike's gypsy story intrigued me, so I'd befriended her. She showed me her collection of occult books. They included the prophecies of Edgar Cayce and studies of reincarnation by the University of Virginia. Prominent among them was the *I Ching, Chinese Book of Changes*, which impressed me with a foreword by Carl Jung. Much as I liked Mrs. Fichter and reading her books, my ulterior motive was to talk to Rae.

But *no dice*. She'd avoided me until this magic moment under the great oak's canopy.

There I was, on my way to do a mystical retreat in the woods, and there sat Rae, her intense gaze and provocative smile quickening my pulse. Unbidden, she rose from the group to glide up to me.

"Hey Ron," she cooed as she put her hand on my shoulder, halting me in my tracks. "Where're you going in such a hurry?" She tugged playfully at the strap of my rucksack. "Hey, you've got quite a load in there."

This was the first time she'd even addressed me by name, much less touched me. As an aspiring yogi, I struggled to keep my raging emotions under control. She was a serious test of my willpower.

"I'm going to live in the woods for a few days," I told her.

"Cool." Rea eyed me with even more interest. "Come sit with us first."

Her invitation took me off guard. I wavered in my determination to charge straight into the woods. Inspired by the life of Buddha, I wondered if this girl could be a cosmic challenge from Mara to throw me off the path. Although I should keep my mind free of worldly attachments, celibacy, recommended by orthodox Buddhism, struck me as unnatural.

Esoteric Tantra, however, intrigued me. It skillfully used sex, transforming the poisonous emotions: greed, pride and anger, obstacles on the path, into their antidotes, making them steppingstones to enlightenment. That was my chosen path.

Rea took my hand and led me to the tree. Despite the younger kids playing at the edge of our circle, the others began passing a joint around.

"Wanna hit?" Rea passed it to me.

Should I accept? Sure, I'd offer the smoke as a Tantric sacrament to the primal gurus. As I exhaled, I felt Rea's hand clasp mine tighter. Moments after we'd sat down, Rea climbed onto my lap, pressing her body to me as if we'd been a long-term couple.

This drama was unfolding exactly as I'd long prayed it would.

My karma had ripened, rewarding my patient but lonely meditation practice by drawing Rae to me like a divine gift. She would be my long-sought consort to practice Tantric sexual yoga. Yab-yum, or yin and yang, were the universal dualities thus brought to compatible union.

We kissed long and deep between tokes, taking turns exhaling smoke into each other's mouths. The neighborhood kids all but vanished as our hands explored each other's bodies under our clothes. Her budding tits stiffened, flushing hot in my hands. Proof that my touch excited her, making her open-mouthed kissing more intense and breathless, which stiffened my rod. She grasped that staff of life, comforting me as I tightened my sphincter like Tantra recommended to conserve my seed for the long haul, delayed orgasm.

"It's getting dark," she said.

"Come with me to the Fort," I offered.

Still locked in a tight embrace, we arose as one creature and walked into the already pitch-black forest. The West Enders cultivated patches of luminous moss on trees along the path that gave off a faint, spooky glow. Used to finding my way in the darkness, I guided Rae to the log at the base of our tree. There we sat kissing and making out for another hour in sublime privacy.

"Spend the night here with me," I whispered.

"My parents will be worried. I'd better go." Touching my lips with her fingers, she added hope to my heart. "I'll meet you here tomorrow, I promise."

"I'll be waiting."

She stopped me from walking to her front door.

"Don't let them see you with me, Ron. I'll come tomorrow like I promised."

She gave me a parting kiss before she ran inside. An enormous chunk of my heart went with her, but lightheaded with joy, I slipped back into the shroud of trees. Swift and sure, my hands found the notches in the bark to climb to the platform. Sleep fled from me that night. My wakefulness fueled my meditation on the uncanny synchronicities that crop up in the mystic dance of life.

My world had changed. Unloved and alone only hours before, I felt connected, like I belonged with this girl who represented my fulfillment.

Dawn came, then noon. Finally, the dusk of evening enveloped me once again. Stoic, I stayed on my lonely perch among rustling leaves as the boughs swayed, creaking with every breeze. Rea didn't appear. Had she and her loving touch been a mere hallucination? No, the faint musty-sweet smell of her body remained on me. Her parents must be giving her trouble. Going to her could backfire.

My mind was in a turmoil of desire. I forced myself to wait, to stick to my faith in her promise and our projected destiny. *If you love someone*, I'd often heard, *let her go*. If her love was meant to be, she'd return to you. I tried to believe that naïve saying. It was pure torture, but I focused all my erratic concentration on Tantric yoga. Chanting mantras, I visualized the iconic deities in yab-yum sexual union. Although without the guidance of a qualified guru, I did my best, praying to unseen powers to bring my *Shakti*, my Dakini, whether she be Rea or another sublime feminine being, back into my loving embrace.

Things aren't always as they appear. Daka and Dakini, the male and female guides along the path, can manifest in unexpected forms. Rea could be more than a mere girl. It behooved me to envision her as the earthly transformation of a celestial Dakini. Tilopa, the founder of the Kagyu lineage, experienced paranormal powers through sexual union with his celestial Dakini.

Even if Rea wasn't an actual, sky dwelling Dakini, she would be my earthy Tantric consort. Either way, we'd make magic together. I'd carry her off to a commune somewhere, somewhere better than Joe Sage's place back in Taos. Or maybe we could swing by there. Maybe Joe would repent of how he'd run me off and welcome me back with open arms. I'd forgive him. We had to treat each other with respect and compassion instead of harsh condemnation.

Visitations

"OOOOOODIN!" The call echoed through the late-night forest, rousing me from sleep upon my lofty perch. Again, the voice rang out: "OOOOOODIN!" Someone was hailing me, shouting Odin's name to announce his approach, as was our custom in the West End. It was a tradition borrowed from the movie starring Michael Douglas, *The Vikings*, which fit in well with our youthful delusions of grandeur. Answering the call helped a visitor navigate through the darkness without wimpy aids, like a flashlight, which interfered with honing our night vision. Crawling to the edge of the platform, I returned the call.

"OOOOOOODIN!"

His answering voice got louder as he broke into the small clearing below. Monkey like, he climbed up the notches and onto my perch. I recognized the legendary Mike Dee himself, a welcome companion to boost my flagging spirits.

Mike was a founding member of the SSVA, the *Super Salacious Villains of America*, Wood Dale's answer to the West End gang, and inseparably linked with them by solemn treaty. I looked up at Mike, a square-jawed, regular sort of guy who looked like he stepped out of a

Norman Rockwell painting. He seated himself cross-legged in front of me before stating his business. He seemed to be brimming with joyful news, yet he brushed my questions aside, choosing instead to build up the suspense by exchanging pleasantries, asking me how I liked living up in this aerie he'd helped build and how my spirit quest was going. Finally, he blurted out: "Ron, I'm joining up!"

"Joining what?

"The Army! You know how I've lusted after adventure, to prove myself in life and death situations and see what I'm made of. Well, I'd better get overseas before that Asian war is over. In the great shape I'm in, I'll be an elite paratrooper soon, jumping into the jungle, ready for hand-to-hand combat, like those exalted heroes we've read about. Did you ever finish those books I lent you?"

"But Mike, this isn't the same as the crusade against Nazism or the Japanese Empire. Ours is the wrong side in Vietnam, morally wrong, man. The Viet Cong are the defenders of their hearth and home against our alien conquest. We've taken that war over from the Goddamn imperialist French, who treated them like shit."

He gave me a bemused, tolerant smile. "Look, Ron, I got nothing against the Viet Cong, worthy adversaries they be, but it's in our basic makeup as men to be warriors, to put ourselves in harm's way for the sheer guts and glory of it. I remember you talking about it that way too, Ron, a couple of years ago."

It was true. Before I'd read more and gotten radicalized against our country's policies, I'd been a staunch believer in the anti-communist cause and just as anxious to dive into a hail of bullets to be a hero.

Mike warmed to the subject, trying to convince me he was right. "Men die or get killed at home, whimpering in bed all the time without living up to the glory that is their birthright. Seeking to prove our valor is the destiny we ought to embrace, our way to Valhalla."

Seeing I was unconvinced, he tried another tack. "It's like this, Ron, if I don't go and grab at my share of glory, someone else will be sent in my place who might be a draftee, someone who didn't want to go. I'm helping somebody stay out of Vietnam. Anyway, if I don't get over there soon, I'll miss my golden opportunity to experience combat. This is my once in a lifetime chance to be in a real war!"

Although I sympathized with Mike's sentiments that he'd chosen the wrong cause, on the side of oppressing a popular revolt against tyranny, appalled me. He didn't seem to care about the effects of his adventuring on other people's lives and the planet at large. Keeping my voice as calm as I could, I tried to persuade Mike of his error, but he brushed my objections aside.

"Too late, Ron. I already signed the papers. There's no turning back now, even if I wanted to. Jesus, man, this is the best decision I ever made in my gosh-darn life."

He would be yet another body fed into the war machine. Too many of the guys I knew, even ones who should've known better, were signing up for the war. They were all adventurous young men, no different from me, being siphoned off to fight an evil war in an exotic faraway fantasy land. We needed them to fight against the establishment for a better future here in this country. I wanted adventure too, but I felt a duty to the larger world and needed to fight for the right cause.

We talked long into the night. As a faint glow heralded the approaching dawn, Mike bid farewell and clambered down, vanishing into whatever fate the jungles of Vietnam and his own karma held in store for him.

At daybreak, Rae's brother, the other Mike, dropped by the treehouse. I imagined he came as an emissary from her and held my tongue, waiting for her message, but he talked of everything except what I longed to hear.

Finally, I blurted out, "How's Rae? Has she said anything to you?"

His blank face was clueless. "About what?"

The novelty of my presence in the woods wore off after a couple of days. Fewer visitors arrived bearing magnanimous offerings of food for my sustenance. I sallied forth and bought a few loaves of rye and whole wheat bread, simple fare, as the ancient yogis survived on.

My meditative focus returned. I seemed to be making progress with Dream Yoga, one of Naropa's Six Yogas, becoming conscious that I was dreaming while asleep and not wake up, called lucid dreaming in the West. On the Tantric path, it was a step toward gaining a foothold on the other side to reach spiritual freedom on the astral plane. When certain I was not awake, in a dream, I conducted experiments: facing down enemies, dancing through clouds of bullets or arrows without harm. Nightmares lost their terror as I knew them to be empty shadows of waking life, which was itself but a passing drama that I should confront head-on. But my dreams told me nothing of Rae, whom I still hungered for.

Another day dawned, and another, sweeter voice hailed me from below.

"Hey, Ron, come on down!"

Standing below my platform was Rae. It was no dream. She'd appeared in the flesh, causing my pulse to quicken to a joyful beat. I'd almost given up on her. Climbing down, I attempted to embrace her sweet-smelling body.

"Not now," she admonished me with a frown, grabbing my hands before they reached her waist. "Let's go. There's someone I want you to meet."

I clammed up to see what she had in mind. As if I were a dog on a leash, she pulled me back to her house, where we got into her dilapidated car. She drove to a playground in Elmhurst, the whole way carefully avoiding any physical contact with me.

She never mentioned our magic night. Sitting beside her, I almost wondered if she was the same girl whose passionate kisses had aroused me. Had I dreamed it, or was this present moment a dream? After parking, she took my hands, her earnest eyes probing mine.

"Ron, there's a guy I want you to meet. I'm sure you'll get along with him." She looked at my hands in hers, and then, after sucking in a deep breath, blurted out. "He's my steady boyfriend. See?"

So that's it? She only brought me there to introduce me to her REAL boyfriend. Still, I held my tongue, surprised, yet still hopeful there was a place for me in her heart, or at least her bed. Maybe she wanted to include me in a threesome. Maybe the celestial Dakinis were toying with me through her, evaluating my self-control, gauging my spiritual readiness for the next step on the mystic path. If I kept my equilibrium, they could initiate me into divine wisdom, such as the great yogi Tilopa experienced.

A curly-haired guy drove up in a Volkswagen bug and parked beside us.

"Ron, this is Roger."

"Good to meet you, Ron." He pumped my hand with vigor, making me wonder what Rae had told him about me. Then he embraced Rae, lifting her off her feet and kissing her with as much passion as I had a few days ago.

"Come on, guys," Rae called, still nestled in his arms. "Let's swing!"

Unsure of my role, I followed them across the park. Rae sat on a swing that Roger pushed higher and higher, making her squeal with delight. I sat on the one beside them, going up and down with less enthusiasm.

Watching Roger cavort with Rae was like an out-of-body experience, as if I'd entered his body and was acting through him as my doppelgänger to play with her. I took it as a lesson in the transient nature of love and life itself. Yet, I remained hopeful that she'd eventually include me in some wild, wonton sex that would enhance all our lives. Why else had she brought me there but to share our passion in a holy trinity?

Immersed in each other, they paid scant attention to me and my hopes faded as time went by. Beaming, like he was doing me a big favor, Roger finally offered to drive me back to the woods. His and Rae's plans wouldn't include me.

Devastated as I was, I kept my emotions in check, my face a wooden mask. But finding myself back in the tree, as if I'd never left, the whole experience struck me as fucking hilarious. I couldn't stop laughing until I wore myself out. Sober again, I took serious stock of my situation. There was no more fooling myself. I would never find my wild Dakini here, among my familiars.

My meditations seemed to have borne some fruit, so my efforts weren't wasted. Flashes of intuition and what I took to be scenes from past lives came to me in vivid color. I felt prepared to resume my quest to find worthy companions, comrades who would help me transform our grubbing materialistic society into a more open-hearted Aquarian ideal. A place where we could fit in without the million compromises with our integrity, even simple ones like cutting our hair. Long hair had become our flag, our uniform, our self-identification as harbingers of a blessed new social order. In Chicago's hip districts, I hoped to find fellow travelers to make all our dreams come true.

But leaving these woods would be leaving my true home. I loved the scene of wild nature around me. Silent and unmoving, I watched families of raccoons stroll past my perch, mother possums with kids clinging to her hair, climbed the tree close beside mine. Those familiar neighbors warmed my heart. Waking up to birdsong without an alarm clock telling me I had to rush to a job where red-faced managers hurled abuse at me had become my new normal. As much as I loved it, it was time to leave the woods for a more active role in my fate.

Part Two
Street Freak

Chicago Bound

At the edge of the woods, I ran into Lee Swanson. "Hey Lee, I'm off to explore the hippie scene in Chicago."

"Good thing I caught you. By the way, I heard they don't call themselves hippies anymore. It's *freaks* now." He gave me a conspiratorial wink. "Pretty freaky, huh?" He laughed at his joke. "Anyway, listen up; I got a proposal for ya."

Redheaded Lee was a more recent resident of the West End neighborhood and a peripheral member of the Woods Runners. Although ambitious, an organizer, a guy with something always up his sleeve, he didn't join any of the riskier nighttime pranks, like beer and copper heists. His goals shot higher. He tried to pull us into up-scale social networks, like lobbying churches to transform unused basements into folksy coffeehouses, youth hangouts and venues for garage band concerts.

We both agreed that we were in the Age of Aquarius, a time of revolution, as crucial to history as 1776 had been, but his ideas were more pragmatic than mine. Whereas I saw inevitable blood in the streets as we confronted the power structure, Lee envisioned a gradual changing of the guard as our generation overwhelmed and outlived our elders.

He led me to his house, where he had an office set up in his parent's garage. He pulled an olive drab bundle out of a closet and threw it at me.

"It's an Army surplus duffel bag," he said. "It includes a down sleeping bag, a mosquito net and a hammock. A much better way to haul your gear than that *beat to hell* knapsack. You've got more room in it too."

"Thanks, Lee." I pulled it apart to examine. "Too bad I didn't have that mosquito net the past few nights, got eaten alive, but I won't need it in the city. I'll leave it and the hammock with you."

The duffel bag was easier for me to manage on the road than the blanket roll I'd used the last time I sallied forth into the unknown. It gave me space for more clothes and the nice warm sleeping bag in place of my worn-out woolen Army blankets. It was a godsend as winter lay before me.

Lee fixed me with a serious look. "Ron, I'd like you to be my eyes and ears. Give me reports on the hip scene in the city or wherever the hell you end up. Nothing too regular, just tell me what you find out about crash pads, communes and organizations like the Yippees, so I can help broaden our horizons out here." Lee sounded like a military officer briefing me on an upcoming mission. We all had grandiose plans, and I respected him for it.

"Sure thing, man, I'll be on the road a lot, but I expect to swing back here from time to time."

"All the better. What you told me about Drop City and Taos was terrific. There's a lot happening in New York that I'm interested in too if you get out that way. The more connected we are to the bigger scene, the sooner we can build that fantastic new society you're always talking about. Rock concerts, be-ins, that's the social impact on culture that'll create real change more than attacking the entrenched political system head-on."

"Maybe we need to do both, Lee. The revolution ought to be

multi-faceted to last. I'll see what I can find out for you." Of course, I intended to keep in touch and paid close attention to what might be worth passing on to him. Unfortunately, in the whirl of events that became my life exploring the urban scene.

With a buoyant *bon voyage*, I shouldered my new duffel as euphoria washed over me. It'd been almost three months since I'd done any hitchhiking, long enough to reevaluate the pitfalls of the wandering life and put the grand adventure into a more favorable light.

The open road lay before me on a beautiful summer morning. I was back in the real world with only a vague sense of what I was looking for. Crossing Grand Avenue to Lake Street, which was a busy artery direct to the downtown Loop I stuck out my thumb. It was Rush Hour, and I soon got a ride.

The driver was a pudgy, nerdy looking fellow with inflamed, red acne as bad as Lee, sprouting all over his pasty face. The front seat was full of his crap, so I settled into the back. He pulled away from the curb and started yakking.

"Hey man, know of any *hot to trot* hippie chicks around here? Do ya, huh? I'm horny and need a good fuck!"

"Hmmm?" I pretended I didn't understand what he meant. That sad sack turned my stomach, but he'd probably never gotten laid, and I'd try to be compassionate.

"You look like a hippie," he continued. "You ought to know something about where to find chicks." He winked at me in the rearview mirror.

My hair had grown out over the summer. In his eyes, I was just the sort to help him procure a *free and easy* woman with no moral hang-ups. Free and easy, the essence of joy, exactly what we all craved in our partners to enliven our wretched lives. What's wrong with that?

"Come on, you know the kind of chicks I mean, man. Hippie chicks like to fuck, right? I hear they're all sluts, whores, whatever. Is that true?"

Pitiful, the way he talked about women. Sluts and whores were disparaging terms reserved for sexually available women. People don't call men whores, no matter how many women they fuck. A guy like him would never think of sticking with such a tarnished gal after relishing her body. No, he'd marry a prim, uninitiated one, conditioned by her over-protective upbringing to hate sex. Horrible karma!

The sexist double standard stereotyping women, who are nothing if not men's other halves, into *good* and *bad* categories, struck me as evil. I'd listened to *heroes* returned from Vietnam, bragging about how they used and tossed aside *gook* women, without any concern for them. To come home *from the bush* to what they lauded as a pure, white, *round-eyed* girl who'd waited patient and unsullied for her warrior's return. No prude, myself, I was all for freewheeling sex, but snide moral superiority nauseated the hell out of me. It was my duty to straighten out this be knighted wretch.

"Man! Don't talk that kind of shit about women. You've got to treat every kind of chick, right? Be nice to them; appreciate her generosity if you get some. I mean, what's in it for her?"

"Yeah, right." That killed the topic for him. I'd burst his bubble. He drove on in silence, exuding disappointment while I mulled things over. Was I all that different from this guy? I and every other heterosexual man were looking for the same thing, to get *laid*, but I didn't want to be so crude and selfish about it. There had to be something in it for the woman, too.

Okie and Blondie

The guy dropped me off in Oak Park, where I caught the El train to the Chicago Loop, transferred to the northbound subway, got off at Division by the Mark Twain hotel and walked into Old Town.

Old Town was Chicago's famous hippie quarter. While the main action was on the coasts, far away in New York and San Francisco, things had gotten more *real* in Chicago after the Democratic Convention, when the Yippees took over and confronted the cops. As I walked up Wells Street, guys became freakier with long hair, beads and buttons bearing slogans like "Make love not War" and "Speed kills," but I wasn't a tourist. I needed to make friends and find a place to stay. Everyone I asked repeated the question to himself as if thinking aloud.

"A place to crash, huh?" They'd scratch their shaggy beards a moment. "Well, gee, I don't know right now, man. Sorry, can't help you."

Lincoln Avenue sliced diagonally northwest from where the north end of Wells stopped, and the hippie district expanded along it. *Head Imports* and the *Feed Store* served as points of contact along that strip. Farther along, tucked under the noisy el tracks by Wrightwood, was *Alice's Restaurant-Revisited*, named for the Arlo Guthrie song. It stood beside the offices of the *SEED* underground newspaper. Someone there ought to help me find a place to crash.

Freaks bought stacks of the *Seed* wholesale and sold them for the marked price of thirty-five cents a copy, earning fifteen cents apiece. If nothing else panned out, I'd try selling the *Seed* too, but the office and restaurant were empty at that early hour, so I started back toward Head Imports.

A disheveled fellow in his mid-twenties reached out to hail a bus bound for the stop a block beyond him. As I came abreast of him, he slipped off the curb and fell directly in front of the bus. I reached out and grabbed him by the scruff of his neck and yanked him back onto the sidewalk with inches to spare.

The bus screeched to a halt. The wide-eyed driver swung the door open, his voice quaking as he screamed, "Is he all right?"

The stumbling man answered with a slurred western accent, probably drunk. "Yeah, man, I'm all right," he hesitated. "This time."

"Jesus," the driver exclaimed. "You scared the bejeebers out of me, man. Better be careful. You still want a ride?"

"Nope." He shook his head and waved the driver off. "I'm a-gonna catch my breath here and talk to my new *pardner*. Thank you, sir!"

I guessed by partner he meant me. As the bus pulled away, he said, "You *shore* saved my ass kid, I owe you one."

"That *was* close, man. You missed a date with the mortician."

He laughed. "*Shee-it*. I really didn't wanna ride that ol' bus anyhow, I ain't got nowhere to go, nowhere *at-tall*." He looked me square in the eye. "How about you, boy? Maybe we ought'a team up. I'm new in this here town and need to find a place to flop." Standing on unsteady legs, he looked me over with narrowed eyes. "How about it, man? Any objection if I tag along?"

"Nah." I shifted the weight of my loaded duffel to my other shoulder. "I'm looking for a place too."

46

"Well, put 'er there, *Pard*." He held out his hand and shook mine while pounding my back with the other. "Just call me Okie. That's where I'm from, and gosh-darn glad to be outta there."

That was the first time I'd heard the term Okie, which I guessed meant Oklahoman.

"We ought to look out *fer* one another," he continued. "I *been a thinking* I ought to get me out of this here Chicago, had nothing but bad luck since I came. Now that I met you, my luck has changed. So, I expect I'll stick around."

Although I wondered if he might prove to be a liability, I voiced no objections. Okie kept gushing his thanks for saving his life and how he was indebted to me and would be my friend through thick and thin. It seemed a bit more than I wanted, reminding me of the Chinese proverb about how saving someone's life made him indebted for life, almost the slave of the benefactor, but what if Okie only wanted to *sponge* off me?

If he were a longhair, I'd trust him more, but he was a down and out hillbilly. Maybe it was the memory of my grade school chum, the Kentucky kid who'd pulled a knife on me at the school bus stop. I'd only said I didn't believe some bullshit he told me, no good reason to stab his only friend. A guy had to be careful with people but not get paranoid.

As we walked down Lincoln to Wells, Okie rambled on about anything that popped into his head while I mumbled in reply. Maybe I was his first human contact on his solitary journey. I needed a friend, too. It was nice to have someone to talk with.

After so much time alone in the woods, living rough, without a chance to do more than give myself a quick rinse from a garden hose, I was probably as rank as Okie. You get used to natural bodily odors after a few days on the road, but I looked forward to a nice shower as much as a place to flop for the night. We needed to expand our society to find that.

We passed the narrow redbrick Piper's alley with its upscale boutiques, its slick, glib, tacky merchandise capitalizing on overpriced psychedelia. I called the owners of the establishments the hip-wa-zie, a play on bourgeoise, but Okie didn't get it. Across North Street were clubs featuring go-go dancers silhouetted in the window before a quaint little courtyard with an ornate birdbath. Across the street was the Purple Cow dairy restaurant, famous for great shakes, then *Ripley's Believe it or Not* museum of the weird. Farther down Wells was the *Climax* psychedelic shop. We continued around the corner to the *Hungry I,* which had a great big unblinking eye painted on the door, where you could eat your fill for a buck and a half. It was good money in those days, but well within our price range.

"Let's eat," Okie said, pulling my sleeve.

"Sounds good, man. I've been living on bread and water the past few days."

Stuffing our faces to full satisfaction on the smorgasbord, we'd be ok for another day or two if necessary. As the day dragged on into the late afternoon, the street filled up. People passed out ads or propaganda for a variety of events, concerts, restaurant openings, or exotic ideologies. One fellow stood out. Dressed all in black, like a crow, he had a pointy black goatee that made him look like the folk singer Mitch Miller. A gold chain hung around his neck from which an upside-down crucifix.

"Good day to you, fine gentlemen." He spoke with an eerie formality while handing us a glossy brochure, printed on heavier, more expensive paper than the broadsheets others passed out, with better art than other struggling cults. "Have you heard of The Process?"

A spooky thrill ran through me as I thumbed through his material. Their official name was the *Church of the Final Judgment.* They sported a crazy pantheon, with Satan as a separate entity from Lucifer, alongside Jehovah and Christ, in a sort of revisionist godhead that reconciled the duality of good and evil, salvation and damnation, found in orthodox Christianity. Curious, with nothing else to do, we accompanied him to their headquarters off Wells. But when he overwhelmed us with demands to join, we backed off. Interested as I was in the occult, the *Process* seemed to be too Madison Avenue slick, out for paying converts who sought another path in reaction to the excesses of Christianity. I saw nothing that could guide the true spiritual seeker and tried to enlighten the fellow, telling him I had the *Dharma* truth, beside which everything else paled. He didn't want to hear that and chased us away to sow more fertile fields.

Okie stuck to me like glue. We were jobless and homeless, free from commitments, and unsure if Chicago was our temporary or permanent harbor. Any strangers we ran into, ideally of the female variety, could transform into friends who could alter our destiny for better or worse.

"Hippies and Okies got a lot in common," he said, nodding like a sage. "Whoever said we're different from each other is full of shit."

"That's right, man. We all got the same basic needs."

"Needs? You bet, *pardner*! One thing I need is to find me a woman. Been awful lonely since my gal gave me the boot back in Oklahoma."

"We're in the same predicament, Partner," I told him the story of hot and cold running Rae, and he clucked in commiseration.

"Women are hard to figure sometimes, *pardner*, but we *shore* as hell can't do without 'em."

Thirsty, Okie and I began crossing the street to the Purple Cow. A car crawled almost to a stop. The middle-aged driver in a three-piece business suit, one of the sightseers who cruised along Wells, *must* have seen me, but as I got in front of him, he hit the gas from three feet away. *Bam!* He slammed into me, throwing me onto the hood of his car. The worried driver jumped out. "Are you hurt?"

"Naw, it's Okay, man." More embarrassed than jarred, I hopped off his hood and scurried on across the street. Okie ran to catch up with me.

"You sure you're OK?"

"Yeah, shit happens. Crazy, huh?"

The incident made me feel foolish, and I didn't want to talk about it. It was a weird coincidence to have pulled my new companion back from a certain bus accident and hours later have my own run in with a car. Existence is fragile.

A guy stood outside the Purple Cow dressed in bell-bottom trousers with Mod blue polka dots on his red long-sleeved shirt. With a shock of yellow hair falling over his forehead, he looked like a grownup version of the cartoon character Dennis the Menace. He laughed and called to me.

"Wow, dude! You sure know how to make an entrance." He extended his hand. "I'm Blondie. Come on in for a drink of cold moo juice on me."

We sat at the counter of the milk bar. Blondie, as our generous, extroverted host, ordered blended yogurt shakes all around and came right to the point.

"Do you guys need a place to stay? No problem if you do, plenty of room at my pad."

Okie and I exchanged glances. It looked like we had a place to crash, at least for the night. Things were coming together for us. Okie's face relaxed, and he seemed to have run out of words, but Blondie rambled on.

"I'm staying up the street with a *gay* black dude, Jimmy. He's way cool. I can talk him into letting you stay there because we're lovers."

Okie shot me a surprised look. Suppressing my own dumbfounded reaction, I nodded back to show I'd heard it too. Blondie didn't strike me as *flaming* gay. I hadn't heard gays *rap* so open and nonchalant about their love life before. Blondie paused for an answer, so I jumped in.

"I suppose we could crash there a day or two. Are you sure Jimmy won't mind?"

"Positive, man, Jimmy's good people. Lots of our friends stay over. It's a party joint."

Okie looked leery. "Hold it, man, I *dunno* about this." His eyes narrowed at Blondie. "Are you trying to pick us up or something?"

Blondie almost choked on his yogurt. "That's up to you, *dude*. I'm not like a rapist or anything. I got plenty of lovers to choose from, way more than I can manage." He winked. "Some high-profile ones too. I even fucked Hugh Hefner after a wild party at his penthouse."

"But he's straight," Okie shouted, flustered. "The owner of the goddamn Playboy Empire, for god sake."

"Well, he's AC-DC, man."

"AC what?"

"Bisexual." Blondie nodded, insistent. "I'm AC-DC, too, man. I swing both ways with chicks *and* dicks. Get it?"

"Shit!" Okie looked at me with pleading eyes. "How about you, *pardner?* Don't tell me you're gay or AC-DC?"

"No way, that's not my bag. I'm totally into women. But each to his own, right Blondie? As long as you guys don't bother us. Live and let live. Right?"

"Well, I suppose we'd be all right if we look out *fer* each other."

Blondie stood up with a big grin and clapped us both on the shoulders. "Groovy, do your own thing, man. Come on, I'll introduce you to Jimmy. Then we need to celebrate with a real drink!"

Jimmy's pad, on the second floor, corner apartment of a posh red brick building overlooking Wells, offered a terrific view of the colorful people parading below. A long couch and a couple of end tables constituted the only furnishings in the living room, set on a tan shag carpet the same color as the walls. Blondie called it beige the first time I heard the name of that color.

"Welcome, boys," Jimmy greeted us with a grin. He proved to be an affable, well-spoken black man upwards of thirty, with short shiny, *conked* straight and dyed black hair. He offered us his shag carpet for sleeping space. "Unless you'd care to join us on my king-sized waterbed."

"We're not gay," Okie clarified.

"Yeah, they're straight," interjected Blondie. "At least for now, but a guy can change his mind, right Jimmy?"

"Whoever you screw is your business and no concern of ours," Jimmy said. "I just enjoy the company of good people, guys and dolls too, so make yourselves at home, boys."

Turning to Blondie, he said, "Dearie, could you mix our new friends a nice cocktail?" Turning back to us, "Or would you rather have a beer?"

I opted for beer. Okie did too. Although I was no clean-freak, I'd detected, or perhaps imagined, the faint whiff of *ass* under the flowery perfume that filled the house. Drinking straight from a bottle rather than a glass seemed safer. The beer helped counter the nausea rising in my stomach.

Dropping our heavy packs in a corner, Okie and I settled on one end of the sofa with nervous relief in our new surroundings. Blondie and Jimmy seemed to be all right, guys. The adage: *do your own thing*, allowing for tolerance.

A couple of young dudes sauntered in from the bedroom, dressed in hot pink women's nightgowns, half-open to bare their hairless chests. Sashaying their hips as if they were female fashion models on the runway, one of them bent his rear-end over, giving us a flirty smile over his back. "Hi, boys, like what you see?" Then he sat too close beside us.

Blondie came to our rescue. "Take it easy on them, Sally. Give 'em time. We don't want to scare 'em off. Maybe, after a while, they'll start to like pretty boys like you!"

Everyone laughed except Okie and me. We dropped to the carpet at the far end of the living room to give them all the space they wanted on the couch.

Jimmy sat on Sally's lap, giving him affectionate kisses and asking him to try on another of the new outfits he'd bought. Massaging Sally's thigh, Jimmy told him: "Leave those poor boys alone. Different *strokes* for different folks, you know." He emphasized strokes, which elicited another bout of laughter. Resigned to be the butt of jokes in this company, Okie and I forced some weak chuckling to be polite.

The other effeminate white boy plopped beside them, pouting until Jimmy began chiding and fussing over him too. Although Blondie told us he was Jimmy's lover, he didn't seem jealous. It was evident that all four of these men were sexually involved with each other. Sipping my beer, I closed my eyes and leaned back against the wall, trying to shut out the flirtatious drama that made me queasy despite my valiant attempt at open-mindedness. Okie did the same.

I appreciated Jimmy's hospitality, but the mannerisms that turned on these guys, attracting them to each other, had the opposite effect on Okie and me. This wasn't our scene. We were visitors on an alien planet. Trying to make sense of our divergent natures, I reflected on the natural impulses of attraction and revulsion, wondering if sexual preferences were innate or acquired. Maybe this was how gay guys felt around girl crazy guys, but we only had to make it through the night. We'd try to find some place else in the morning.

"I'm beat," Blondie said, his hand on the bedroom doorknob. "You cats come on in when you're ready to play."

The others soon joined him. Hot and heavy sounds came from the bedroom. The slurping, moaning, thumping, and banging against walls eventually died down, giving Okie and me a chance to catch some slumber. Thus, we made it through our first night in gay Old Town. Up by midmorning, earlier than his bedmates, Blondie greeted us with his usual high spirits.

"Ever been to Rush Street? Come on, I'll show you guys around."

John Bell

R ush Street seemed aptly named. Businessmen kept glancing at their watches until they grabbed their briefcases and rushed out to catch one of the patrolling cabs.

We found it full of subdued men in suits and ties, reading the Wall Street Journal and sipping coffee or an early cocktail at the eateries that catered to them.

"Check it out," Blondie said, ushering us into a posh establishment. In a whisper, he added, "It's my main hunting ground. I pick up some well-heeled guys here."

But it was too early for that action, and I was underage. He steered us over to a luncheon counter at a crowded but unremarkable diner. Blondie was paying and did most of the yakking as Okie and I tore into a huge stack of flapjacks.

"You know the ancient Greeks and Romans were all switch hitters, man; they said Julius Caesar was husband to every wife and wife to every husband or something like that. What do you think about that, huh? Homosexuals were like acceptable in those days." On and on he went, chattering away on every personal, sexual, historical, and political topic under the sun. Dizzy from the overload, I give up trying to follow his exposition.

Okie stood up and said he had to use *the John*, but he must have grown tired of us and slipped out the back door. *Adios amigo*, I thought to myself with disappointment when he didn't return. He'd grown on me. I'd miss him, sure, but as the Buddha said, *Meetings always end in separations*. Regardless of gains and losses, relentless life charges on.

As the noon crowd thinned out, I noticed a glum black guy sitting on a stool at the far end of the counter. His short, woolly black hair, sprinkled with gray, indicated he was around forty. Dressed in clothes as shabby as mine, he seemed out of place among the better dressed clientele. Listening in on the collage of topics we were rapping, race, sex, and social revolution seemed to perk him up, and he invited himself over.

"Hi, guys, I'm John Bell."

"Groovy to meet you," Blondie said. "Gimme some skin, man." He held out both his hands, palms up, for John to wipe his hands over them with a flourish. It was the elaborate manner then fashionable among hip black youth. "Do you go for men, John?" Blondie gushed, embarrassing me. "I'd love to introduce you to my swinging black friend, Jimmy."

"Hey, man, I'm no queer."

"Neither am I," I said, extending my hand the old-fashioned way. "I'm Ron."

Our renewed conversation began to exclude Blondie, but a well-dressed, middle-aged man came in smiling at him, so he winked at me and went over to his table. He had his own, more profitable, scene to make.

I told John I didn't have a place to crash. He nodded and said, "Me too. Maybe we ought to get our own *crib* together, man."

Crib? That was the first time I'd heard the term, but I figured it must be a *pad*, a place to live.

"Sure thing, John." I said. "We need to make our crib a commune, a place for *our* kind of people to mingle and let their hair down. I've seen communes out west go wrong, man, and I want to improve on the idea. It's important for us savvy open minded cats to form communities with all racial and ethnic groups in open hearted love. Can you dig that?"

"Groovy idea, man," he grinned his approval. "Black, tan and white, everyone has got to crib together. That's the only way to solve the goddamn race problem in this country."

Blacks and whites living together was still something of a revolutionary concept. Rampant prejudice made segregation de facto in most Chicago neighborhoods. Although a few blacks, like Jimmy, lived in Old Town and Lincoln Park, the Southside ghetto contained the bulk of the black community.

John waved me closer and whispered so Blondie, sitting across the room wouldn't hear us. "No *fairies*, man! Dig? We need to limit our crib to straight dudes and foxy ladies!"

Although I liked Blondie, he and his tribe had their own scene. "You're right, John. Us *straights* need our own *happening*." John and I toasted our new enterprise with yet more coffee refills, wiring us for the task ahead. We ought to find an apartment easily in tolerant Old Town or Lincoln Park.

"Apartment hunting is new to me, John. I've only rented flophouse rooms back in New Orleans."

"Well, Ron, that wouldn't do for us. If you get us a newspaper, we can check the listings." John frowned and continued. "There's just one thing, Ron. I gotta be straight with you." I held my breath, hoping it wasn't anything too serious. "Ron, I'm flat broke right now, but I've got big money coming in soon."

That deflated me a little. I'd have to bankroll this project on my own until his cash caught up with him. Being young and inexperienced, I needed a savvy partner. Could I rely on John any more than Okie, who'd slipped out on me? Shit, no, but nobody's perfect, and nothing lasts forever. I needed to be practical and get situated. Once we had an apartment, a crib, we'd find others to share the costs. Somehow, things were working out. I decided to give John a chance, bought a newspaper and got a couple dollars in change for the payphone while the cheerful waiter refilled our cups with fresh coffee.

As he split arm in arm with his friend, Blondie gave me a wink. "Catch you cats later, man." The almost empty restaurant became our office. John opened the paper on the counter to the rental section. Chicago was a big place; the listings went on for several pages. Single rooms looked reasonable. Some wanted a *sober man* at ten to twenty dollars a week, but there was no sense wasting *my* money on that temporary measure. We needed to rent a big apartment on the Northside of Chicago by the month. Under the heading: *Modern Living 1969*, I saw two bedrooms, two baths for two hundred and eight bucks. There was another at a hundred thirty-five for two bedrooms right beside the lake. John said to ignore those larger ads for flashier places. We couldn't afford the extra frills, like elevators, air-conditioning, or extra bathrooms. Just the basic unfurnished space would be cheaper, and we'd take care of making it feel like home on our own. We zeroed in on the cheaper targets, skipping studios. Four bedrooms in North Troy went for a hundred fifteen.

"Well, looky here, Ron," John jabbed at the small print on the paper. "Three rooms for ninety-seven bucks and fifty cents! Then there's this other three-room place for a hundred-twenty-five."

One on North Beacon had four rooms for eighty-seven, another rented five rooms, *adults preferred*, for ninety-five. We stepped over to the payphone on the wall and started dialing. Each call cost me a dime. If no answer or the line was busy, I got my coin back to try again. Running through the whole list ended up costing me a couple of bucks. John told me what to say, and I did the talking, so they'd hear a white-sounding voice.

Some places were already taken. When we got a live one on the line, he asked probing questions about our employment, which neither of us had. We lied, of course, certain that we'd find a gig soon and set up appointments with the landlords.

Full of caffeine and high spirits, we set off to look at the apartments. Yakking our heads off, we got to know each other's stories. John had a lot to say.

"You see, I was just a nineteen-year-old kid when I got sent into that goddamn Korean War. What a fucking hellhole that was! It still gives me nightmares." He shivered a little as he got into his story.

"The Army had just been integrated. You know, they needed our black asses up on the firing line. The Chinese came rolling down on us. No matter how many we killed, they kept coming at us. I'd be lying if I said I wasn't scared shitless." He studied me for a while. "No lie, man, I mean it, I honest to god shit my britches, and I wasn't the only one. Then we had orders to get up out of our holes and counter-attack!"

Although I'd read a lot of combat history, I'd never heard it firsthand. John put too much emotion into his telling for his story to be bullshit. My uncle Ed survived the meat grinder of the Hurtgen Forest, part of the Siegfried Line, and then came the Battle of the Bulge, but he refused to tell me much about it. The only detail he gave me was that they were pinned down under fire for days, having to relieve themselves in their helmets, the same helmets they ate their rations out of.

John looked at me wide-eyed and grabbed my arm. "Shit, man, do you think Americans are always the good guys? Mother fucking no, man! Our officers passed an order down the line before we charged. *Take no prisoners*! Some of them Chinese threw up their arms, trying to surrender as we rushed them. Scared as we were for our own lives, we couldn't stop to deal with them, had to keep moving forward. We just kept blasting them. Murder! That's mother fucking war, man. It's kill, or be killed."

I could only shake my head in sympathy, knowing my words would be inadequate. We walked in silence for some minutes while John seemed to consider what more to tell me. Sucking in a lungful of air, he continued.

"Some nights, I wake up crying like a goddamn baby. You dig

what I'm telling you? It's like I'm still out there, man, sitting in that mother fucking foxhole, smelling the sickeningly sweet smell of blood and bitter gun-smoke. Shit, I lost plenty of friends out there, man."

He dug his nails into my shoulder and starred at me with eyes big as saucers. "I'm still here, ain't I? They can't get rid of old John Bell that easily! Don't know how many motherfuckers I blew away. They don't all die so quick like in the movies. No man. They scream and holler until they gurgle their life away, bodies ripped to pieces, guts and brains spilling out. It ain't a pretty sight. Gives me the fucking wellies remembering it."

Sorry, it's taken, said each of the landlords when we got to the apartments. John wondered aloud if they put us off because he was black, so I went alone to the next one, but that landlord said I looked too young and turned me down. Nothing we could do about our race or age, but at least we had each other. That evening we sought companionship at Alice's Restaurant-Revisited.

Ruby and the Nightriders

A rollicking, good-sized crowd packed the room and filled the tables. "Let's get the fuck out of here," hissed John, put off by the crush. But I spotted a couple of empty seats along the far wall at a table with two women. They were both dressed alike, maybe sisters, in lacy summer wear, as black as their long flowing hair. I grabbed John's sleeve and pulled him along.

"Are these seats taken?"

"Yes," one gal answered. But before we could split, she added, "by you guys!" They burst out laughing, and we sat down.

"I'm Ron, and this is my pal, John."

"Cool," said the heavier one closest to me. "I'm Ruby." She put her hand out, and I bent to kiss it like a nineteenth-century swain. That earned another ripple of laughter. I was on a roll with these chicks.

"I'm Carol," her friend said, stifling a giggle. When she put her hand out for me, it felt cold and stiff. I stopped in mid-bow. It was plastic, a prosthetic forearm! Fuck it. I played along and kissed it, anyway.

"Got you, Ron," she crowed. They exploded in mirth at pranking me. "I'm Carol, the one-armed prostitute, a proud professional lady of the night."

Despite that missing limb, Carol was slim and well-endowed. I liked her looks as much as her spunk. John, getting over his apprehension, slapped me on the back and gave Carol a wink as he addressed her.

"Maybe I can afford you one of these days. Meanwhile, could I get a freebie?"

Pointing her plastic arm at him, she deadpanned. "I could give you a free hand-job!" The stiff fingers didn't bend as she pretended to jerk his cock with her plastic arm, causing us all to explode in laughter.

"You guys are alright," Carol said, still chortling. "But sorry, dude, it's gotta be cash upfront. I don't come cheap and gotta make rent."

We were having more fun than anyone else in the establishment. Music, whether live or juke, came from somewhere, but I paid it no mind. Fleshier than Carol, Ruby's bare belly-roll shook when she laughed. I suddenly remembered a word for fleshy girls: Rubenesque. Rubenesque Ruby had a nice ring to it, and for the first time in my life, I found that body type delightful.

Suddenly serious, Ruby grabbed my shoulder. "Got any uppers?"

"No," I said, trying to figure out what uppers were.

"I really need to *get off*, man. Downers then? You got downers or anything?"

I shook my head no. Without missing a beat, she tossed the question to John.

"No, girl, I'm not a druggie and never carry anything up to this side of town. Like as not, I'd get busted around all you white hippie freaks." Bringing his mouth to my ear, he whispered, "That chick is a *stone* speed freak."

I whispered back, "Maybe so, John, but I could go for her."

Beyond some occasional weed or psychedelics, I wasn't into drugs and had only tripped on acid once. That was a heavy scene, tripping on the open road all alone in Colorado. I'd do it again, but only in a more stable environment.

Ruby made the rounds of nearby tables until someone gave her something. Without even looking at it, she dropped it down the hatch as if it didn't matter what it was. She plopped back beside me, grabbed my hand, and pulled it under her top onto her ample breasts. Wow! Her warm flesh sent ripples of joy throughout my body. There was nowhere else I'd rather be.

After I fondled her for a while, she gushed, "Oh, man! I'm really getting a rush!" I assumed she was enthused about my handiwork. She hyperventilated, repeating over and over, "Wow, what a rush!" But then she said, "I need a downer," making me realize she meant the drugs she'd taken, not me.

She left my warm embrace to make another round of the neighborhood. It seemed there were plenty of free drugs passing around, like cigarettes in the dark and smoky place. She'd take whatever they offered, crossing one drug with another to counteract the effects. Her desperate need for a chemical high, especially if she had to keep reversing it with another, was beyond my understanding, but she returned to my arms. Things seemed to be working out for me, but John got nowhere with Carol. It came down to cash.

"Maybe see you cats another time," Carol said as she stood up. "Nice to see you again too, Ruby. I'm off to try my luck out there."

Lip-locked in a hot and heavy embrace with me, Ruby didn't bother to answer. I gave Carol a polite wave and offered a silent prayer of thanks that Ruby wasn't leaving with her. This night was a dream come true, working out better than I ever imagined. Quite a change from the lonely, love struck week I'd spent meditating in the woods. John seemed at ease for the moment. Maybe he'd stick around too. I'd rejoined human society.

At closing time, two longhairs in tie-dyed shirts popped in and hollered. "Anybody up for a wild ride? We're going to the airport to trip on the lights!"

That had been my dad's thing. He and a hundred other middle-aged men would park for hours along Mannheim Road and watch planes take off and land at O'Hare airport. It bored me to tears when he dragged me along. I overheard people talking about these younger airplane buffs.

"Shit! Did you see their eyes?"

"Big as saucers. Damn! Those dudes are tripping on acid, man."

"Don't go! They'll crash out there for sure."

No way could I imagine driving while tripping, but I'd taken four times the recommended dose on my one and only acid trip while hitchhiking. Crazy as it sounded, Ruby was all for the madcap adventure. I couldn't disappoint my new lady and had nowhere else to go. John's dusky face paled at the suggestion, but we couldn't leave him behind and pulled him along. The only black guy mashed in with a van-full of excited white freaks.

With no seats in the back of the VW van, it filled up like a cattle car, way beyond capacity. The three of us hunkered down together on the floor behind the driver's seat. Hemmed in by the crowd of bodies, we couldn't see much of the colored lights the guys up front swooned over, but it didn't matter to me. Ruby and I picked up where we'd left off, smooching and fondling each other as the van roared into the night, rocking and bouncing. It was beyond me how we didn't crash or get pulled over. John, crouched on the far side of Ruby, glanced around, wary, as we careened too fast around corners.

"Close your eyes, John. Try to get some rest." I was sure that was all he needed, but he sat up wide-eyed the whole time.

Ruby's warm body comforted me. I let my fingers do the talking, keeping her hot and bothered. If we had a little more room, we might have fucked then and there. But I was still a novice, too shy for such public hijinks. Between bouts of making out, we dozed, bouncing against our companions with a rough yet soothing rhythm. The night ended in a purple dawn. The driver parked by the Seminary restaurant on Lincoln and shouted back at us.

"Did you all have a good time?"

The packed-in crowd gave a muted, groggy response.

"Anybody hungry? This is a great place to chow down."

That got better feedback. Damn! A hot breakfast sounded great to me. We stumbled out to make sense of our situation. Ruby and I had gotten some shuteye between dry humps, not enough, but I've always been a morning person. Red-eyed John looked haggard. Ruby, disheveled but upbeat, giggled and chided him.

"You were freaking out, huh, John?"

"I'm not used to being in a large bunch of crazy white people. *That* scares the shit outta me."

"They're not Klansmen," I said. "Just a bunch of wild freaks. At least we had a warm, cozy place to hang out through the night."

John didn't laugh. "Come on," he said with a wan smile. "Let's feed this girl some breakfast, and then we'll find us a place for tonight."

The Seminary restaurant was popular with cops, but the two across the room from us munched their food and didn't bother us. With John broke, paying was up to me. I knew better than to ask whether Ruby had any money. Chicks ride free. After she went to the toilet, John shook his head in approval.

"You did good, Ron. Fat chicks are hotter than skinny ones in bed."

"Yeah, she's a real firecracker. Turns me on, belly roll and all."

John laughed. "Gives you something to grab onto while you ride." He demonstrated as if pulling in the reins of his mount while he jerked his pelvis forward. "Ride 'em, cowboy! Get it?"

The crude way he put it made me laugh, despite my efforts not to. John turned serious.

"We got to find you two a bed for tonight. Your luck will run out if you don't fuck her good and proper soon."

Coming back into the booth, Ruby said, "I need a better place to freshen up. There's a guy I know lives around here. Let's go." She led us a few blocks down Halstead.

A tall, debonair black man answered our knock. He wore a long tan duster buttoned only at his neck, which hung like a cape over his shoulders and down his back. That, with a wide-brim hat tuned up at one side, gave him a dashing look.

"Hi Duke." Ruby smiled up at him. "So good to see you, man."

"Ruby!" He greeted her with a wide grin and open arms, causing a wave of jealousy in me that I swallowed down hard. She'd fucked him for sure, but what right did *I* have to be jealous?

She asked her ever-present question. "Got any uppers, Duke?"

"Still the same old Ruby, I see." He laughed and slapped his thigh. "Bring your friends on in." With a sweeping bow, he waved us through the door. At the kitchen table, he uncapped a medicine bottle to pour out a small handful of pills. "Save a few for later."

Cuba Si

"Where's the bathroom, Duke? I gotta go-now!" After a full breakfast and a walk, nature's urgent call hit me suddenly and hard. After a bigger dump than usual, I almost bumped into Ruby on her way in after me. She no sooner shut the door behind her than she charged back out.

"Jesus Christ, Ron!" she shouted loud enough for everyone to hear. "You can sure stink up a bathroom!"

All I could do was apologize. I hoped I hadn't blown my chance with her. In the living room, John ask Duke if he knew a place we could crib tonight.

"Sorry, John, I like to keep things *just so*. You and your people can't stay here, but I tell you what, there's a dude over on Howe Street who might help. He's one of those Castro loving revolutionaries."

Duke offered to store my heavy duffel in his closet for a few days. It didn't contain much beyond my clothes, sleeping bag and my well-used Evens-Wenz book, and lugging it around was a drag. A profound feeling of weightlessness came over me as I dropped it in his care. With lighter hearts, we continued our quest for lodging.

Howe came to a dead-end at a dilapidated one-story house. A long white banner hung over the porch proclaiming: *Power to the People!* That must be the place.

A thin, wispy bearded man dressed like Che Guevara in a black beret with a red star answered the door. We told him we were Duke's friends and asked if we could crash for a few days. He looked us over a long moment before answering.

"Only for tonight. You dig? I got some, like, *heavy* people coming in." He waved us inside. "Care for some smoke and chamomile tea?"

He came across as a serious yet mellow fellow, rolling a joint as we sat around the kitchen table sipping tea and talking revolution. In a quiet, self-assured voice. He bragged about belonging to the Young Lords, a Puerto Rican street gang that evolved into a Revolutionary organization, in tight with the Black Panthers.

"You better be goddamn ready," He nodded his head in solemn emphasis. "*The shit is going to hit the fan* soon." It was an expression I was to hear with increasing frequency in the coming months.

We went out to check on apartments. Nothing panned out, even when I passed Ruby off as my wife. She got a kick out of that, laughing too loud, which didn't go over well with the humorless landlord.

"Fuck him," she snarled as we walked away. Then she started laughing again. "Did ya hear that?" She elbowed John, who shrugged his shoulders. "Ron called me his wife." She smiled, giving me the eye as if the idea amused her. "Jeez! Think I'd say yes if he asked me?"

John grinned back at her. "Come on. Don't you just love this crazy dude?"

"Shit, I don't know. What about lust? That's way better than some creepy-ass love."

"Right," I said, unsure what else to say, but I had to come up with something. "Shit, yeah, Ruby. What the hell good is love without lust, anyway? I'm definitely in lust with you, babe."

Ruby shot me a crooked smile. Without warning, she stuck her hand down my pants to give my dick a nice squeeze. Wow! It turned hard in an instant. I loved a forthright woman. She sure knew how to keep my interest. Things would work out for us; all we needed was a place to make it happen.

By late afternoon, we returned to spend the night with the Cuban. There was only one big bedroom in the small ramshackle house. In a show of unexpected generosity, he offered it to Ruby and me. For himself, he pulled out a mattress on the back porch while John flaked out on the couch in the living room. When I thanked him, he smiled and shook his head.

"Power to the People, man! We're all here for each other. Dig? You and your lady could use a little privacy."

The poor water pressure in the shower came out lukewarm. Ruby and I made the best of it, my first time showering with a woman. Ruby was only my second sex partner, and it had been months since Joanne went back to her husband, but I said nothing about that as we jumped naked into a real bed. She popped her last *upper*.

"Fuck me, Ron," she yelled far too loud as she pulled me on top of her. "Goddamn it, man, give it to me! Come on, harder, faster, fuck me!"

Jeez, she'd freak out our friends, or even the whole neighborhood! Ruby was a wild force of nature, unlike any girl I'd known. With her enthusiastic encouragement, I overcame my gentle start, and I rammed into her while she bucked up against me with surprising ferocity. All too soon, despite my effort to hold back, I exploded and felt my dick softening.

"Did you come already?" she rasped. Before I could answer, she flipped us over and rode me hard, a cowgirl on a bronco, her tits and belly-roll bouncing up and down, desperate to *come* before my dick became useless.

"Squeeze my tits," she commanded. "Oh, yeah, now bite em... harder, hurt me, goddamn it!" Her fingernails tore into my shoulders. She threw her head back and emitted a throaty roar befitting a tigress. I'd not seen such a climax–a vision of the blood-drinking goddess Kali in a furious trance, trampling her dying Lord Shiva. *Om Mahadevi!*

Not quite sated, she rolled off to my side. Her billowy tits heaved, like undulating waves on the cosmic sea as Ruby caught her breath beside me. I didn't know whether I should apologize for my hasty orgasm or say nothing and just hold her. Finally, she sat up and scolded me.

"Sorry, Ruby, but I only need a breather before I'm ready again." She had to have fucked enough guys to understand our biology. What she said next blew me away.

"The boys at school called me a real whore after they fucked me."

"Oh, no, Ruby, I ..."

"Shush!" She touched my lips with her fingers and then sat up to look down at me with her lewd and crooked smile. Her voice turned husky. "That's all right, Ron. Fuck, it really turns me on. All that soft romantic shit doesn't work for me. See? I am a whore." She said it so matter of fact as if whore was the most natural thing to call oneself. "I'm proud of it, too. I love sex."

"Well, I don't want to hurt you, Ruby. I've always been told women need to be treated gently by a restrained, romantic man."

She giggled. "I don't want a damn chick, you know! Think I'd let you hurt me? I'm a fucking masochist. I need some pain to feel a rush, to be alive!" She lowered her eyelids and ran her fingers down my chest to circle my navel. Her husky voice lowered. "I want a real man, not a fucking pussy." She grabbed my cock and milked it. "So, give it to me rough, stay hard on me, dude, and you won't regret it!"

Her raunchy speech worked magic. My dick came alive for her much sooner than I expected. Seizing the moment, she jumped astride me again. The second time outdid the first. I released my pent-up emotions and gave my all, manhandling her without restraint. Flipping her into new positions, different angles, that produced new exciting results for her and me, too.

Keep in control, I told myself, enjoying the sight and feel of her ecstatic response, such heady pleasure that I almost gave way too. Only after she had several shuddering orgasms, following one after the other in rapid succession, did I let myself go. My sperm seemed to explode from every cell in my body. *Fuck yeah!* Simultaneously with Ruby, I went over the top.

Exhausted and sweaty after our shattering thunderstorm, Ruby passed out in my arms. I held her to my chest like a child, as if I could protect her from the world and even from herself. Sleepless, I rested in passion's afterglow, playing with her long black hair. Joyous, tender emotions mixed with a confusing kaleidoscope of emotions. She aroused raw sexuality that felt natural, like putting on well-fitted gloves. Ruby wanted sterner stuff, and I needed to whip her in line, get her off drugs, and keep her hooked on me.

Who was this wild woman who proclaimed herself a whore and a masochist? If she was a masochist, did that make me a sadist? I had to admit I enjoyed the role, but only as an erotic game to play with her, without the approbation society put on it. She had to be at least three years older than my seventeen years. I pondered our twists of fate. What had Ruby had been through to shape her desperate need for drugs? Would she burn as bright without them? I hoped so, because like a moth to the flame, her fire attracted me. She was dynamite with a short fuse, but I didn't want to tame her, only to push the chemicals out of the picture. Maybe I could *fuck* that shit out of her head.

Morning After Blues

The Cuban was sitting up on his mattress reading the latest issue of the Chicago SEED. He couldn't have slept much, so I apologized for the noise Ruby and I made in the night.

"It's all cool, man, don't sweat it." He touched his forehead in a salute. "You're a lucky guy. She's one wild chick, isn't she? Glad you two got your rocks off."

What a big-hearted guy. He served us more chamomile tea, but we wouldn't impose on his frugal breakfast.

On our way back up Halstead to the restaurant, I spotted a sign over a small brick building, the Chicago Zen center. I decided to investigate. Some people thought Zen meant behaving oddly and doing the unexpected, but I'd read enough to know that was only a cartoonish pop-culture take on a much deeper spiritual tradition.

"Wait a minute." I opened the waist-high iron gate and marched up the short brick walkway through a tidy lawn lined with flowerbeds to the heavy black door. A middle-aged Japanese man in black robes answered the bell.

"Can I help you?"

"Yeah, I'm curious about Zen meditation. Can I come here to try it sometime?"

A young close-cropped American in street clothes came up behind him and took over.

"We're not open today. Our times are posted on the door. We have zazen, or sitting meditation twice a week, with special meetings on Sunday."

Zen would have to wait until I'd gotten settled in. Back on the sidewalk, my companions waited with obvious impatience. Ruby demanded, "What're you talking to them weirdos for?" John sounded peeved. "Come on, Ron, we're starving!"

Back at the Seminary restaurant, it was again up to me to pay the bill. With her stomach full, Ruby's other needs came to the fore. "I gotta find some uppers," she said far too loud.

"Shush," I warned her. "Cops come in and out of here all the time."

"Fuck you, Ron. Let's get outta here then."

We wandered over to Wells, where we spotted a pale, rail-thin white guy, whose whole body jerked in flamboyant spasms as he paced the sidewalk, jiving with a couple of Puerto Rican guys. An obvious speed freak, he dressed in an unbuttoned pin-striped blue and gray suit jacket that didn't reach his wrists and with no shirt underneath to cover his hairless chest. He made an incongruous sight, even in Old Town.

Ruby ran up to embrace him, gushing her litany of desire. "Got any uppers, man? I need a real good supply."

The speed freak winked at his companions as he put his arm around her fleshy middle and chuckled. "Come with me, sugar. I'll take care of ya." He slid a hand under her top to grab a tit as he led her away into an alley. "Oh, yeah, girl, I'll take care of you *really* good."

"Where ya going, Ruby?" I demanded.

Speedy leered back at me. "Me and Ruby got some negotiation to do." His grimacing friends backed up to him as though part of the package. "We'll mix our business and pleasure, just like we always do. Right, babe?" He evil-eyed me as he reeled her along.

"Fuck it, Ruby, don't go!"

She half turned and called back to me, "See ya around, Ron. Be cool. Okay?"

I started after them. "Fuck it! You don't need that shithead!"

John grabbed me. "Don't try to stop her, man. She won't come and believe me; those boys will cut you up." He pulled me into a café where he let me spill my guts over a cup of Joe.

"Fuck that bitch, John! Last night I'd been too much of a goddamn gentleman. Now look how she treats me! I want to fuck that bitch hard and ruthless now. She needs that more than some fucking speed, and so do I!"

John was a good listener, nodding in agreement. "Guess you love that hot, big titted mama, don't you, Ron?"

His words jarred me out of self-pity into the revelation of what a hypocrite I was. Love? That misused word rarely meant altruism, caring for someone with no strings attached. Lovers want to possess the object of their desire, a selfish, spiritually unworthy emotion, and yet there I was in its grip. I wanted to keep Ruby just like I'd wanted Joanne and Rae or any number of other ill-fated infatuations. In our pitiless fast passed world, love, our *oh so necessary* carnal, human love, had to be grabbed at the moment or lost forever to dreams and nightmares. Fantasy was never enough for me. I needed to touch and feel.

I cared about Ruby. Yes, I would miss her wild spirit as much as her voluptuous body. We humans are more than cerebral creatures, and I would not deny that essential ingredient, LUST! Full of confession, I hated to lose her massive tits, her jiggling belly-roll, and sweet ass. Fat chance I'd succeed in fucking her drug needs out of her. John was right. Chasing after her would have been useless. Chances are she'd overdose, end up on a mortician's slab someday. Such a fucking waste, but coming clean would be up to her.

Our time together was far too short. There were others out there, but Ruby's raw wildness was hard to match. She had to learn to temper her fire, or burn up.

A year later, a friend ran into Ruby and happened to mention my name.

"Oh," she responded. "You know Ron? We hung out. He was an all right dude, except he was into all that spiritual crap."

At Loose Ends

John sighed. "We ain't getting any luck finding a crib up here on the Northside, Ron." He opened the fresh newspaper to the rental section. "Let's try our luck in Hyde Park. The University of Chicago is down there." He nodded, smiling encouragement at me. "It's closer to *my* people on the Southside, too, but not right in the damn ghetto. Hyde Park used to be a high-tone area, rich. Now it's filling up with hippies and students, our kind of people."

I'd been to the Museum of Science and Industry but never explored more of south side Chicago. From the 51st Street El stop, we walked east. Black men in fedoras and long coats stood along the sidewalk, opening their coats as we reached them to expose shiny trinkets that hung within.

"See here, man," they whispered. "I got gold chains, watches, jewelry, cut-rate stuff. See anything you like for your gal back home?"

It had to be *hot*, stolen merchandise. The patrol car parked across the street didn't faze them. I wondered if they paid off the cops or just brazened it out. The atmosphere changed as we walked along 55th Street, which became the broad, parklike Hyde Park Boulevard.

A few multi-racial couples strolled, hand in hand, or pushed baby carriages. That idyllic scene gave me hope for Chicago's transformation. Hyde Park appeared to be an integrated island of *hip* liberal whites and blacks. Run-down mansions of the long departed pampered rich were being transformed into multi-family apartment houses. Some of them had wide front porches, perfect for hanging out with friends and beer.

Our first stop was a bookstore where John thought we could find information posted on a bulletin board. We came upon a scene of chaos or opportunity. Coins covered the floor. Whether from a robbery or a clumsy accident, the change drawer had spilled from the cash register. It represented manna from heaven to us. A middle-aged woman called to us over her shoulder as she ducked into a back room.

"Just a minute! I'll be right with you."

"Grab some," John whispered. I began grabbing handfuls and shoving my pockets full. John didn't dive in himself but critiqued my performance.

"Forget the dimes and nickels, man. Go for the quarters and half dollars!"

Too late. The clerk ran back from whatever emergency had called her away and she shrieked at me. "How could you do this to me? Give it all back!"

I fished out a shallow handful of coins from my pocket and handed it to her.

"Give me all of it," she insisted.

"That's all I've got," I lied, backing out the door.

I felt guilty, taking advantage of the poor lady's predicament. Maybe she'd have to make up the difference to her boss. Assuaging my conscience, I told myself we were redistributing the wealth as if this little bookstore epitomized the capitalist establishment. Anyway, I'd gotten too many dimes and not enough quarters, amounting to less than three bucks.

"Some take," John mocked.

"Well, I didn't see you stooping to grab any."

"Because I'm black. Dig? They'd drop a more serious charge on my ass than a white boy like you would ever get."

The appointments we'd set up didn't pan out any better than up north. John said he could find us a crib in his south side neighborhood, the ghetto, but as a white guy, I wouldn't survive the gangs. "They'd cut you up in no time," he insisted. Black disenfranchisement caused a homicidal backlash of anger that no paleface could ignore if he wanted to keep in one piece.

"Hey," John said, pointing at a theater marque that proclaimed a movie named *IF*, starring Malcolm McDowell in his first role. "What a weird title that is. We ought to take us a break from all this walking around."

We mixed in with the crowd to kill time. It proved to be a fictional story of a student revolution in a stuffy British private school. It took our mind off our predicament and brought home, more than all my reading, how fortunate I was not to grow up in that hierarchal country. A few surreal sequences seemed as dreamy-weird as my own life had become. Sad to say, that movie was the high point of our fruitless excursion to Hyde Park. Leaving the theater, we rapped with someone who pointed us to a crash pad. Unfortunately, the place was crowded as well. John didn't trust it, and we split.

With no particular place to go, John and I rode the El across the length of Chicago. At the end of the line, John and I got off one train and boarded another, traveling back and forth on an endless loop for an eternity. The demarcation lines between day and night blurred. His money still hadn't materialized. The costs of daily living, eating one or two greasy spoon meals a day, diminished my funds and affording an apartment became less likely. We managed brief snatches of insufficient sleep huddled on the rocking, *clickity-clacking* train. John droned on about how *bad* we needed our crib until he lost consciousness. Then there were the nightmares he'd warned me about.

"Ahh! Get off me, goddamn it!" He jerked up straight and lashed at the empty space before him, looking bug eyed at the blank faces of the other passengers. His face relaxed when he noticed me beside him. He exhaled a long sigh, like a deflating balloon, shook himself and chuckled, trying to laugh it off.

"Them goddamn Chinese soldiers are jumping into my foxhole again. *Ha-ha*, those ghosts are still trying to kill me." The Korean War ended in a truce seventeen years ago, but for John, it replayed in his head every day.

Shadows chased me, too. Hallucinatory images blended with my waking reality. Solid shapes took on weird forms, like I was tripping on acid. The present intertwined with beguiling memories of what should have become my future. All the love I'd ever wanted tormented me in dreams of my lost paradise.

Tike's yellow hair shimmered under the bright New Mexico sun. She smiled her love at me while nursing baby Zon at her overflowing breast. Beside us, raven-haired Joanne winked and nodded her assent.

"Go ahead, Ron. We're one big family here."

Tike's pert nipples oozed her bounty of milk. They tasted so sweet in my mouth. She threw her head back, laughing, "I have plenty for both of you!" I felt her hot breath as she kissed the back of my neck while I licked her excess nectar.

The booming thunderclap of Joe Sage's voice interrupted us.

"Your Karma will follow you!"

WILL FOLLOW YOU! The words echoing loud in my brain jarred me awake. I blinked, refocused my eyes to find myself back in Chicago. Beside me, John's stubbled salt and pepper head swayed with the train's rhythm. It had been a dream, an echo of my lost Eden, a remembrance of the brief happiness I tasted only three months ago. The memory of how Joe Sage, the *mad monk* of Taos, drove me from our love family was still fresh and painful, a wound that refused to heal.

Initially, Joe accepted me with open arms. I was a hard worker who tried to ignore his irrational mood swings. But that ill temper drove away Joanne, my first love. Finally, I just had to open my mouth and disagree with him in a meek, quiet voice. That's all it took for him to kick me out. Everyone else, including Tike, just sat there, too cowed to stick up for me. Joe's overreaction made no sense. I was still trying to figure out what I could have done or said differently, but at seventeen years of age, I had no idea how to stand up to Joe.

John and I finally stepped off the El to wander the still empty streets of Old Town. We'd become urban nomads, refugees from the American Dreamscape, hunting a place to live or even just to lay our heads. We were homeless in Chicago, hoping to build our own utopia, an open, loving, forgiving culture with new companions. The Age of Aquarius was only a dream. It was up to us to make it reality.

Bone tired, we plopped on the cool, green grass of Lincoln Park to warm ourselves under the slow rising summer sun. John insisted on leaning up against a tree, as if on guard duty, while I flopped flat. Drifting in and out of sleep, I raised my head to see John's chin fallen onto his chest. God, he needed sleep. Then, through bleary eyes, I watched the scene unfolding around us. White, black and Puerto Rican bodies wandered by, wearing new mod styles or the bleached and tie-dyed fashions of *Stone Freaks*.

A trio came our way. Two dark featured Hispanic dudes, immersed in conversation, they passed a joint between them. The pale, blonde, frizzy haired woman ambling along at their side stood out. She swung her hips with a wide, undulating gait that reminded me of a South Asian Temple Dancer. Her skimpy blue blouse covered only part of her ample bosom, while her flat midriff gyrated, belly dancing above low hung jeans. Spotting me gazing at her, she took the joint, inhaled deep and headed our way like a succoring angel.

"Wanna hit?" She offered me the joint as if it was a sacrament, and I received it as such. Being glassy-eyed enhanced her celestial beauty. After a toke, I tried to hand it back.

"No, man, you keep it," she said with a regal, blitzed out smile and swiveled her way back to her group. I passed the joint to semi-conscious John.

A profound feeling of limitless love and bliss radiated through my body; I saw the world with new eyes. The dreamy girl was an angel dispensing divine revelation. All these strangers cruising by seemed more beautiful, generous bodhisattvas in the making. They were linked to me in the most intimate, spiritual way. Through eons of incarnations, we'd all nurtured, loved, and served each other as parents and lovers by turns. These passing human shapes were all *our* people. Although John and I were homeless, we were where we belonged among them. They, too, were fellow travelers on life's wild ride to the far side. Arriving there, even death would welcome us into further dimensions.

My mind returned to Ruby with great tenderness. Although a druggie who chose a mad *rush* over me, she'd enriched and blessed me with the experience of her body and the heady taste of her wild, untamed energy. My initial anger at losing her gave way to gratitude.

But what would become of her? Without a dominant partner to master her, one who kept his erotic sadism within safe bounds, she'd crash and burn like a shooting star. She needed a bodhisattva lover, someone like me, of course! Maybe her masochism, with a controlling, sadistic edge, would be her path to divinity. She was beyond my control, but I offered a prayer to the unseen forces who aid us all.

John leaned over me. "Everything cool with you, man?"

"Yeah, John. Wow, that was some grass. Huh?"

"They might've put something in it."

"Just watching that chick walk over here was like, amazing! Gave me a contact high before I even had a toke."

"We just gotta get us a crib, man, a place for *us* to chill and bring chicks. Dig?"

We drifted back into semi-consciousness. Suddenly, John's panicked face reappeared above me as he shook me awake. "Come on, Ron, I lost it a minute. We could have been jumped! We gotta get. Now!"

"What's the rush, man? We got nowhere to go."

The sun was low on the horizon, but I didn't see any reason to get up yet. Maybe he'd had one of his nightmares. Zombielike, we rose from the ground. Our bodies cooking up an adrenaline stew to keep plodding along to where we knew not. But once up, it surprised me how refreshed, almost clear headed I felt. Maybe it was true, sleep was only a slice of death, cheating us of valuable time that slipped through our fingers like sand through an hourglass.

The Mexican Dude

Alice's looked dead. No unoccupied chicks, like Ruby or Carol, the one-armed prostitute, to welcome us to their table. Disappointed, we wandered back down Lincoln, where fortune, in the form of a pretty woman, smiled upon us. Although she hung on the arm of a long-faced bearded man who carried a bag of groceries, she hailed us in good cheer.

"Hi, guys! Come smoke a joint with us!"

They led us to a cozy one-bedroom apartment overlooking Lincoln. A little Mexican guy sat rolling a joint with two skinny white freaks in their early twenties. We joined them in a circle around a low coffee table on the carpeted floor.

Lighting up, the Mexican said, "I sing my special song for you. I call *Happy Marijuana*." He exhaled a lungful of smoke and then performed the simple tune as he passed it around. It sounded like a childish birthday song.

"Happy Marijuana, happy marijuana, happy marijuana to you!" He chuckled, immediately firing up another joint while continuing to sing. After that one finished making the rounds, tears welled up in his eyes. He hugged his knees to his chin in a fetal position. Although still in his early twenties, he seemed to age before me as if in a surreal movie. He rocked back and forth as he transformed into a broken old man.

"I got something to tell you, man." he spoke in a sort of trance. "What happen in my country last year? I've seen so much blood, so much murders. You know? The Falcons, man, they killing us!"

The Falcons? I rewound my memory of last year's news. The *Falcons* were the right-wing paramilitary in Mexico, tools of the State, and unofficial dogs of war.

The *whole world was watching* in 1968, the year before, when the Yippees confronted the Chicago police at the Democratic Convention, but it wasn't only in the States. People were standing up, demanding accountability from our governments, the freedom to speak out. Popular uproar exploded in Czechoslovakia, France, and Mexico.

Mexican students hit the streets, chanting and waving banners after the Army closed the National University. It looked more hopeful than it had in Czechoslovakia, a Russian satellite that sent out tanks to quell demonstrations. Mexico should be different because it claimed to be a democracy and would host the Olympics, but the government responded with a massacre. Their Falcons opened fire on the students with machine guns, killing others execution style, up close and personal.

"They said only forty-nine killed," the little Mexican said. "Shit, man, you can't believe the fucking newspapers. I've seen hundreds lying dead in the street!"

We *Norte Americanos* sat there; some of us too stoned to respond and the others unsure what to say. Our wide-eyed blond hostess finally blurted out, "That could never happen in our free country."

"What do ya mean?" I countered. "It already has!" Realizing they had no grasp of history, I filled them in. "Countless times they've shot down labor union people, like the Ludlow massacre in Colorado and at the Haymarket right here in Chicago. What do you think happened on a smaller scale at the '68 Convention?"

Gazing across the room, as if into a time-space warp, the teary-eyed Mexican told his tale of woe. "Like, I've seen it all, you know, the blood, the dead bodies on the fucking street, man. I've *seen* 'em!"

He'd fled from the horror to find refuge in *Gringolandia*, as he called it. He only wanted to hear the vague assurances of love and peace from flower children, sing his simple songs, and smoke enough dope to hide the awful images that raged inside his skull.

The Mexican's story was one more incentive for me to fight back against the machine. Our government pulled the strings on how other countries clamped down on their people, creating cheap markets to enrich those at the top. We needed a fucking revolution!

John nudged me awake, whispering, "Time to go." On automatic pilot, I followed him to the street. Then my brain clicked back on.

"Did they kick us out?"

"I was getting bad vibes, Ron. We weren't welcome."

"Shit, John! We could've stayed 'til morning. They all looked zonked to me."

"It didn't feel right."

"Why so, John? The chick stayed in the bedroom with her boyfriend. The skinny guy crashed in the corner near the Mexican. It was safer than anywhere we've been." It dawned on me how paranoid John was. Maybe partnering with him wasn't to my best advantage.

Outside, John nudged me. "We ought to go check out places in Wilmette, in the northern suburbs, lots of hippies there."

The Blackfoot Girl

Our perambulations took us to Clark Street, where a short, squat chick with long black hair in her early twenties stepped out of a Mom and Pop store, struggling with an armful of groceries as she fell in beside us.

"Hey, boys, want to help me with these?" Her oversize belly hung over her belted shift, making her a much rounder and heavier version of Ruby. Her light bronzed skin gave her a Native American look.

"Sure," John said.

"I'm not far up the street. Where you guys going anyways?"

"Nowhere, in particular. We don't have a place to stay."

"Cool," she smiled and gave me the eye. "You can crash at my place tonight. It's kind of small but warm."

I smiled back at her, but tried to keep my demeanor neutral. She had a faint rancid smell about her I'd noticed with some overweight chicks. It turned me off, although I didn't want to offend her.

"I'm Clara from Montana. Ever been there?"

John shook his head. "No, but I've been to California, Japan and Korea."

"Nope," I told her. "But I wandered through the Indian

reservations in Arizona and New Mexico." Acting on my hunch, I asked. "Are you Indian?"

"You guessed it! I'm a member of the Blackfoot Nation."

"What a coincidence. I lived with a Blackfoot Indian in New Mexico named Joe Sage. Ever hear of him?"

She shook her head no.

"Joe founded our commune, which he called the Family. We were all in an open marriage with each other. The others, mostly from Haight-Ashbury, were great people, but Joe was always stomping around, angry all the time, hard to please." I debated telling her more, but decided to keep it under wraps. My feelings about Joe's crazy personality and the Family wavered between guilt, anger, and the sorrow of lost love, too hard to articulate.

We carried her load of groceries upstairs to her tiny unkempt studio apartment on the third floor. John and I took turns in her shower, a very welcome delight that we needed. Then John gravitated to a chair by the window. He seemed taken with the view of the street below while our voluble hostess focused her attention on me. She filled me in on Blackfoot customs in a direct and personal way.

"In our tradition, a girl's father teaches her all she needs to know about sex." She shot me a coy, sideways glance. "He becomes her first lover." She nodded, insisting on the veracity of her words. "He breaks her cherry, gentler that a boyfriend would, like my daddy did." She laughed, nervous, as if unsure how I'd respond.

Her story made me squeamish, but I doubted she would make up something like that. I hid my surprise, wondering whether a father's incest with his daughter was an *official* Blackfoot tradition. Joe Sage had a huge sexual appetite, which he lauded as a sign of vital health. I'd heard the tribes had orgies on the long winter nights back in the old days.

"Maybe your dad was just a dirty old man?"

"Oh, no, he was a good, kind man, acting out of love. It wasn't just me, you know, all my girlfriends got broken in by their dads." She gave me a cheerful wink. "Who better to break a girl's cherry than her own father? Right?"

The Victorian attitude of seeing rape, unwanted sex as *a fate worse than death* always bothered me. It remained with us as part of our sexual double standard, but Clara didn't seem traumatized. She hadn't been raised to view herself as a victim, to categorize her sexual experience as a wrong done to her by someone she loved, and yet, there was a limit to how open-minded I could be. Incest just didn't seem healthy, not from a genetic perspective, at least. But I believed in surviving and healing from our psychic harm.

Trauma is an integral part of life. From the moment of birth, when we're yanked out of the birth canal, to being bullied by strict, unyielding parents, teachers, military officers, or random bullies, we all get a share of it. There's no escape until death, so we may as well try to make peace, even learn to enjoy some of the drama as a challenge. Anything that didn't kill or maim us could be overcome by opening our minds to face our true, cosmic identity. We were all divine, eternal beings who could laugh at the temporal dramas.

John, a few feet away, fidgeted at the window. "I'll get some air. Be right back." Clara's story might have sickened him, or maybe he wanted to give us some alone time.

Clara made her move. She pulled off her top, exposing sagging breasts, and lay back on her bed in the warm room. "Come on, Ron," she beckoned me between her legs. "Let's get busy!"

My feelings were conflicted. Pity overwhelmed my lust, inhibiting me. I saw her more as a victimized sister than someone I wanted to fuck, yet she needed love and was *not* my sister. I was supposed to be a compassionate yogi, not a selfish prick. Overcoming my qualms, giving her a rocking good time, hurt no one and would be an act of selfless love. Whereas I'd found Ruby's belly-bulge under her large top-rack erotic, Clara's butterball and rancid scent put me off. I'd have to think of Ruby to get my dick hard for her, and that struck me as less than chivalrous to her. In my mind, a guy should focus on the lover or lovers he's with, not some absent fantasy.

Another idea popped into my head. John hadn't gotten laid yet. A good fuck would do both of them good. When he came back in, I stood up and waved my hand over her body, offering him the half-naked girl.

"Hey John, this sweet girl needs love." Clara giggled, jiggling her flesh. She seemed to like the attention. "I had Ruby, remember? It's only fair for you to get some."

"What?" John's mouth popped open and his eyes bugged out. My generous offer, worthy of a bodhisattva in the Jataka Tales, must have overwhelmed him. I turned to Clara, suddenly realizing that I ought to have asked her first. Times had changed since the days of ancient India.

"You don't mind, do you, Clara? John is my partner, and we gotta look out for each other." Clara, serene and wordless, shot us both a coy smile. I interpreted it as an eager affirmation of all I'd said, but John's reaction surprised me.

"God, what do you think I am, anyway?" He stomped back to his chair by the window, on guard against phantom enemies.

"Come on, John!" I tried to mollify him. "You know I didn't mean anything bad by that. We're partners, right? I would've shared Ruby with you, too, even though I was crazy about her, speed freak that she was." I thought up more arguments. "Sex is sacred, you know. It makes our tough life worth living. Sharing Clara between us would be Holy Communion. Dig what I'm saying? If you join in, we'll make a holy trinity."

Clara pulled me back on the bed, giggling, and snuggled up to me. Her warm, naked body looked ever more appealing, although her scent still held me back. I'd fix that.

"Why don't you take a shower with us, girl?"

She glared at me, offended. "Fuck you, Ron. I showered an hour ago." She sat up, cupped her sagging breasts, and lifted them at me like a gunslinger at High Noon. "See these? If neither of you guys can appreciate that you've got a horny woman here, ready to go, you're just a couple of limp dicks."

She made her point. I debated whether to overcome my qualms and show compassion by satisfying her. My knowledge of Tantric sex was theoretical; I needed more practical experience.

"Aw, shit." John harrumphed, came over and squeezed onto the single sized bed beside us, but unlike Clara and me, he kept his clothes on.

As if comforting a patient, I just held her in my arms, wondering if I was virtuous or too damn prissy to initiate sex. I left it up to her, but still upset with me, she turned to John and pushed my hand away.

"Come on, Johnny boy," she whispered in his ear. "I bet you got a nice hard dick for me." I heard her unzip his jeans, but then the sound of snoring arose from him. She clucked, disgusted. "Man, I really hit the jackpot with you dudes this time."

Cuddling Clara's hot, fleshy body between us in the overheated apartment, we didn't need a blanket, but with so little sleep over the past few days, John and I were dead to her. None of us got any sexual satisfaction that night. Awaking with my usual morning hard-on, I felt guilty about ignoring Clara and rubbed against her.

"Ah, let me sleep. You boys had your chance. I gotta get up to work soon."

"Come on, Ron." John waved me up. "We gotta go too."

As I got dressed, I told Clara, "We could come back tonight."

"Don't bother." She pressed her face into the pillow. "I don't need your fucking games."

"Look," John said. "Your studio is way too small, anyway. We need a bigger place."

"Well, okay. Why don't you guys come back when you've found someplace and are ready for me? You'll find out what a hot mama I am."

Her words made me regret I didn't give her what she needed from me. My compassion needed a lot of work.

Wilmette Sherry

We trekked back to Duke's to pick up my duffel bag, but I found my Tibetan Yoga book missing after a thorough search.

"Hey, Duke, are you reading my book?"

"Shit, no, I didn't touch your stuff. It's been right there in the closet since you left."

"I stuck it in the very bottom of my bag. It's not there now."

I'd grown attached to that book, but as hectic as my life was without a place to call home base, there wasn't time to read, anyway. This was my chance to practice openhanded generosity as I lightened my load. I only hoped Duke would get something out of it.

Exiting the Wilmette train station, we turned right through a quiet park. A slim, well-dressed girl sat alone, her heels tucked underneath her on the grass. She wore black-rimmed glasses and had a small bust. Without a strand of her coiffed brown hair out of place, she looked like she might be on a lunch break from an office job. Her intense gaze strayed from the book in her lap to scan passersby with curious interest.

John surprised me by taking the lead, approaching her with a cheerful greeting. She smiled and nodded when he asked if we could join her. I wasn't sure if she was being polite or bored enough for our company. After some small talk with John, she zeroed in on me.

"Do you meditate?"

"Sure, what makes you ask that?"

"You have that faraway look like you're seeking distant horizons. It's very becoming."

"Sounds nice. No one ever told me that before."

"I'm Sherry, by the way. Like the drink."

After I mentioned my interest in Tibetan Buddhism, we had a real conversation going. She was well versed in comparative religion and Madame Blavatsky, the nineteenth century stimulus to New Age religions. I spoke of my solitary meditations in the woods and travels in the Rockies. John regaled her with a dramatic telling of our recent adventures in seeking a *crib*. He fixed her with an earnest look.

"Ron and I are gonna get a commune going and share the rent. Could be right here in Wilmette. Maybe you'd like to join us?"

Sherry nodded and then added, "Let me show you around town. Ever seen the Baha'i temple?" She knew a lot about the faith, explaining that it accepted all religions as compatible, sincere attempts to awaken spirituality. Neither of us had ever been to Wilmette, and Sherry proved an excellent guide. We walked around the ornate domed Bahai temple. A surrounding ring of reflecting pools multiplied its image, like pictures I'd seen of the Taj Mahal. Sherry gave us the rundown on the place.

"It's built directly on the opposite side of the world from the holiest Bahai spot in Iran."

"Wow," John said. "It really dazzles in the sunlight."

We had a fun morning; however, finding an apartment eluded us. Sherry remained cheerful and joined her fortunes to our wandering band, on a journey to everywhere or nowhere. Sitting on the train back to Chicago, Sherry even offered to share her stash of acid with us.

Acid? In tailored skirt and nylons, she looked too square and well dressed to be a hippie.

John raised an eyebrow. "I ain't never took no acid before."

"Don't worry," Sherry said. "We could all trip together. It would be a wonderful bonding experience."

Wow, I wanted in on that. This would only be my second acid trip. My first had been a quadruple dose while I was all alone on the open road in Colorado. John looked askance as I tried to describe the wonder of it, saying, "Man, I don't need none of that shit!"

Sherry gave my hand a squeeze and looked into my eyes. "That must have been *heavy*. This time you'll be with friends instead of all alone with your mind blown."

The dynamics of our little group seemed compatible. John indicated his attraction to Sherry but wasn't making any overt moves on her. She was cordial to him, but focused more on me. Poor John, I didn't want him to feel left out. After all, I had to practice what I preached about generosity and overcoming jealousy. We needed to be a noble experiment and push our boundaries beyond ordinary, limited love. Our future together looked bright, except that I was running out of money and still supporting John.

We took the train back to the Chicago Loop. On the ride down, John wondered if he was ready for psychedelia. "Grass, beer and wine are enough for me, man. I don't know about that acid shit."

Sherry smiled and winked at me as if to say we'd drop it without him. I smiled and winked back.

The three of us slid into an empty booth in a homey looking joint. It reeked of deep fry cooking that fired our appetite for dinner, although it didn't clear my brain of worry. My wallet wasn't as fat as it had been a week ago, and we still hadn't found a place to live. I'd been avoiding a confrontation but had to speak up.

"I'll be broke soon," I announced. "When's your money gonna come in, John?"

"It's cool, Ron," Sherry said, grabbing my forearm. "I can pay my share."

"Thanks, Sherry, but it's about time John chipped in."

John frowned, inhaled, and let out a deep sigh. "Okay, man, I'll check on it."

"You better." I stared at him until he stood up. "Here's the dime."

As he went to the phone booth beside the restrooms, I apologized for being tough on John.

"Sorry, Sherry, but running from place to place with hardly any sleep for days, I'm burned out."

"Take a hit, Ron." Sherry leaned across the table and slipped me a tab. "I already popped mine. Looks like John isn't ready, and you need a new perspective." She was right, so down the hatch it went.

John came back looking sheepish. No bread yet. Maybe he was just a deadbeat, sponging off me to the bitter end. Fuck it, I had to wise up and look out for myself. After days of facing the world together, cutting him loose felt harsh, but we were getting nowhere. The waiter brought our food, and I put off the unpleasant task of confronting John.

More customers walked in, filling the tables. The middle-aged waiter in a stained white apron had his hands full. A heavyset man in a blue uniform with a holstered pistol sat up at the counter. Whether he was a cop or a security guard, his presence set me on edge.

After eating, John looked into my eyes. "Aw, goddamn it, Ron, you're tripping already! We were supposed to do it together, man!"

John's anger irritated me. We shouldn't be talking about this in a public place, especially with a cop in the room, but we had no private space. I kept my cool and tried to smooth it over.

"You didn't seem ready for this, John, but drop a tab now. We're only a little ahead of you."

"That's not the point," his face screwed up in righteous disgust. "What kind of partner are you, Ron?" He kept going on about it, pissing me off even more as the acid took effect. Wild sensations inundated me through all my portals. The room, along with the people around me, took on weird shapes. The walls rippled as if breathing in and out. Faces around me elongated, appearing kind or hostile by turns, sending paranoid chills through me. I didn't need to hear John's crap too.

"John, either take your hit right now or let it fucking go! And don't you call me a lousy partner. I've been supporting you all week!"

John's mouth moved in reply, but the sound was off. My attention scattered as color and sound swirled around me. I seemed to smell colors, especially red and green, which erupted from pieces of fabric, or a stripe on the posted menu. Images carried me to vivid memories of my forest bower and Christmas decor. But through it all, I couldn't allow myself to be ripped off. In a dangerous city like Chicago I shouldn't panic, so I put on a bold front and acted as if I had it all together like a rational guy.

Sherry's dilated eyes watched us in awe. Mine must have looked like hers. She said nothing and there was no sense dragging her into my stupid quarrel with John.

Suddenly, a holy light began shining around us, permeating the restaurant and everyone in it, including the cop. Divine blessings were at hand for all of us if we would but open our hearts. Our little drama felt so petty in the broad cosmic scheme, inspiring me to act on loftier, crazier thoughts. I picked up the bill and held it out before John's angry eyes.

"Look at this, John; I've been paying your way, haven't I? It's only money, sure, but we grub so hard for it all our fucking lives and our precious time keeps slipping by." I nodded with emphasis. "My eighteen-year-old cousin died of heart cancer only a few days after the diagnosis, just before that stupid moon landing that she never got to watch. Dig it? We're all only a heartbeat away from the great beyond. Every single moment, we get closer. Are you ready to die with this fucking shit on your mind?"

That shut him up. He'd told me about all the horrific deaths he saw in Korea, and his mind seemed to fly back there. I overheard the customers around us whisper. *He's tripping, alright.* Conversations ceased. It was so silent I could hear my heart beating out a drumroll in our drama. The waiter stood watching us with narrowed eyes. We were exotic hippies putting on a show for these straight, middle class folks. Perfect. Like a sermonizing preacher, I ramped it up for them.

Walking up to the cash register, I slapped my wallet on the counter and laid out my remaining bills and pocketful of change. Maybe twice what our bill required, but it amounted to less than we'd need to put down on even the cheapest apartment. That option, getting a crib and starting an urban commune, had evaporated. No matter how idealistic we tried to be, it always came down to cold, hard cash. It was the bottom line of our survival.

I held the bills up in my hands like an offering to gods and men. "See this." I swiveled around as I addressed everyone. "It's only colored paper; that's all money is. I worked my ass off for it, but it has less value than our human dignity."

In my LSD induced vision, a dollar bill changed value from a one into a ten or a twenty. Unable to make out the right amount, I handed the whole mess to the befuddled waiter. "Take all you need," I told him.

With a concerned frown, the waiter pushed my fistful of cash back. John, with an equal look of concern, stepped up and counted out the necessary amount, putting the remainder back in my wallet, and shoved it deep in my pocket. Neither of them attempted to profit from my sacrificial state, proving their integrity. I'd made my point. Maybe the presence of the cop, still munching his fries as he half turned to watch us, had something to do with it, but I shot them all a benign smile. These people seemed full of potential, true beings of light. As I began expounding on compassion and selfless giving, John and Sherry hustled me out the door.

Out on the sidewalk under the late afternoon sun, glass and steel buildings seemed to melt and vibrating into weird shapes. Metamorphosis was upon us. My body felt alien, more like a car I was driving, certainly not my permanent home. Maybe I was on the verge of a transcendent vision, but at the same time, I felt more distant, aloof from those around me.

Everything in my life was transient. People came and went.

There was no one I could hold on to for long. Walking that lonely path seemed to be my dharma, the divine plan for this lifetime. By clinging to companions, I'd fall short of my destiny, my best chance for enlightenment in this lifetime. Anyway, John was dragging me down, leeching off me. I couldn't keep supporting him.

"I'm almost flat broke, John." After speaking those words, which sounded like they came from somebody else, a dark cloud of urgency came over me. "We'd better split up for a few days so I can take care of it."

Looking befuddled, John asked, "A few days?"

That morning had been brimming with possibilities for us three wanderers. The acid blew away my rational thought process. Yet even in my stoned state, I wondered if I was pushing things too far. We might never see each other again.

John picked up a scrap of paper from the sidewalk. *Got a pen?* Sherry gave him one from her purse, and he scribbled. "Here." He handed it to me. "I don't remember the phone number, but that's the address of a pool hall on the south side. The guys who hang out there are a rough bunch, but they know how to reach me."

He put his hand on my shoulder and fixed me with a serious look, as if probing my soul, trying to determine if I'd gone insane. "Be careful going down there, man. It's the fucking ghetto, gang turf."

Sherry, as tripped out as I was, stared glassy eyed at me. In our day long acquaintance, I had gotten no solid details about her. Whether she was playing hooky from college, a job, a husband, or lived with her parents was a mystery. We'd been hitting it off so well; it would be crazy to walk away from her too. For a moment, I questioned what I was doing, but decided she would be safer with John than me. John had been my constant companion for a week, and despite being penniless, he'd proven himself an honorable guy. Anyway, he liked her, and I wouldn't screw up his chance at finding love.

My whole being was becoming translucent, turning into the Vajra Rainbow body the Tantras speak of. I had to focus my full attention on attaining that exalted state because, as a mere mortal, I could do nothing to help anyone.

Those two were the most important people in my life, but the cosmic light seemed to place me at a crossroads of destiny. Acid does that. Opening my arms, I gathered these beloved comrades to me in a group hug and felt their hot breath and the boom-boom of their hearts beating in sync with mine. A fountain of great love bubbled up within me.

Maybe I was misreading the psychic messages from on high, or maybe I should have asked them both to come along to fetch more money from my stash. Crazy. It never crossed my mind. Spending the night in Fischer's Woods was all I could offer them, anyway. Hoisting my duffle bag, I strode to the Lake Street El station.

To the Southside

The acid wore off by the time I awoke to birdsongs and rustling leaves. I found myself alone in the gently swaying tree house in Fischer's Woods. All seemed well until I remembered John Bell and Wilmette Sherry. The events of the day before came back. With a fresh and clear mind, I realized that I'd fucked up. It was one thing to leave John, but Sherry! Tripping on acid, she needed me as her copilot, and I'd abandoned her on the streets of Chicago. A wave of guilt spun my mind dizzy as I wondered how she managed.

Sherry would be good company; I'd have to make it up to her. Had she stuck with John or returned to Wilmette? With or without John in the picture, she and I might partner up. My thoughts about John remained confused. I'd been supporting him, he'd given me companionship, and we shared some heavy experiences, but I couldn't keep paying his way. It wasn't his fault. The ghosts of Korean battlefields still haunted him. I'd give him one last chance. If he didn't cough up some cash, I'd have to shake him loose.

Climbing down from my perch, I went to Lee Swanson to update him on my reconnaissance of Old Town's hip scene. I didn't have much to tell him. I'd just been wandering the streets with John in a fruitless search for a pad.

"Blacks call a place to live a crib," I told him, then gave him the latest copy of the SEED and the colorful brochure from the Process cult that merged God, Satan, and Lucifer as co-equal deities.

"I've already got that issue of the SEED, Ron. Can you get me some more insight into the Yippee and SDS Revolutionary groups?"

"Sure, Lee. Sorry I kind of got busy running in circles and didn't run into any of them, but after I go get some more of my savings, I'm heading back to find them."

I hightailed it over to Wood Dale for more cash from my stash. Mom, overjoyed to see me, gave me a hug, but my closet hiding place was empty. Despite her promise, Mom had deposited the rest of my savings in the bank beyond my control. It was her tactic to get me to return to my senses.

With pleading eyes, Mom begged, "Why won't you settle down, Ronnie? You could still get your job back at Beeline. Once you're eighteen, you know, the savings account will be yours. There's enough to buy a used car. Think of your future!"

My future lay far away from this place called home, but that was impossible to explain to Mom. My goal to start a commune in Chicago and join the Yippee revolution was undimmed; I just needed more time to explore the scene and figure it out. She handed me ten bucks, all she claimed to have on hand. When that ran out, I'd have to get by selling the SEED and other underground papers on the street. Other Freaks got by like that, and so would I.

Worried about how Sherry and Jim were doing, who suddenly loomed as my dearest companions, I cut my visit short to get back to them. But back in our Old Town haunts, I couldn't find them. My friends were nomads, moving targets. Walking those familiar streets, hearing only the hollow echo of my own footsteps, I missed them even more. People need each other, even if the give and take in the relationships aren't mutual.

The scrap of paper John wrote on was my only clue. I hoped he left a message for me at the pool hall. He warned me it was in territory hostile to the whites, turf of the Devil's Disciples and Blackstone Rangers. I stepped out of the el station, the only white in a sea of the blacks. People eyed me with palpable anger. I thought I'd mastered the southern drawl when I was down in New Orleans two years before, but the ghetto jargon, delivered in rapid, run together words, was another matter.

"*Gimmeyomoneyman!*"

"What?" I couldn't process that long, run together word.

The teenager repeated, "I say Gimmeyomoney, man!"

It didn't make sense until I replayed it in my head. He grabbed my shirt. I broke away and kept going. He ambled after me at a slow, deliberate pace. As if he had all the time in the world to nail me. I sped up, brushing past more young men in twos and threes at every other corner until, at last, I found the address of John's hang out.

Three tall, muscled men in white sleeveless tee shirts, what we called *dago tees,* stood blocking the door of the ramshackle pool hall, eyeing me with intense suspicion. My palms were sweaty, and my heart thumped loud as a church bell. I wondered if I was committing suicide. They challenged me as I charged up.

Where the hell you think yer goen', white boy?

Without answering, I barged into the cool, dark room that smelled of cigarettes and stale beer. Beyond several worn and chipped pool tables, the bald bartender beheld me with crossed arms and scrunched eyes. He looked no friendlier than the others, but I better understood his measured words.

"What the hell you doing here, white boy?"

"I'm looking for John Bell."

"Huh?" he blinked. "John Bell? What you want wid him?"

"Uh, I'm supposed to meet him here."

"Well, I don't know nothing 'bout that. He ain't been here in quite a spell. You best be gone before you find yourself some trouble."

The other men followed me in. Surrounding me, they discussed the situation. The barkeep condensed and explained their words in clear English. Finally, he wrote a number.

"Call this number. He just might be there." He pointed to the phone on the wall beside the bar. I dropped on a dime, conscious that all eyes were on me, and wondered if I was being set up.

"Hello there," a deep, sugary sweet voice answered. "Can I help you?"

"I'm looking for John Bell."

"Well, *he-he-he*, this is John, and who are you, my man?"

I didn't recognize the voice, but I played along. "This is Ron."

"Hel-lo, Ron. Where are you calling from?"

"I'm at the pool hall, the address you gave me."

"Very well. Wait right there. *He-he*, I'll be along shortly."

It didn't sound at all like the John I knew. Paranoia overwhelmed me, certain these guys were setting me up, but I kept my face blank. It could spell trouble if they knew I was wise to them. My only smart move was to scram while I could.

"I'll just wait outside," I told them and backed out. Once on the sidewalk, I broke into a trot back the way I'd come. More than ten blocks lay between me and the el station, a gauntlet of alert, hard-faced black youths again confronted me with rapid-fire demands.

Hey! Gimmeaquarter, man.

You got my money? What'ch you doing here, white boy?

I kept moving. A couple of the more aggressive guys followed me, and several more lounged ahead in the next corner. They had me trapped, like meat in a sandwich.

Then a breathless ten-year-old boy ran up beside me. "Mister!" He waved at me, but I suspected he was in cahoots with the others and didn't answer. "Mister, listen, you in big trouble, they gonna get you. Better take that bus!"

Swinging around, I saw a green and white CTA bus barreling along. Just in time, I jumped directly in front and held up my hand. It screeched to a stop, and I boarded.

"Sorry," I told the older black man driving. "I don't have any change, but those guys are after me. Please, could you get me closer to the el station and away from here?"

The kid yelled up to the driver's window, "That white man is in danger!"

The sympathetic driver shook his head, chuckling. "You know you're in the wrong part of town for a white man, son. What were you thinking?"

The thugs stared hard at me through the windshield, but to my great relief, the driver shut the door before they boarded.

"Thanks kid!" I called through the window, praying those goons wouldn't take it out on him. He rejoined an older woman, probably his mother, on the other side of the street. I sat behind the affable driver.

A nervous chill that ran through me and I panted from the exertion of running while lugging all my gear. My shoulder felt kinked and raw from where the strap rubbed it. I had time to contemplate the situation I'd been in. It could have been much worse. I could have been robbed, beaten, cut up, or killed if the kid hadn't helped. It didn't matter if I was a racist *honkey*. Just being white made me a target in the ghetto, but I didn't hold it against them. Segregation stuck them on the wrong side of the color line. Those boys were disenfranchised with few opportunities in their neighborhood. That's why we needed to build a radical community and fight back against our raciest, capitalist, warmongering society. Naïve talk of peace and love wasn't enough. We needed action.

After only a few stops, we reached the el station. "Thanks, man," I told the driver as I jumped off. "You saved my life."

White cops, the first I'd seen all day, sat in a patrol car outside the station, ignoring the black men in long coats selling hot merchandise. Chicago cops were infamous for taking bribes, and I assumed these black entrepreneurs were paying them off. Although I viewed these upholders of a corrupt *Law-n Order* as the enemy, in the unnatural racial tension, they gave me safety.

Chicago's Hyde Park

F ive long-haired white guys about my age squatted on the curb in animated conversation. Drawing near, I caught a few words of a blond boy's rant.

"Shooting up Vietnam like we're doing creates nothing but bad karma for our country." That was my opening, and I barged right in.

"You're right, man. We have to stand up to the establishment, fight back against the racist war machine."

The speaker introduced himself as Lonzo. We were at the 53rd Street shopping center. They seemed to be my kind of people, so I called out to them.

"Hey, any of you guys know of a place I can crash tonight?"

Lonzo stood up and put his hand on my shoulder. "Follow me." He led me to an unfurnished, wood-paneled apartment a couple of blocks away. A short-haired, denim clad blond guy greeted me with a brother's handshake, our thumbs interlaced.

"This is Bill," Lonzo introduced him. "Bill, Ron's looking for a crash pad."

Bill sized me up with a good-natured grin. "Come on in, man. You found us."

After dropping my duffel bag in a closet with tremendous relief, I trooped back to the parking lot with Lonzo. The fluid group was down to three, plus me. Their conversation had progressed to Greek philosophy.

"Yeah, Socrates hung out on the street just like us," I told them. "His classroom was the marketplace. This shopping center is the modern version of that. A common space for people to meet, share and interact is essential to build a progressive community."

As if on cue, a blue and white police car pulled over to our curb, and the cop stepped out. Lonzo and I stood our ground while the others took to their heels. The cop confronted us.

"You kids should all be in school."

"I'm a legal drop-out," I told him.

"Yeah, well, I could run you in for vagrancy then."

"The streets belong to the people, man." I pointed to the logo on his car. *We serve and protect.* "That means us; we're citizens of a free country."

He snickered. "That's for tax paying *decent* citizens, not you dirty, long-haired punks. Get in the car; I'm taking you two down to the station."

Hoping to open his mind, I gave the cop my rap about Socrates.

"He's one of the pillars of our civilization, and he hung out in the marketplace, just like us, but today you'd bust him as a vagrant. Hemmed in by private property instead of public space, where we can mingle, we've become a culture of isolation."

He chortled and spat into the gutter, "My job is to enforce that isolation. I don't care what your Socrates has to do with it."

At the station, he made me call home. I dialed, and he grabbed the receiver from me as soon as Mom answered, but I could hear her voice.

"Is this Mrs. Schulz?"

"Yes."

"I have your son here at the Chicago police station."

"Oh, my god! Is everything all right? Is he in trouble?"

He told her I was okay. He just needed her confirmation that I was emancipated on my own with her permission. He put Lonzo through the same exercise, and that checked out too. After he hung up, miffed at getting cheated out of his chance to send us back to our parents or lock us in a cage, he delivered a stern lecture on getting a job and staying off the public streets.

"What is it with you hippie punks? Both of you need haircuts." A malicious smile crossed his face. "And I'd be happy to give you one, too."

It was standard procedure to shave the heads of long-haired prisoners processed into Cook County jail. It was only hair, but a nation's flag is only cloth. Hair was our flag, a sign of our tribal identity. We had to let our *freak-flag* fly as the saying went. It took so long to grow my hair to a decent length, and I'd hate to lose it.

"Tell you what," the cop said, shaking his head. "I'll give you a break this one time, but I'm cutting you loose with a warning. If I catch either of you punks hanging out on the street again, I will bust you for vagrancy. Understood?"

We nodded, no sense aggravating him. We were the disinherited children of our money-grubbing society, with no stake in it unless we cut our hair and conformed to the status quo. As we left the station, I nudged Lonzo. "That's how society ceases to evolve, man. It traps us all in a straitjacket of conformity."

"Fuck yeah," Lonzo said, pulling his flannel shirt together and buttoning it over his tee shirt. "It's getting chilly. We'd better coffee up at the diner and stay out of sight!"

Lonzo and I rejoined the other guys who'd returned to hang out at the curb. The aroma of fried chow wafted from the diner, enticing us. "Come on," he said, charging in. We slid into a booth, safe from the vigilant eye of Officer Law and Order, which we corrupted to *Lawn Order*.

"What'll you boys have?" asked the cheerful redheaded waitress, handing out menus. She looked to be about fifty, in a pink uniform with a white apron and a tiny blue trimmed cap that sat atop her giant bouffant hairdo.

Although hungry, we were all low on cash and just ordered coffee, the poor man's affordable rent for a warm place to sit. She patrolled the half empty joint, refilling our bottomless cups at no extra charge. All the while, she kept up a lively banter, asking her regulars how their kids were doing in school and whether they expected a severe winter that year. She must have assumed us younger customers were all broke because on her second pass, she leaned over and whispered.

"We've got yesterday's pie at half off. I could cut you each a double portion." She gave us a broad wink. "No extra charge. We're going to toss it soon, anyway."

After our hassle with the cop, her maternal concern boosted our spirits. She seemed to enjoy our presence, laughing and joking with us as she did with her *straight* clientele. When she brought the bill, the pie wasn't even on it, only coffee. As the other booths filled up with the dinner crowd of paying customers, the manager came out to help. He gave us the evil eye.

"How long have those long-haired punks been in here?" he asked the waitress, loud enough for our hearing.

She frowned at him. "Maybe a couple of hours, but they're not bothering anyone."

"Yeah, well, they're taking up space." He stepped over to us. "You guys scram. You're bad for business."

"Hold on a minute!" A guy in a business suit sitting in a booth across from ours called out before we stood up. I'd noticed him watching us for some time. Suspicious of *straights* in suits and ties, I wondered if he was an undercover cop or maybe just a horny gay man.

He stood up and told the manager, "Let 'em be, Frank. I'll buy these boys a meal so they can stick around a while." Turning to us, he said, "I enjoyed listening in on your conversation. It's a cut above what I'd expect from a bunch of dropouts and street kids."

106

He let us order the daily special and singled me out.

"Come sit with me over here." He pointed to his booth.

Lonzo nudged me and whispered. "Be careful, man. He could be a fag."

Whether or not he had sexual designs on me, he didn't look dangerous, and we were in a public place. Anyway, I'd been starving since my last real meal the day before and welcomed the free food. As I sat across the table from him, he fixed me with a curious look.

"I'm a psychologist at the University. You seem to be a particularly interesting character."

"Really?" I wasn't sure if he was just buttering me up for seduction or if that was an honest compliment. Either way, I played along. After being denigrated by the cop and all the crap I had to put up with daily, it felt nice to get some praise. Even if it was phony praise, it lifted my spirits a notch. I'd take what I could get.

"Yes," the psychologist continued. "I'm researching the societal problems affecting modern youth and the causes of their alienation from mainstream society. I think you'd make a good subject for my study."

He took off his black horn-rimmed glasses, wiped and adjusted them before looking through them at me like a wise owl. "If you don't mind, of course, I'd like to study your responses. That would greatly assist my work."

They were standard word association exercises and inkblot tests. I'd already been put through that drill several times by school psychologists. Then, in a lower tone, so others couldn't overhear, he asked a series of probing questions about my sex life.

Do you prefer sex with men or women? What is your favorite sex position, on top or bottom? Have you ever gotten oral sex? From a man or woman? How often can you ejaculate in a single day?

With no secrets to hide, I gave him honest replies. I had no interest in men. However, I was open to sharing a woman with a man, orgy style. That idea aroused me, whereas fumbling with a man's body put me off. He began furiously jotting that down in his notes. Maybe he was looking for material to write a pornographic book.

He asked about sexual positions. I could feel my face redden as I admitted my lack of experience. It was limited to the face-to-face missionary position, and most recently, with Ruby, the woman in top position. I confessed that I'd been unlucky in love.

"You're still young," he said. "Good looking too. Girls will be all over you in no time."

That made me feel better. My luck keeping a girlfriend had fizzled when Ruby dumped me for a drug dealer. Taos had been my sexual invitation, the high point of my life so far. I filled him in on that.

"How about hallucinogenic drugs like LSD? Have you ever, ah, *tripped*, I think you people call it?"

"Sure, the first time was on the road in Colorado."

"Colorado? What brought you out there?"

I bragged about handling four times the recommended dose of LSD alone on the road. The psychedelic trip was a mystical experience for me on my way to check out the Rocky Mountain communes.

His eyes bugged out in awe or disbelief, but he didn't interrupt as I rambled on about my adventures in Drop City and Taos with Joe Sage's group marriage. Broadening my scope, I took the opportunity to discuss the dawning of the Age of Aquarius and the prophecies of Edgar Cayce. His owl-like, open mouthed expression made him look amazed at all I had to say, as if he'd never heard it before. That struck me as odd, as these subjects popped up in magazines and on television talk shows with frequency.

After an hour of grilling, I begged off. It had been a long day and a longer week spent sleepless on the streets of Chicago. I was glad to return to the crash pad.

Tripping Again

"Welcome home, Ron!" With a big smile on his face, Bill handed me a tiny white tablet. "Like some acid? I got a pal with a chemistry lab whose mission in life is to turn people on. Pretty groovy, huh? I got plenty for everybody."

I hesitated. Last time I tripped, I'd left my erstwhile companions, Sherry and John, under the hasty presumption that I was on the verge of spiritual enlightenment. Psychedelics seemed to hold some promise of being a gateway. If I could only keep my focus, I'd cross into the spiritual realm. That didn't occur as I'd expected on my last trip, yet I felt confident I was making spiritual progress.

This new offering of acid seemed portentous. I made an instant vow to use it to probe deeper into the psychic mysteries. My weariness vanished as I popped it down the hatch, ready for my third acid trip. Almost immediately, Lonzo popped in, shouting with excitement.

"Hey, Ron! Did Bill give you some acid too? Cool, man! Wanna come to a party with us? Should be chicks there."

"No, but thanks, Lonzo," I said with more resolve than I felt. "It's tempting, but I have to get serious if I'm ever going to open my chakras, not waste my trip listening to a lot of mindless chitchat from chicks."

"Heavy duty, man. Good luck with that."

They all trooped out. As the acid took hold, I was alone in the empty house, dark except for the single candle burning before me on the floor. I braced my legs in the lotus posture. Chanting mantras, focusing on my third eye. I attempted to conjure mystic powers, which, inherent within all of us, appear as chaotic, fearsome aspects of our subconscious mind. As if on cue, terrifying images began popping out of the dark recesses of the house. Using what little I'd learned of Tantric practices, which uses the virtual reality of intense visualization, I put on a bold, accepting front to welcome those fearsome images *like old friends.*

Wraithlike beings with angry exaggerated features, fangs, and protruding tongues floated around me. They were terrifying, but I reassured myself that I'd taken spiritual refuge in the Triple Gem: Buddha, Dharma, and Sangha. Breathing slowly and deliberately through my nose was the key to calm and embolden myself. That helped me confront and seize control of these monstrous apparitions.

I'd read about the Tibetan Chod Rite, which is best performed in a graveyard surrounded by corpses, which I tried to imagine all around me. The ritual terrified me enough when I performed my version of it without being high on acid.

With a spirit of sacrificial generosity, I mentally offered my flesh and blood to these ravenous apparitions. For this corporeal body I dwelt in was not the whole of me. The bodhisattvas' unconditional love transcends the categories of friend and enemy, those who help and who do harm. All have been our dear mothers in countless lifetimes. That boundless love blasts away karmic blocks to our spiritual evolution.

That's the theory. The ideal intention of loving selflessness clears away the negative karma holding us back as mere suffering mortals.

Generosity allows us to arise, transformed into the divine beings we are in reality.

Although I knew they were products of my imagination, my imagination exploded tenfold under its psychedelic influence. Terror raised the hair on my neck even though I assured myself that these phantoms could not harm me, not unless I lost control and surrendered to fear. Uncontrolled fear, I'd read, could spiral into panic and a total nervous-mental breakdown.

Hehehehahahahuhoshushushushishu. A sound like helicopter rotor blades vibrated in my head. It seemed familiar. Then a childhood memory resurfaced. At age six, the surgeon put a black mask on my face, putting me under anesthesia before I went under the knife for a hernia operation. *This* was the same auditory hallucination that had accompanied my loss of consciousness then. But there was more that came back to my memory.

The sound heralded the opening of a portal. A mass of rapidly pulsing threads of energy, which my child's mind had interpreted as a fast moving multi-legged spider. It had come charging at me until it devoured me into unconsciousness. Remembering that gave me courage that I'd again reached the portal and was on the brink of a successful crossover into the psychic realm.

Pham! Shouting mantra aloud kept me focused, blasting opens my nervous system. Conquering my fear by keeping an accepting, inner calm, I confronted the wild frontier of my subconscious, or whatever you choose to call the hidden parts of us that override our rational thought. The wrathful images then dissolved into smiling Buddhas. My flesh seemed transparent. Within my body, I could see my *Nadi* channels blasting open. Through them, Buddha's light and energy flooded into me. Waves of joyous blessings rained down, welcoming me as a conqueror of obstacles.

Exhausted, I drifted into a wonderful dreamland. Little by little, the acid faded into mundane reality. At dawn, I awoke, confused about who, what or where I was, yet with a deep feeling of accomplishment.

Lonzo bounced in from the all-night party with exciting news.

"Ron, you'll never fucking believe this, man! I told this girl at the party about you. Her name's Bonnie. She said, 'wow, man, I gotta meet that crazy dude.' What do you say to that, huh?"

Part Three
Revolutionary Love

Cupid's Arrow

"She'll be at the Point," Lonzo said.

"Where's that?"

"Promontory Point. It sticks out into Lake Michigan, a beautiful place to get high and watch the waves roll in. You'll dig it there."

It was Wednesday, September 24, 1969. As the sun climbed above the horizon in the morning sky, Lonzo led me to meet the mysterious woman. Meditating on acid all night blew my mind wide open to the possibilities. That a chick wanted to meet me after hearing a few tidbits about me from a guy I'd only known for a day amazed me.

Maybe I'd made a bigger impression on Lonzo than I realized, or else he built me up to this girl for some ulterior reason, like getting her off his back. It could also be a practical joke, so I kept my expectations in check.

We walked east along Fifty-Fifth Street to where it dead ended at Burnham Park. A tall blond woman stood at the back of the parking lot. She was no ugly duckling and flashed me a welcoming smile. Two young longhairs stood beside her. At our approach, they extended their hands.

Lonzo reached out. "Gimme some skin, man!" We took turns sliding the palms of both our hands across theirs, them reversing down to up for them to do the same. Lonzo turned to the woman.

"Ron, this is Bonnie from New York, the one I told you about."

"Hi, Ron." She ran an appraising look over me. When she took my hands in hers, I felt an instant jolt of electricity between us. Her open, smiling face also seemed to recognize something in me, as if we had a past together that we'd forgotten.

Turning on my charm, I said, "Gee, you look familiar. I wonder if we've met in a prior life."

Her smile grew wider. "Lonzo's told me so much about you, Ron. I feel as if I know you already. I'd like to hear more about your trip to the communes out west. You want to bring it all back here, huh?"

Bonnie's frizzy reddish blonde hair unhaloed her head, reaching out like a lion's mane to her shoulders. A golden Star of David nestled above the pert melon sized mounds of her breasts, proclaiming her membership in the storied tribe of Abraham. The star gave me a clue about what Lonzo may have said to interest her. He and I had discussed Nazi Germany and the Holocaust, comparing the genocide it unleashed then to the horror our own fascist government was perpetrating in Vietnam. That could have aroused Bonnie's interest in me. I knew much more than the average guy about the Holocaust.

As a nine-year-old in 1961, I'd followed the trial of the war criminal Adolph Eichmann in Israel, filling a scrapbook on the testimony which sparked a lifelong interest in the struggle for human rights against intolerance.

Bonnie's brash confidence accentuated her physical assets, making her more alluring than a woman of comparable beauty.

Her two male friends, introduced as vagabonds like the rest of us, were in excellent spirits. They laughed and slapped each other on the back. One of them reared back and shouted to the heavens. "Oh, man! We'll have another great party tonight!"

"Yes, Ron," Bonnie's softer voice purred close to me. "Yesterday, we pooled our money to rent a room at the Mark Twain Hotel. Tonight, we'll get washed up, celebrate and, ah, *sleep* in comfort." She narrowed her eyes, and her voice lowered to an even sexier purr. "You can join us if you'd like."

"Of course, yeah, I'd love to." I began to sweat and gulped a lungful of air to offset it. My wildest dreams were coming true. I'd better not screw this up.

The girlfriend of one of the guys arrived, chattering with excitement. He turned to us and announced the good news. "Linda's parents will be out of town for the rest of the week!" A chorus of *Yippee* rippled through our boisterous group before he continued. "She lives in this huge mansion, much bigger than the hotel we booked. I vote we move the party there. What say ye all to that?"

"Too bad we pre-paid the hotel room," said the other guy.

Lonzo concurred. "Yeah, they won't refund our money, but shit, we'll have Linda's place for several days. Well worth the tradeoff." The vote for that change of venue was unanimous.

Bonnie pulled me aside and stood on tiptoes to reach my ear. "What do ya think, Ron? We'll have the hotel room all to ourselves!"

"Great!" I grinned back at her, hardly believing my luck, which I ascribed to my acid fueled karmic breakthrough the night before. "We don't need all this whooping and hollering. Do we?"

She gave me a sly grin. "No, I think we can make our own." That wowed me.

"You know, Bonnie, I feel like we've met before."

She grinned wider and took my hand. "Maybe it's kismet. I feel the same about you. Come on, let's walk and talk."

We strolled away from the others to Lake Michigan. Alewives, an invasive species of fish, washed up on the shore by the thousands every year. Despite the rotten stench of dead fish littering the shore, the Point presented a scenic view of the roiling lake. Bonnie and I began dodging the spray from waves that splashed against the concrete breakers.

Ahhhh! Bonnie shouted and dodged behind me as an even bigger wave crashed in too high, soaking me. She started laughing. "Gotcha! Wow, man. I bet that was cold. I just love the Lake. Don't you?"

"You bet," I agreed. "Too far to see across. Lake Michigan is the next best thing to the Atlantic Ocean. You're from back there, right?"

"Yeah, but I've only been to Long Island beach once. I'd like to see the Pacific someday. How about you?"

"Not yet. I haven't seen either coast. Maybe we ought to head out there."

She gripped my hand tighter when I said that. Within minutes of meeting her, this amazing girl had spun my life around, pushing all other concerns to the sidelines. But I knew better than to take my luck for granted and rush things. She went on at great length about something called egg creams.

"Oh, Ron, it's the most amazing thing you'll ever taste. Made only in New York City, can't find it here in Chicago."

"What is it, eggnog?"

"It's much better than that. I simply cannot describe it." Without missing a beat, she moved the conversation in a personal direction.

"By the way, I'm Jewish."

"I know. I like your Star of David."

"Those *goy* guys thought it was just a plain old star."

As an avid reader, I already knew that goy meant *gentile*, a non-Jew, but this was my first actual conversation with a Jew. Bonnie's *otherness* enhanced her sexy mystique. I wondered if it worked the same magic for her. She must have read my mind.

"Did anyone ever tell you your baby blue eyes are sexy, Ron?"

"Not exactly, Bonnie." I lied because I didn't want to ruin this. "You're the first."

She giggled. "I can't believe that. Lonzo tells me you know a lot about Jewish history."

"Yeah, I'm into history, big time. I believe in reincarnation, too. History isn't just about kings and generals. It belongs to all of us, our never-ending story."

She burst out laughing. Maybe I'd said too much.

"Wow, Ron, that's cool. I, too, feel we have a personal part to play in history."

We stood there, holding hands, gazing into each other's eyes. She spoke first.

"Ron, you're my *schmuck*. My *Meshuge bokher*. Know what that is?"

"Is it Yiddish? I know some German. *Schmuck* is jewel, but I think you mean it sarcastically like my grandmother would. Right?"

"And *Meshuge bokher* means crazy guy! Yiddish is close to German, Ron, with some Hebrew mixed in. That's what I'm gonna call you now, my crazy *goy* guy."

"Guess that makes you my crazy chick, Bonnie."

"*Du meshugener! Ikh hab dir lib!*"

"Wait-wait," I told her. "The first part sounds like 'you crazy,' and the last part is 'I have love for you.' Right? Germans say *Ich Liebe dick*. It sounds like I love dick!"

"*Du meshugener!*" Bonnie repeated, laughing. Then, in a quiet voice, she added, "I think maybe I *could* love your dick too. We'll see about that."

Bonnie's face flashed seriously. She grabbed my elbow and drilled me with an intense look before asking a surprising question. "Ever hear of the Motherfuckers, Ron?"

"What?" The strange question took me off guard.

"The Motherfuckers." She said the word so matter of fact like it was the most natural thing to say. I wasn't sure what she expected to hear.

"Ah, it's, well, something bad. Worse than calling someone a bastard or a no-good son of a bitch. Right?"

She chuckled and punched my arm. "Not that! You silly goy boy. I mean the revolutionary collective, the *tribe* of motherfuckers in New York City! As in *up against the wall, motherfuckers!*"

That revolutionary rallying cry had come to my attention only recently. Her face again serious, she added, "I'm a motherfucker."

That floored me. Motherfucker was *not* a complimentary term, something you'd call yourself. But people were challenging negative labels and biases, taming slanderous words by owning them with pride. Some radical gays had called themselves *queer* and Blacks, who once preferred the more *polite* term Negro, which is simply black in Spanish, took proud ownership of their color. Swear words, too, were coming into mainstream use and losing their sting. Latin should be no better or less vulgar than Anglo Saxon. Why should we prefer saying *excrement* to shit or *intercourse* to fuck? I'd become used to hearing Motherfucker spoken with a fond smile.

"So, what's your motherfucker thing all about?" I asked.

"We're anarchist revolutionaries, rising from the underclass to form a Revolutionary tribe. We dropped out of the consumer rat race to live by our wits. Our Freak Revolution goes much farther than that naïve peace and love shit those spoiled middle-class hippies envision."

The smile spread across her face vanished into a serious frown. "My motto is: *Flower power won't stop fascist power.* Dig it? We have to stir things up to create change. We publish the *Rat Subterranean News* in the East Village. It educates and agitates the masses in the fight for social justice. Ever hear of the *Rat?*"

"I heard of the *East Village Other* but never had a chance to read it."

"Oh, you silly country boy!" Smiling again, she put her arms around me and squeezed. "You Chicago guys really are hicks in the sticks. The *Rat, Subterranean News* is our underground paper that, like, synthesizes our politics with the hip lifestyle. We take it up a notch from the *Other*, which is more artsy-fartsy like your Chicago *Seed.*"

Her eyes softened. She pulled me down onto one of the rock benches that lined the promenade, and her lips met mine. Her warm embrace gave me a sensation of instant calm, just what I needed to ground me in this world. Still punchy from tripping all night, I had to convince myself that Bonnie wasn't an acid fueled hallucination, born of the longing for my lost love back in New Mexico, which I'd been dealing with. She was real, a flesh and blood woman holding me in her arms. It augured a fresh start, a new, more fulfilling chapter in my crazy life.

A vague image sparked in my mind. Her warmth. Her natural, musky, un-perfumed smell resurrected a scene from a long-forgotten memory, like a past life or a dream. Another woman, so like her, sat with me on a park bench in a leafy urban park setting. She wore a yellow star on her arm. That's all I saw in an instant flash, but it merged with a cartoonish red dragon. That dragon had appeared repeatedly during my last acid trip, biting the end of its tail that looped in a circle around it. It seemed to imply that the past, present and future joined into a continuous, repetitive cycle.

Bonnie had to be my karmic connection, the fulfillment of what we had done in the past into an eternal NOW. She felt so familiar because we'd been together in a past moment, decades or even centuries ago. Fate joined us together again to fulfill our continuing destiny. That I'd been given the acid the night before was no accident but a psychic preparation for this fated rendezvous. I felt like both a participant and an observer in this unfolding story, curious about how this divine act would play out.

Egg cremes? I wondered if they tasted better than Bonnie's salty sweet mouth as our tongues wrestled and our lips nibbled. We smooched much longer than I'd ever kissed a girl before, at least in my current lifetime.

Bonnie pulled away. She sat up straight, shoulders back, and looked deep into my eyes. In an instant, her demeanor changed from lover to serious businesswoman.

"You see, Ron, we motherfuckers aren't just mobilizing the Proletarian class." She hesitated and bit her lip. "Do you know what that is?"

"Sure," I answered. "The industrial working class."

"Bravo, Ron!" She beamed. "You've read some Marx, I see."

"Sure, Bonnie." I needed to show off and be the teacher's pet. "The Communist Manifesto thrills me; I mean, my hair stood right up when I read it the first time, and the second time too. Last year, I struggled halfway through *Das Kapital,* and wow, it's some heavy shit. I agree with Marx about capitalism, but..."

I had to phrase my words carefully to avoid freaking her out. The whole world was in the throes of the Cold War, which, in a sense, was a continuation of the Great Game played by the imperialist powers of the last century. Politics can be brutal, the right and wrong can change sides, but we need to play the game or be swallowed by those who play to win. Somehow, we have to promote positive changes in our wayward society.

"You see, Bonnie, Marxism in Russia and China haven't lived up to the promise. Have they?" She didn't react, so I continued. "Maybe Stalin, Mao, even Lenin, betrayed their high ideals, sold out the righteous cause to keep in power. Theory is hard to implement in the real world, but we keep trying. The future of our people, our planet, depends on it."

"Right on, Ron! That's why I'm an anarchist. Do you know what the Lumpenproletariat is?"

"Ahh, I remember reading that word, but not sure what it meant."

Ah-hem. Bonnie cleared her throat, preparing for another lecture. "The Lumpenproletariat is the criminalized dropouts from the proletarian class. Strict Marxists, not me, would call them antisocial counterrevolutionaries, who tend to have no class consciousness, just out for themselves. However," her lips pursed, modeling a strict disciplinarian. "I disagree with that presumption because we dropouts *are* the Lumpenproletariat."

She paused and then reeled me in for another, even longer kiss before proceeding. "Doctrinaire Marxists overlook the dispossessed who try to escape the grind of wage slavery. But we anarchists see their potential because they never sold out to bourgeois values. If

educated and organized, they could join the revolutionary vanguard."
Misty-eyed with the passion of her words, she pulled me to her again.

Bonnie continued her lesson, punctuated with bouts of kissing, a
marvelous teaching style. I'd met the Revolution in the person of this
sexy chick who had the hots for me. My life was coming together like
clockwork, back in synch with my cosmic destiny. Things could only
get better.

Wild Fling

Taking the el, Bonnie and I got off at Division and Clark and stepped into the Mark Twain hotel to drop off our packs. It was still too early to check in, so we walked north on Lincoln to meet her friend at the funky second-floor apartment where she used to stay. A heavyset woman in a loud orange, yellow, and red Hawaiian muumuu let out a piercing shriek as she opened to us.

"Bonnie, I wondered what became of you!" She wrapped her ample arms around her. "We thought you went back to New York City."

"Not yet, Lucie, but I'm thinking about leaving soon."

Ignoring me, they launched into a rapid-fire exchange, gushing nostalgically over their greatest of all cities. It was a tribal identity thing I would have to endure whenever New Yorkers found each other. Finally running out of steam, Bonnie turned as if she suddenly remembered me and put her hand on my shoulder.

"This is Ron." She smiled as she pulled me front and center to give Lucie a hug. "What do ya think, Ron, wanna go to the Big Apple with me?"

"Sure, never been there and got nothing holding me here."

"Great! You'll love it. I'll show you around and introduce you to the Motherfuckers. They'll love you."

We'd only been together a couple of hours and already had travel plans. New York City! Lucie's apartment was only a block north of the iconic Biograph Theater at 2433 Lincoln. It was where the famous bank robber, John Dillinger, saw his last movie in 1934. I couldn't help but admire Dillinger and wanted to share his heroic Robin Hood mystique with Bonnie.

"Look at this, Bonnie!" Pulling her along to admire the art déco Chicago landmark, I launched into the Dillinger legend, getting excited as I rambled on.

"I think Dillinger is the perfect example of your criminal class becoming revolutionaries." I stuck my finger into the bullet holes that still graced the telephone pole in that alley. "The Woman in Red set him up for ambush here. The FBI shot him as he fled up this alley beside the theater. Bystanders dug out the bullets for souvenirs before John's corpse was even cold. Dillinger was a popular folk hero during the Depression. Along with Pretty Boy Floyd and Bonnie and Clyde, but they were all killed in shootouts with the FBI. Damn capitalist lackeys!"

Bonnie shouted. "Oh, wow, Ron!" I thought I'd gotten to her with my rap on Dillinger, but she pointed up to the marquee.

"Look up there! The Beatles' *Yellow Submarine* is playing! Did you ever see it?"

Bummer! She hadn't even listened to my Dillinger spiel. "Nah," I told her, letting all the air out of my sails. "That's just a silly cartoon, not my thing."

She put on a stern face, then giggled. "You're too gosh-darn serious, Ron. Lighten up, will ya!" So now *I* was the serious one? She dragged me up to the ticket booth.

"I've seen it lots of times, Ron, but it's such a gas. I can watch it over and over."

Okay, if it made Bonnie happy, that was good enough for me.

The tickets cost a buck twenty-five apiece. My funds were getting low, but I trusted in my changed luck, even springing for a bag of popcorn and cokes to share with Bonnie. We settled into the half empty theater to watch the Beatles' *Yellow Submarine*. It hadn't struck me then, but it was the first time I'd taken a girl to a movie, making it my very first *traditional* date. It was a stupid cartoon, but she was right. I needed to mellow out. Even hard-core revolutionaries like her needed fun.

Back at the hotel, we tore off our clothes and hopped in the shower. It had been days since either of us had more than a quick rinse over a sink. Luxuriating under limitless hot water, we soaped and scrubbed each other, then jumped into bed for our first glorious fuck.

We'd had enough foreplay in the shower and got right down to business. Bonnie gave as good as she got. We rolled out of bed onto the floor, laughing ourselves to tears before we got serious and, with less haste, started over. Nibbling her neck, I pumped slowly, moving her from side to side, trying different angles, and judging their effect on Bonnie's moans. Her panting, throaty gasps told me I'd succeeded. She quivered in my arms.

Oh-yes-yes-yes. Don't stop! Ohhhh, yeah, ohhhhh-ahhhh!

Holding back my orgasm until that peak moment, I rammed her faster-harder, letting my demon go, until I gushed my last reserves of strength into her depths. As that tide washed out, a powerful wave of surrendering love swept in. Finally spent, my vision faded into a whiteout as I collapsed onto the soft comfort of Bonnie's pillowing bosom, her arms enfolding me as my consciousness sank into a long denied and much-needed nap. Neither of us had slept the night before, but it couldn't have been too long before Bonnie began tickling my ear.

"Ron, I'm famished. Let's go eat!" Down the street at the *Hungry I*, we romped and devoured huge portions of the buffet. Then, hand in hand like lovers in the movies, we window shopped along Wells, gazing more into each other's eyes than store windows. At the corner of North Avenue, we came alongside another couple on a stroll.

The dude was a biker in black leather, musky aromatic chaps over denim. Macho tattoos featuring skulls, chains, and horned devils enhanced his brawny arms with medium length, greasy blond hair that peeked out from under a blue bandanna that covered his head pirate fashion.

His knock-out chick was a bronzed brunette, her slim tanned belly enticing below a skimpy halter-top that begged me to uncover the pendulous wonders within. She smiled a crooked grin, so *wicked*, as she looked me over with her sparkling black eyes that burned to my core, arousing me despite my satisfaction with my beautiful emerald eyed lady.

Should I feel guilty? Hell no! Bonnie's fingernails dug into my palm in a delirium of desire, her smoldering eyes on the dude. I wasn't alone, but in a lusty partnership. His chick snuggled against him and whispered into his ear with her eyes still fixed on me. He turned and grinned at us.

"Hey! You guys look pretty groovy together like you're crazy in love." He nudged his companion, who giggled like a mischievous schoolgirl. "Just like we are! Right Babe?"

Bonnie and I glanced at each other. Love? Neither of us had spoken that word in our brief time together, but *sure as shit*, we were head over heels, high on amour.

He winked. "My lady wants to know something, man." He scratched his chin as if unsure how to phrase it. "Let's switch up and, ah, kiss each other's old lady? I mean, for luck and all. Would you cats dig that?"

Bonnie gave me a furtive glance, followed by a *why not* shrug that belied her pale face blushing crimson. She gasped as she allowed him to sweep her right up off her feet. Yeah, she was digging it alright.

The biker's saucy brunette, still keeping eye contact, threw her arms around my neck. As I swung her up, her legs grabbed my waist. My blood pumped a drumroll in my ears. My flesh tingled as she stuck her eager tongue in deep. Her black eyes pulled me into their depths, launching me into a search for her ancient yet ever youthful soul.

Bonnie's soft moans of pleasure, limp in the biker's arms, woke a twinge of jealousy in me. But what right had *I* to feel jealous, immersed as I was in the charms of *his* lady? We were all co-conspirators in open, joyous, freely expressed lust, not at all furtive and with no sense of betrayal. For the benefit of these cherished friends of the moment, I tossed my selfish jealousy onto the sacrificial pyre, transmuting it into open handed generosity.

My heart thumped my love for both Bonnie and this other woman. But I felt a different kind of love for her man. As opposed to the more sensual, erotic pleasure I felt for both of our ladies, my feelings for him felt more like a self-recognition, as if I was looking into a mirror and seeing his face.

He was me as I was he, and we were all together—with our fair ladies. He enjoyed watching his gal with me as much as he enjoyed pleasuring mine. Sharing our women made us soul brothers, a sacred experience, however long the moment lasted in our transient world.

Too soon, the brunette released me. Our eyes remained locked as she stepped backward to her man, stealing away a piece of my freely given soul.

Red-faced and perspiring, Bonnie re-materialized at my side, seizing my hand. Her quickened pulse told me she'd gotten as big a *rush* from this as I had. She kissed me, desperate as a drowning woman, with more intensity than before.

Tempted as I was, I didn't press my luck by suggesting that we invite this couple up to our hotel room. Mesmerized, we both stared at these divine beings. The black-eyed beauty draped herself back over the muscular shoulders of her blond Adonis. He wore a satisfied smirk that matched his lady's. Then he swung his partner around and gave her ass a resounding smack that elicited a delighted giggle from her.

"She's such a bad-ass girl! Ain't she?" He winked at me and then raised his arm in a farewell salute to both of us. "Nice running into you 'all. Take it easy, now."

They sashayed up the street toward the lake. I watched, and sure enough, his lady's eyes flashed back over his shoulder to meet mine dead on, causing a renewed explosion in my head. Bonnie's head turned too. I felt her stiffen with a spark of jealousy that added fuel to her passion, that edged up to anger. To channel that energy back to creative lust and forestall danger to me, to us, I whispered in her ear.

"That was fucking amazing, wasn't it, sweetheart?"

I'd never before called a girl sweetheart. Corny or not, voicing the silly endearment sent a nice, warm glow through my body. Bonnie's eyes got misty. She seemed to lose her balance and fell against me, giggling into my chest. "Oh, you silly, silly goy-boy!"

Switching partners jazzed us both. Great sex thrives on open borders and exuberant fantasy, best nurtured beyond the narrow confides of strict monogamy. This experience reinforced my conviction of that. Bonnie and I were partners in love *and* lust, allies exploring the possibilities of sweet wild *sex*, where dreams and fancies intersect with the hard realities of changing fortune. For I'd gone too long without love and knew better than to cling to a woman who might vanish from my life in an instant. The old saying held true: I had to charge ahead as though I knew what I was doing for as long as my luck holds up.

We were both so turned on that we scampered back to make more love on our rented bed. Panting beside me after that latest encounter, Bonnie whispered in my ear.

"Let's go to Alice's Restaurant tonight."

Flush with satisfied love, eager to show each other off, Bonnie and I put on the still damp duds we'd rinsed out in the sink to sally forth as clean as could be. While Bonnie wore her sensible hiking shoes, I decided to toughen my feet, going barefoot, to prepare myself for the hardships of the revolution while also purifying my yogi spirit. *No shoes, no shirt, no service* was not then in effect. Countless tiny shards of glass were always present on urban sidewalks. Some embedded themselves so deep into my calloused feet it would take years to work their way back out. The pain sharpened my pleasure at our simple joys.

I felt so fucking alive! Just seeing Bonnie glowing beside me was all I'd ever need.

It was a decent size crowd at Alice's, and Bonnie knew several of them. *I heard you were going back to New York, Bonnie*, was a regular greeting. She'd been telling them that for weeks.

A boisterous, drunken girl in long braids shouted for all to hear, "You Motherfucker, Bonnie! Goddamn it, we'll miss you." That elicited a raucous laugh from all of us.

Two girls she didn't know came to our table with a kitten. "She's the last of the litter. Please take her before my old man drowns her. If you do, I'll give you a couple hits of acid."

It smittened Bonnie. "Oh, she's so cute. What do you think, Ron? Oh, please say yes!"

"The hotel won't let us take it up. No pets allowed."

"We could smuggle her in! Tell me you'll do it, and we'll drop the acid together."

A kitten was the last thing we needed, but she won, of course. I'd be crazy to upset my wild, dreamy gal. She repaid me with a lingering kiss, and as a celebration of our togetherness, we each popped a tab of acid into the other's mouth.

Two older, down and outers in patched and threadbare clothing that I assumed were beatniks joined us. With mock seriousness, one of them spoke to me as Bonnie and the cat girls looked on.

"You got quite a lady there, man." He winked at Bonnie and turned back to me. "You better eat her pussy really good to keep her satisfied, you know."

What the hell? I didn't know how I should take that remark and expected it to offend Bonnie's feminist sensibilities. Not that it was a strange topic in all male company. Many of the guys I hung out with extolled the virtues of cunnilingus, but inexperienced as I was, I worried how my new gal would react to such crude discussion.

The other beatnik chimed in. "Do you ever lick her clit? Get right in there, man, and eat her pussy like this." He demonstrated for everyone at our table, wiggling his stuck-out tongue with an obscene yet comical, wide-eyed expression. "Keep doing that until she screams and hollers, man, that'll super satisfy her."

"Don't talk your vulgar shit here," I told them.

"Hey," said the second one. "I'm just trying to help you make her happy, man. You gotta eat a woman's pussy to keep her around these days."

"I said knock it off." I glanced at Bonnie for confirmation that I'd done right, but she shot me an exasperated look like *I* was the one out of line.

"Just let him talk, Ron," she hissed. "You silly goy country boy. And pay attention!"

Everyone laughed, making me even more self-conscious. So, *I* was the prude. Despite hearing so much on the subject, I'd had no direct experience of giving *or* getting oral sex. The matter hadn't come up with my three lovers, including Bonnie, only hours ago. They'd all been in their early twenties. To an inexperienced seventeen-year-old like me, they were savvy *older* women. I couldn't sabotage myself by letting on how naïve I was. At some point, I'd need hands-on female guidance, but making a fool of myself *down there* terrified me.

The acid started taking effect.

Blood Atonement

The terrified kitten cried despite all the love Bonnie showered on it. Refusing milk, it clawed her hand until she clamped its paws in a firm grip. Mummy-like, it struggled on. I had to tell her straight.

"We can't bring that thing up to our room until it settles down, Bonnie."

"Don't worry, Ron!" She shot me an evil look. "I told you I'll take care of this."

"Ah, I guess we'd better scat," said one of the cat girls. It was smart of them to shove off in case Bonnie realized what a mistake she'd made.

For the umpteenth time, Bonnie told everyone at our table, "Ron and I are heading to New York in the morning!" She giggled. "*Up Against the Wall, Motherfuckers!* He's joining my collective."

"Woooooow, maaaan, thaaaat's heaaaaavy." The beatnik's words dragged out like a long string of spaghetti. They seemed to echo from a faraway tunnel.

The acid had taken over. Everything shifted into slow motion. Familiar objects and people took on exaggerated, outlandish shapes.

Sight, sounds, and smells came in through previously unknown portals throughout my body, as if my nose, eyes, and ears were not enough to take it all in. But this being my fourth trip, the unusual mindscape was becoming familiar.

The beatniks, who laughed at the slightest provocation, waved their hands over Bonnie and me. "Fear thee not, oh Bonnie!" One proclaimed with a sarcastic intonation. "We impart our blessings upon your bold new enterprise."

Only the day before, we citizens of this expanding Universe had all been strangers, yet we chattered away like long-lost friends in a dingy establishment in a big city of a populous nation in an overpopulated world that spun around a star in a solar system that was but a speck in a vast galaxy within an even greater cosmos. *Fucking heavy, man,* was all I could say about it.

The ancient Buddhist teaching from the Heart Sutra popped into my head. *Rupam shunyatavam, shunyatavam rupam.* I loved the Sanskrit sound of it. *Form is emptiness, and emptiness is form.* The words took on deep relevance as once solid shapes shimmied and shifted like molten plastic around me. The faces of people became ever stranger, elongating into threatening shapes like in a carnival funhouse. Even Bonnie's face morphed into an evil witch, which my observant brain struggled to deny. A sudden wave of terror washed over me, and I felt lost and alone. The lyrics from the Doors album, *Strange Days,* rang in my head.

People are strange when you're a stranger/ Faces look ugly when you're alone/ Women seem wicked when you're unwanted ...

No, I rebelled against my despairing pessimism to remind myself that Bonnie had popped into my life only that morning. So much had occurred in that brief time. After our furious lovemaking, she seemed an essential part of me, as had Ruby and others before her. Their phantom forms still hid in the depths of my heart, but I needed a flesh and blood woman beside me. I grabbed Bonnie's hand like a lifeline and pulled her to me.

"Are you *getting off* too, babe?"

Bonnie didn't voice an answer, only smiled like an insane woman with fanged teeth and huge dilated eyes. This acid was heavy shit.

"We'd better get back," I told her. Taking charge, I pulled her up and led her out.

After the warm afternoon, it was already cold on that September night. We hadn't dressed for it. A chill wind blew off the lake, and the street funneled it right at us. Bonnie snuggled against me, holding the kitten inside her thin blouse. It meowed, loud and inconsolable. A discordant, nagging tune to our journey home.

Home? It was a cheap hotel room, our temporary refuge, until we reached Bonnie's fabled Gotham City. She wasn't a stranger there. Her *motherly fuckers* would welcome us to our new, rightful place in the Revolution.

The familiar route down Lincoln became an exotic landscape. The sidewalk, sprinkled here and there with bits of broken glass, sparkled under the streetlights. *As above, so below*, came to mind as the dirty ground turned into a starry sky. We space travelers voyaged on. LSD opened a panorama whereby the past intersected with the immediate present in a single fabric.

Bonnie transformed into the first image I had of her, the cocky Warsaw Ghetto fighter. And me? I took the *rap*, bearing on my shoulders the German crimes against them. As a wannabe Tantric Bodhisattva traveling through time, I'd have to take responsibility for the awful karma created in our past lives and tear it into Shunyata, the emptiness of self. Yes! For the love of this wild, beautiful Jewish woman beside me, my mystic offering would atone and transform evil into positive love. Together, we'd burst beyond our fleshy limits into spiritual dimensions. Explaining all this to Bonnie was impossible.

Her concern was the meowing creature she held to her breast. We had to silence it to sneak past the hotel clerk. He stood behind his desk beside the elevator. Under his hostile glare, we crossed the short hallway from the glass door. The tiny lobby had no furniture to hide behind. Waiting for the lift, the kitten broke free and yowled, busting us. The mean faced man roared.

"You can't go up with that damn cat!"

"It's only a kitten and just for tonight," Bonnie pleaded.

"Those are the rules. Take it out, or I'll call the cops. I'm sick to death of all you damn hippies sneaking stuff in."

I took the kitten from Bonnie. "You go up; I'll take care of this."

It slashed the back of my hand before I swaddled it tight and ran out to the deep-fried aroma of Sammy's hotdog and burger stand in the alley. A lengthy line of Black men stood waiting for chow. *Anybody want a cute kitten?* I pleaded with them but got no takers.

An ever more frigid wind blew in off the lake two blocks away. On my bleeding bare feet, I walked up and down the street, hawking the cat. Impossible! I should never have let Bonnie accept it. I'd have to abandon it or spend the night shivering outside.

Some bodhisattva I'd turned out to be, but I couldn't forgo lying in the arms of my dear Bonnie. It struck me that I was in the same moral conundrum many Germans found themselves in during the Holocaust, following repugnant orders. Was I any better than they were? Fuck no. Circumstances trapped me, like all mortals, in a no-win situation.

Hoping that someone would rescue the loud meowing thing, I set the kitten on an overflowing garbage can behind Sammy's in the alley. At least it was warmer than the cold ground. The greasy food waste attracted rats, a cat's natural prey, but the tables had turned. It never had a chance; the girls' old man would kill it if we didn't take it.

With a troubled conscience, I returned to our warm hotel room. Bonnie peppered me with questions. "What did you do with my baby?"

Her baby! Guilt, magnified tenfold by LSD, weighed heavily no matter what I said, so I lied to spare her feelings.

"I gave it to someone. Hey, we're going to New York. Right? It's better for the poor baby to stay in a nice, warm home than out on the road with us."

An awful image hit me. That *nice warm home* it got could be the belly of a rat. My evil karma was multiplying on me.

She collapsed in my arms, sobbing. "You're my guy, my *Meshuge* Chicago country boy. Take care of me. Will ya?"

Hammer blows of intense emotion banged in my chest as I squeezed her tight. She was *my* baby, my tough revolutionary motherfucker baby. I wanted her; I needed her. No way could I pretend indifference.

As we showered, I watched blood from the small cuts on my feet swirl red trails down the drain. An LSD inspired drama ran in my head like a movie. My mind conjured up bleeding bodies, images of mass graves, murder in which I was both a victim and perpetrator. To expiate the vision, I hugged my sopping wet lady. We toweled off and dropped into the sack. This was the first time I made love on acid, and everything was intense. Whispering endearments mixed with fantasy, I spun her a tale drawn from my exploding psychedelic imagination.

"We were lovers in a past life."

She laughed. "Wait, stop! Really? I wanna hear this, you *Meshuge* guy."

"The first time I saw you, you reminded me of a Warsaw ghetto fighter whose picture I'd seen in a history book. Somehow I knew you. It just hit me, don't freak out, but maybe I was a German trooper, a fucking Nazi enemy in that life. But damn it, I fell in love with you. You flipped me, made me change sides. After they pulled you out of a bunker, a prisoner and, and..."

Trying to follow the thread of images racing through my mind, I wondered if I should unload all this crazy gibberish on her. Exploring the dark side of consciousness was a *thing* with me, but I wasn't sure how she'd take it and didn't want to freak her out. I hoped to inspire her with who, just maybe, we could have been in a past life.

She shook me back out of my head, "Come on, Ron, what do ya mean, enemy?"

"Maybe I was drafted into the German Army, just like the guys now being sent to *Nam*. Maybe there was no place like Canada I could run to."

"Okay, so you were on the wrong side. But a fucking Nazi soldier! So how did we become lovers? It doesn't make sense."

"Life isn't fair, neither is love," I said, feeling inspired to wing it. "But love conquers all. Right? You conquered me then, too, even if I was a Nazi goy. Cool shit, huh?"

That bit of tribute to Bonnie's charm made her giggle. And so, I rambled on, deep into the realm of bodice ripping Harlequin romances, which flirted with sadistic and masochistic themes, feeling certain I'd score some points with her.

"You fucking hated me as a cruel Nazi beast. Of course, you were *my* prisoner. But then you captured my heart. I became *yours*. I hated me too, so I pulled you away from the shooting range and ran away with you to the forest."

Bonnie's eyes softened. Warm and doe-like, she snuggled against my chest while I continued spinning the yarn.

"When I tried to kiss you, you fought me, bit my lip. You looked at me with such intense hate, but I was willing to die at your hands. I took my dagger from its sheath. There was a big swastika on it. I put it right in your hand, the blade pointed at me. *Kill me*, I told you, and it looked like you would. My neck was ready for you. I'd let you sacrifice me for my love. Dig? Instead, you kissed me back, and we made love."

"Shit, Ron, you'd really let me kill you?" I could see that it turned her on.

"That's my crazy love for you, babe."

"But, Ron," she sniffed. "I don't want to kill you. I want a happy ending!"

"Okay." I nuzzled her neck, which made her shiver. "This *here and now*, this is our happy ending with a *new* beginning. See, Babe? We've come back, reincarnated in this world to remake history with our crazy fucking love. Get it?"

Bonnie got it. Excited, she took charge, pulling me back into the saddle to resume our passion play in earnest. Maybe I wasn't so crazy after all. This wild fantasy turned her on. And who knows, it might even be true.

Wow, she repeated over and over, whimpering and moaning like a kitten. She was *my* kitten, *my* baby. With our copulation, we'd joined into a single organism. An exploding orgasm shot my goyish seed into her Yiddish womb. In my delirium, I imagined it would germinate a fresh dawn of humanity. A baby, hers, and mine could result.

The idea turned me on. Oh yea, I could see myself as a father, a dad, doing the job right, correcting all the stupid mistakes my parents, all our ancestors, had made. That Bonnie was probably on the pill didn't jell right away in my tripped-out brain.

In the post-orgasmic white dawn, we drifted into our individual acid dreams. Mine became a nightmare. I saw the kitten's big eyes meowing as I abandoned it. It morphed into a child, a Jew, pleading to live. I saw myself in a black uniform, standing above a ditch, holding a rifle on the kid, unwilling but fated to shoot. Words flashed thru my fevered brain:

Mutiny... failure to obey the command of a superior...

To disobey the order to shoot would be mutiny, even treason. My erstwhile comrades, my brothers in arms, sworn to defend the Fatherland, would shoot me too.

Then shoot goddamn it!

The face of my commander, contorted in rage, became my father in this life. As I watched, his face aged. He became older, ancient. His head sprouted horns, which transformed into a Viking helmet. He'd become Odin, or Thor, god of thunder, his blasting voice accusing me.

You have betrayed your Volk, your race, your blood...

The big-eyed child was gone, but the deep trench remained. I tumbled in. The cartoon image of Lewis Carroll's *Alice in Wonderland* became my reality. I fell, spinning head over heels, down into the rabbit hole. On the way down, I passed vague images, snippets of dimly remembered events infused with a wild imagination. They flew by me too fast to grab onto.

Wham! I made a hard landing, awakening back into my new present, my 1969 Chicago wonderland. I awoke in a sweat on a comfortable bed. It took a moment to reorient myself from the vivid dream to current reality. I couldn't tell if all the history I'd devoured put me in the dream scene or if it was a true, deep memory of a prior life.

One thing was clear: none of us were innocent. I, along with every other creature on the planet, was tainted with evil karma. My past life karma was probably no cleaner than the evil I condemned in others. It was impossible for any of us, smug vegetarians included, to be free of complicity in our society's crimes. Not unless we stood up to *them*. Bonnie and I would fight back. Her motto was *Flower power won't stop fascist power*. Violence against our criminal government was an act of transcendent love.

I gazed at Bonnie facing away from me on her side of the bed. The rise of her hips and the swell of her bosom entranced me. She acted like a tough rebel woman, but on acid, she'd needed my protection. She needed me, and that was all the assurance I needed.

As I drifted into dreamless slumber, I wondered if my LSD fantasy had a grain of truth in it. Making a baby together would connect our mythic past to a positive stake in the future.

The phone rang, jarring us awake.

The Wake-up Call

R*ing-ring. Ring -ring!* It took me a moment to recognize the sound as a telephone and another to realize who and where the fuck I was. It was Thursday, September twenty-fifth, 1969.

Augh, Bonnie groaned beside me. "It must be my friends." She reached for the receiver on her side of the bed. "Hello?" She listened for a second, then swung her arm over her back toward me. "For you, Ron."

"Me? No one knows where I am."

"Hi, Ron! How ya doing, man!" The enthusiastic voice sounded familiar, but my mind hadn't reoriented after my LSD voyage.

"Uh, who is this?"

"This is John Bell, man, your *partner!*"

It took a few seconds to process the name through the Rolodex in my head before it came back to me with a sinking feeling in my gut. I kept my voice flat.

"Oh, yeah. Hi John."

"I'm down in the lobby, Ron. You gotta come down for them to let me in."

He must have tracked me down through the guys in Hyde Park.

John and I had spent every hour of the last week together. It had been an adventure, a bonding experience, except that John was flat broke, and we'd been spending *my* money. I couldn't deal with him just then, so I came up with an excuse.

"Ah, John, I'm with my chick right now."

"Oh, you with your 'ol lady, huh? Is that Ruby, that tubby little speed freak?"

"No, another chick and we're, like, *happening* here."

"Oh, I see. You're getting it on, huh?"

"That's right." I tried to think of an even more solid reason to dodge him. "Let me check with her if it's okay." I nudged Bonnie back awake and, with my hand over the mouthpiece, coaxed her to yell. "Don't go down!"

"Hear that? Not now, man."

"Well, gee, I don't know how long I can hang around–" I broke in with a curt unwelcoming edge to my voice. "Maybe see you later than," and hung up. Dropping back to snuggle Bonnie's warm body, I fell asleep.

An hour later, I splashed water on my face and my mind cleared to remember John's call. Then I remembered Sherry. I'd left her with him during our acid trip. I should have asked him about her, how she'd managed. That was already four days and two more acid trips ago. I told myself John would have kept her safe. Maybe she was with him down in the lobby. *Fuck!* I should have gone down.

Too late, that episode of my life was over. We all had to move on. I felt the sands of time slipping through my fingers. I was spending the last of my savings that I'd slaved so hard for and still hadn't found a place to live. All that seemed about to change.

Bonnie and I were together, leaving Chicago bound for New York. That eclipsed everything that had gone before. After our long night tripping on acid and each other, we got off to a late start, but there was no hurry. With a wide grin on her face, Bonnie sat up in bed and embraced me.

"That was some crazy shit you came up with last night, Ron. Do you really think we were lovers in a past life?"

"Gee, I don't know. It all just popped into my head, but it could be true. We fought the fascists in our last life, that's deep in our character, spontaneously manifesting now again. We're back, loving each other and fighting for justice again. Groovy, huh!"

"Well, up against the wall, you motherfucker!" Bonnie jumped up and pressed me against the wall, kissing me long and hard before continuing. "You belong with us motherfuckers now, Ron. We're forging alliances with the Black Panthers and Young Lords. That's what brought me to Chicago, but I can't wait to get back to the East Village. You'll love it there too." She kissed me again and pulled me into the bathroom.

Once more, we luxuriated in the shower, soaping off our love juice from the night before. Then we aroused each other one more time. It was almost a thousand miles to New York. It might be our last chance for a long while to make clean love in a shower.

Only minutes before checkout time, we skipped down into the dark subway on the corner and took the train to find the Interstate. South of Chicago, Bonnie and I struggled to get our bearings in the confusing maze of ramps at the I-80 cloverleaf.

"This looks like the best spot for us to stand," I said, hoping we got a ride before the cops hassled us. We set our packs down and thumbed passing cars. After a dozen passed by, an old beat up Chevy pulled over. Two clean-cut short haired guys sat up front with a pretty woman in the middle. All appeared to be in their early twenties. The driver called out, "Where ya going?"

"New York City," Bonnie yelled as we scrambled to hoist our gear and run up to his window. The driver raised his eyebrows and looked at the woman. "What do ya think, Hon?" She nodded, and he turned back to us. "Okay, we'll take you there."

Wow! Such instant success blew my mind; Bonnie was my lucky charm. She slid into the back seat, then I sat beside her with our packs on our laps.

"I've never been to New York," the driver said as he merged into traffic. "Neither have I," said each of the others. In fact, none of them had ever been beyond Chicagoland. They were locals with a capital L, busting out of their shells to join us. Bonnie filled them in on the enticements of her hometown.

"You guys will absolutely love New York! Just wait until you taste an egg crème, man. It's the absolute best!" She raved on about the vibrant music scene and social life, especially in Greenwich Village, the best part of the city, until she finally ran out of steam.

After a long inhalation, the driver's words came slow and deliberate. "I'm Fred," he pointed to the other guy. "He's Jack, and Shelly here is our girlfriend. I mean, she's with both of us."

"Way cool, man!" Bonnie congratulated them. It surprised me because they looked so straight. Shorthaired working-class types, not flamboyant, self-identified *freaks* like us. Then I realized I was selling them short, typecasting them. After all, I came from that same proletarian mold, post-World War Two Americana.

"You see," Fred continued. This trip is a nice break for us. It takes our minds off our troubles before we have to get back.

"Yeah." Jack shook his head in somber affirmation. "We all went to school together, and gee, we both fell in love with Shelly. Why fight over her when we can just let it be? Except we all got sick."

"What kind of sick?" I asked.

They all looked at each other. Shelly shrugged, and Fred answered. "We just got our diagnosis. It's VD. We were all bummed out, on our way to check into the hospital and start treatment. But when we saw you two standing there, it was like a sign that we needed to do something impulsive. So, we decided on a road trip. To clear our heads before we have to get back and deal with this thing."

"*Tsk, tsk,*" Bonnie oozed sympathy. "What a dose of bad luck. Huh?" A ripple of weak laughter lightened our mood. "But I hear penicillin works just fine. You guys will be okay."

Her positive attitude about it impressed me. I wondered what kind of VD they had. But I didn't want to confess my ignorance by pumping them for details. Modern medicine seemed to have it under control, which was good because life without sex would be unbearable.

Brimming with the optimism of our own adventure, Bonnie and I cheered them up with tales of our magical meeting on the shores of Lake Michigan and the miles we'd both traveled on our own before that. Within minutes, we wanderers became close confidants. Hitchhiking can bond strangers into instant friends.

"When we get to New York," Bonnie told them. "I'll buy you egg creams and introduce you to some *heavy* people. Did you ever hear of the Motherfuckers?" They hadn't. She filled them in on the revolutionary aims of her political collective, even going into the history she hadn't told me yet.

"It sprang from an earlier guerilla theater group called Black Mask. They hit the scene in 1966 but didn't grow until last year." She shook her head and closed her eyes like she was reaching for memories. "More and more of us started wising up, becoming politically conscious, and organizing against racism and the neo-fascism of the war machine."

Even I was impressed at how she belted out her call for revolution. Bonnie's voice became ever shriller. Her passion inflamed her, taking me with her into the wildfire that consumed me. I hung on her words as she continued.

"Hippy freaks began getting busted by the pigs. They screamed at them. *Up against the wall, motherfucker!* It was the repression that radicalized them, me too! Fuck the pigs! They gave us our new identity. We are proud to be called motherfuckers. Dig it?"

Her audience remained awed and silent. I dug it, but I worried Bonnie could be laying it on too thick for our new friends. Finally, Fred emitted a nervous laugh, while Jack seemed absorbed by the passing scenery. But Sherry, who hardly ever said a word, had turned around in her seat and watched Bonnie intently as if mesmerized by her performance.

Bonnie broke the rules of prim and proper *ladylike* behavior. She was no wilting wallflower but a hard charging gal who drew attention to herself. In Chicago, I'd noticed that admiration from other women too. I imagined they flocked to her because she spoke to a creative, adventurous spark they'd been told to hide deep with themselves. Sherry's eyes remained fixed on Bonnie as her speech reached a crescendo.

"We need to tear down the walls between us. To break free of the fucking death culture that puts us in a goddamn straitjacket of conformity. We Freaks have gotta take our country back and, and..."

She seemed to be reaching for elusive words, but then she caught herself and burst out laughing. "Well, shit, you guys know what I mean!" That broke the spell, and we all joined in for a rip-roaring belly laugh.

It was pitch dark by the time we reached Pennsylvania. We stopped to take a piss in the middle of a forest. As I emptied my bladder into the bushes, Bonnie hugged me from behind. Trippy, how totally at ease we felt with each other. It was a nice, romantic, heartwarming moment.

"Maybe I could play fireman with your hose," she offered, which set off a ripple of laughter from our friends pissing nearby. "You're too late, hon. That's the last of it." As I put my dick away, she pointed over my shoulder at the full moon and shouted, "Look, Ron!"

I'd lost my glasses. Squinting at the full moon, I thought I saw straight lines that crisscrossed into a Star of David, like what Bonnie wore around her neck. "Isn't that a great omen?" She said before kissing the back of my neck. If Bonnie saw it too, maybe I wasn't hallucinating. "Sure is," I agreed. "We're blessed by cosmic forces on this journey, babe."

A few miles farther on, our driver said he needed a rest. All three of them slumped together in the car while Bonnie and I cuddled in our sleeping bags beside a picnic table. With the faint purple light of hazy dawn, we got back on the road but didn't get far. Our pale and drawn driver pulled over again at a quaint little grocery store surrounded by pine trees near the New Jersey line.

"Sorry, guys, I'm real sick. Guess we gotta drop you and get back."

"That's okay," I told him. "We appreciate how far you took us."

"Thanks," Bonnie said as she reached over the seat and gave each of them a hug. "Ron and I hope you guys feel better soon." Our time had been short, but the farewell put at a lump in my heart.

"Too bad I didn't think to get their address," I told Bonnie as we watched them drive off.

"Crazy guy! What makes you think we'll ever go back to Chicago? New York is our home now."

Maybe so. Bonnie and I would create a brand-new chapter in each other's lives, and we were giddy with anticipation. She would introduce me to a broad range of comrades who shared our revolutionary vision. Her mysterious motherfuckers would enlist me into their struggle against racism and the imperialist war machine. Together, we'd struggle for true freedom, justice and forge the *new Mother fucking* American way.

The future belonged to us; nothing could stand in our way.

The New Jersey Turnpike

Bonnie and I stood in the gravel parking lot of the roadside grocery store. We didn't have to wait long. A pickup rolled up. A trio of burly guys in hard hats and flannel work clothes stepped out and waved us over.

"We're just gonna pick up a few things," said the cheerful driver. "If you don't mind riding in back, we'll take you closer to New York."

They came back out with several six packs of Budweiser. "Here you go." One of the generous men smiled. "Take this for the ride." He handed each of us a couple cans before we jumped in back. Our luck was holding up.

We sped along the highway, bundled in our coats, crouched behind the cab to avoid the whipping wind. The beer tasted good in our empty stomachs. Bonnie only drank a few sips in the time it took me to guzzle my two cans. "Here, I'm done," she said, handing me the rest of hers.

Man, this is living! Getting buzzed, I yelled into the sky. The view of lush emerald forest spread to the horizon on either side of the Turnpike enchanted me. My limited and prejudiced opinion of the whole east coast was that it was an overcrowded megalopolis.

"Wow, Bonnie, I'm surprised to see so much wilderness this far east. I figured they logged it off and filled it with people a century ago."

"They call this the Pine Barrens," she shouted above the truck's roar. "Hardly any people live here, just trees and wildlife."

The ride across New Jersey took longer than I anticipated. On the map, it's such a narrow state. As the miles rolled by, a new concern became urgent. The beer wanted out of me. I told Bonnie, who chided me. "You should have peed back at the store."

Through the window, I saw the guys up front polishing off can after can of beer. They'll *have* to make a pit stop soon, I assured myself. Exits were few, and so far between, each one that came up gave me fresh hope. My bladder strained at maximum capacity. These guys must have whale size bladders. Desperate, I banged on the window, shouting, "I gotta pee!"

They held up their beer cans, gave them a little shake, and said something I couldn't make out. They didn't pull over. I assumed they were mocking me.

Bonnie laughed. "That's what you get for guzzling all that beer, crazy man. Why not let it all hang out?"

"Very funny. I can't hold it any longer."

"Well, go ahead. Don't be some prissy sissy."

Unzipping as I kneeled over the tailgate, I smiled at a car following too close. The perceptive driver backed off as I let loose. To my anguished surprise, the slipstream whipped most of it right back at me. *Augh*, I pinched it off and moved to the side. The car came around to pass us and honked. The merry fellow on the passenger side gave me a thumbs up. I gave him my best shit-eating grin and let out another stream. Again, most of it came right back at me. *Fuck it!* It gave me such relief despite my unwanted bath.

Bonnie laughed with what I hoped was sympathy, and the wind dried me off in minutes. One guy in the cab threw out a beer can, from which a yellowish liquid streamed. It suddenly hit me how they managed their bladders. They'd been pissing into their empty cans before tossing them out. That was a valuable lesson to remember for next time.

At an exit before Paterson, New Jersey, they pulled over and dropped us off. It was still early in the day, and once again, we didn't have long to wait. Lady Luck, in the person of a professionally dressed young woman, pulled up to rescue us.

"Looks like you two need a break. I'm not going too far right now, but I can take you on to Newark in the morning. Are you hungry?"

Bonnie and I shook our heads in the affirmative.

"Come on. I'll take you to breakfast at my place."

"Thanks," I told her. "We haven't eaten since, ah..."

"The day before yesterday," chimed in Bonnie. She wasn't counting the beer, of which I'd had the lion's share.

After we jumped into the backseat, the woman twitched her nose and said, "From what I can smell, I'd say you guys need a nice shower too!"

She meant me, of course. But still tipsy, I'd already forgotten my misadventure in the back of the truck. Bonnie responded. "We sure would appreciate that." She squeezed my hand and chuckled. "It's nice meeting you. Our clothes need washing too, if you don't mind."

Her name was Kathy. She'd been on her way to work as an office secretary but lived in an urban commune she called The Big Purple. She flashed us a welcoming smile in the rearview mirror.

"I'll just be a few minutes late for work. Mike will show you around the house. I hope you'll still be there when I get home this afternoon. We can chat then. You seem like fun people, and you'd be welcome to stay with us a few days."

She pulled into the driveway of a large two-story house painted bright purple. It was otherwise unremarkable in the suburban neighborhood of stately trees and manicured lawns. A long-haired man came out. With his thick red beard and barrel chest, he looked like a Viking.

"What's up, Kathy? Did you forget something?"

"No, I found some cool people." She turned to us as we stepped out of the car. "This is Mike. He'll see that you eat, relax and"—she shot me a serious look—"tell him you guys need a shower. Okay? Sorry I have to run." She sped off to her office.

"Everyone else has already gone to work," Mike told us. "I'll have to leave too, in forty-five minutes. But let me show you around the place. It has all the modern conveniences if you want to launder your clothes.

"Finally!" Bonnie raved ecstatically over the washing machine. "This sure beats rinsing things out in the sink."

Mike and Kathy's openhearted kindness impressed me. Bonnie and I were Freaks who'd wandered in off the road. They'd made us welcome, trusting us on instinct.

"Peace and love, guys!" Mike called as he split for work. We had the whole place to ourselves.

"Wow, Bonnie. We've crossed the country and found cool heads all the way. Pretty groovy, don't you think?"

"Groovy, huh? Well, just wait until you meet our motherfucker tribe. They'll do anything for you because we're all brothers and sisters in the struggle." She reeled me in for a sloppy kiss. "It's happening. Damn straight, Ron. Our whole generation is turning on, breaking out of the stagnant fifties. Fuck the isolation and *up the Revolution!* Dig it?"

I dug it. It warmed my heart to imagine we belonged to an expansive subculture of sympathetic freaks. I felt connected; we were building a big community across the country, even spreading our good vibes around the world. I'd heard about freakish vagabonds venturing out across Europe and Asia, turning people on, spreading the message of love and togetherness and creating hippie havens along the way. Sure, there was risk, danger everywhere. Most of it was caused by artificial class and race boundaries. But that was our struggle, to tear down those mother-fucking walls!

We stripped and put all our clothes in the washer and ran it while we showered. It had only been twenty-four hours since our last loving shower at the hotel in Chicago. My prior hitchhiking experience was never as fortunate as this. Being with Bonnie meant everything, a guy alone, without a chick, could go days without a ride or such generous hospitality.

"Let's show our appreciation," I told her. "I'll wash you dry."

Still naked, we attacked the mountain of dishes piled in the sink. Then we mopped the kitchen floor and vacuumed the living room, finally putting clothes on when they came out of the dryer. Bonnie and I made a wonderful team. These domestic chores, while joking and laughing together, felt more like fun than work. Playing house could become a *thing* with us.

When the three resident women came in, they went, *Wow, look at our home!* Amazed at how we'd cleaned and straightened it up.

"You guys didn't have to do all that," Kathy told us, contradicting the pleased smile on her face. "You're our guests." Then she turned to me. "Go hang out with Mike and Bill. Us girls have this now." They shooed me out of the kitchen, keeping Bonnie to help them prepare dinner. Although Bonnie claimed to be a liberated woman who railed against the sexist concept of men's versus women's work, she said nothing, eager to bond with her *sisters*.

Lounging at the kitchen table, drinking the coffee and tea that the *girls* brought out, Mike and Bill, the only resident men, explained how their collective life operated. All the people who lived there worked at whatever straight jobs they found and chipped into a common kitty for rent and expenses. There were, they assured me, plenty of decent paying jobs around, and guys didn't even have to cut their hair, like I'd had to, to get a job back in Chicago. Most local employers had become *cool* with that male fashion trend that refused to abate.

"Why don't you two stay a few days?" Mike coaxed us over the rice and veggie dinner the gals had whipped up. "You seem like ideal people for us."

"It's a big house with several spare rooms," added Bill, who was holding hands with a grinning Kathy. "We'll help you find jobs; you'd fit in and get a kick out of this community."

Everyone else agreed, welcoming us as prospective housemates. I was sold on staying a while, but not Bonnie. After a good night's sleep between clean sheets in a room to ourselves, we woke to a generous breakfast of eggs, toast, hash browns, and god knows what else.

"We're way out in the *burbs* here," Kathy said, "but if you really want to go, I'll take you to the subway station in downtown Newark."

Bonnie perked up. "Yes! I'm familiar with the connection to the Manhattan system. We'll be in the village in no time!"

Mike continued to beg us to stay. "If you ever decide to come back," he said, scribbling on a slip of paper. "Here's our address." Pocketing it carefully, I promised I'd be back and meant it.

As it was Saturday, none of them had to work, so the merry band saw us off with a tearful farewell of hugs, handshakes, and backslaps before we loaded into Kathy's car. To leave these new friends so soon filled me with genuine sadness. The homey atmosphere, lively conversation, and a stomach full of delicious food tempted me. If alone, I'd stay, but I'd committed to Bonnie. She and her mother-fucking family would be my people henceforth.

The Big Village

The graphic news footage showed blood on the street, flowing from the crumpled bodies of Black teenagers. Shops burned into ruined hulks. Armed soldiers patrolled glass and brick littered streets swaggered over a conquered American city.

That was the image I still held of Newark. The 1967 riots seemed like yesterday, and I expected a scene of ruination but found an ordinary bustling city. Newark merged into a vast Megalopolis with all the eastern cities. Its subway station was the farthest link connecting us to that most mega city of them all, New York.

Kathy pulled over to the curb. "I'm going to miss you guys. I *do* hope you come back to the Big Purple. You've a lot to offer our growing commune."

She was as misty eyed as Bonnie, who'd begun digging her nails into the palm of my hand as we got closer to her city. Both of us brimmed full of anticipation for what lay ahead, mixed with the sadness at what we were leaving behind. After a last farewell hug, Bonnie and I dove into the dark subway.

Giddy Bonnie was in her element. She still carried subway

tokens that bought our passage through the turnstile to the platform by the tracks. As we settled into seats on the almost empty train, she rhapsodized on the glories of her beloved city.

"Oh, Ron, isn't it grand? I've missed it so, a city of true artists. This is *our* city now."

After a few stops, the car filled to standing room only, butts in our faces. Then we crossed a bridge. Sparks flew past the window as we careened around hairpin turns with a deafening screeching of wheels, much louder than any of Chicago's trains.

My startled reaction wasn't lost on Bonnie. She shot me a gotcha smile. Chicago was Hicksville compared to this monster. She'd brought her Rube to the big city. None of the other passengers even looked up from their numb passivity. New Yorkers seemed to cocoon themselves into an internal reverie that isolated them from the sensory overload of their surroundings.

At last, we climbed up into the not so fresh air and the unnatural darkness of downtown at midday. Too little daylight filtered in between the megalithic buildings that reached for the sky. Only a few blocks in Chicago's Loop resembled that, but New York's manmade canyons stretched for miles. Bonnie pulled me to a hole in the wall joint. It sold magazines and sundries as well as egg creams. She'd been mooning over them since I'd met her.

"Oh, Ron, you simply have to try this!"

She ordered two, her treat. The guy behind the counter knew her as a steady customer. As he whipped it up in a small blender, he listened to Bonnie speed-rapping about their wonderful city and how you *just can't* get an egg cream anywhere else in the world. He commiserated with her about the barbaric outlands beyond the pale of this city's refined culture.

"I've never even been out of the city," he said with apparent pride. "Why bother? Everything worth having is right here in the greatest city in the world!" Spoken like every New Yorker I'd met thus far.

At last, the glass was in her hand. With delicate sips, Bonnie savored every molecule, as did I. Yes, it was tasty. A cross between eggnog and a malted milkshake, but I'm no finicky gourmand and wouldn't swoon over it.

"Wow, Bonnie, this is the *very best* drink I've ever tasted in my whole life!" She didn't catch the sarcasm.

We strode through streets still bustling after the morning rush hour and took another train to the Village. At last, we came to what looked like a boarded over, run down storefront with peeling paint. We'd reached the mysterious motherfucker headquarters. A meeting was underway inside.

A semi-circle of eight bedraggled long-haired men and four hard-faced women, all in patched and worn jeans or bib overalls, sat on folding chairs. They confronted a perky young dishwater blond woman in a trim skirt and nylons, bright red lipstick, and painted nails. Dressed for success in the straight world, she was gorgeous, but looked out of place or out of class. She embodied a high-profile managerial type, whereas her audience could only be laborers, or maybe funky artists. The well-coiffed lady pled her case in an authoritative tone.

"Yes," she said. "I'm not ashamed to say I'm a liberal. Just because *we* work within the system does not make our ultimate goals any different from yours. We are all on the same side. We, too, want to end poverty and racism and bring the War that is killing so many of our boys to an honorable conclusion. Please try to understand our strategic position. Your confrontational tactics are making things worse, alienating middle-class people who have money and *could* be sympathetic to our cause."

That sullen audience only gave her contemptuous snickers. I felt sorry for her but had to admire her pluck. She was probably a representative from another community organization. According to Bonnie, New Left groups had been trying to tone down or tame the Motherfuckers, or the *Family*, as they called themselves. The Family favored outrageous street actions. They had taken over the Fillmore East Auditorium, liberating it for free concerts. *A free exchange of goods and energy*, as I later read in The *East Village Other*.

Bonnie led me to a pair of empty seats at the far end of the table and whispered greetings to her friends on either side. They nodded with stern, impersonal expressions, which contrasted with her effusive joy to be back among them. From the bored look on these Freak faces, the meeting seemed to have gone on too long. A bearded Freak wearing a pale blue top hat above frizzy auburn hair stood up and turned to Bonnie.

"I've had enough of this so-called meeting!"

Bonny squeezed my hand and said to him, "Let's go upstairs."

"Great."

Bonnie and I followed him up two flights of grimy, debris littered stairs to a dingy apartment. The door was open for air in that sweltering environment. An unkempt young woman stood cooking at the stove beside the door. Another woman sat on a chair on the landing, holding a baby. A man appeared from within, and spotting me, barred our way.

"Who's he?" He demanded of a flustered Bonnie.

"Him? He's with me. A comrade from Chicago."

"You just can't bring some fucking guy in here, Bonnie. Nobody knows him!"

"I do! He's a friend."

With an exasperated sigh, he yanked her inside while the guy we'd come up with pushed me back into the stairwell. "Sorry, man. I guess you have to await the verdict." He left me under the watchful eyes of the chick with the baby, who guarded me with a bemused smile while he trudged up another flight of stairs. Inside, I heard an intense shouting match from which Bonnie's strident voice rang clear.

Bonnie emerged at last, tight lipped, looking as if she'd survived a tongue lashing. She grabbed my elbow. "Come on, Ron. Sorry, this isn't what I expected."

We beat a retreat to the drab living room of a nearby apartment building. A neutral zone for unvetted visitors like me. The walls were decorated with pages torn from the *Subterranean Rat* and the slogans of sundry leaflets.

WALL STREET IS WAR STREET.

POETRY IS REVOLUTION.

BURN IT ALL DOWN.

ALL YOU NEED IS DYNAMITE.

Below, the cartoonish drawing of a squatting American Indian stood the pronouncement:

We are a new music...

A free Music ...

By a new people...

Expressing a new reality...

Other graphics featured M-16s above the slogan *Armed Love*.

There was no celebration of peaceful hippie flower power here.

"What do ya say, Ron?"

"Wow, this is cool shit."

"I mean about not being allowed inside right away."

"Well, I understand the need for security. But I tripped on acid with you. That's like truth serum. I'm a pretty unlikely undercover pig."

"Things have gotten heavy since I left New York." She shook her head and sighed. "People got busted. Now everyone's afraid of undercover agents. The Pigs are even infiltrating the Black Panthers; nobody knows who to trust anymore."

"Your recommendation should be enough. Don't you think?"

"Maybe after the meeting, they'll come get us." She yawned and glanced around the disorderly room. "Like I've been telling you, Ron. The Motherfuckers will love you once they meet you." She flopped on a threadbare couch, and I sat beside her. Plopping her head on my lap, she droned on about art, of all things.

"Did I ever tell you that ordinary life is the purest essence of art? Not that expensive elitist shit they hang in *museums of death*. That's fake art, Ron! Bourgeois people are hypocrites insulated from real life. They fuss over their spoiled sham artists. Fuck them! Revolutionaries are the true artists of REAL life."

I agreed with her about the phoniness of so-called modern art. We had a lot of ideas in common. But no one shares *everything* with someone they love, no matter how much they want to. I was hooked on Bonnie, but she was just as hooked on her city and rad collective family. Thus far, I didn't feel like I belonged there. Whether we were perfect soul mates or not, I didn't want to lose her. The problem was if or how we could make a life together.

A grungy longhair popped in the door, eyeing me before asking Bonnie, "Is he cool?" Bonnie assured him I was. They fell into the tiresome *glad to be back in New York* routine. Ignored, I stood up and leaned against the wall to wait them out. Then the guy asked Bonnie a question that blew my mind.

"Do either of you want some smack?"

I shook my head no, but Bonnie hesitated. That worried me until she finally said *no*. Heroin, smack, was the *Man's* counter-revolutionary poison. In the *do your own thing* hippie subculture, one met all kinds, but in the rarified air of hard-core revolutionaries, I never expected this. I hoped that the whole Motherfucker organization wasn't composed of junkies.

For the first time in my life, I watched someone cook up a white spoonful of heroin over the flame of a cigarette lighter and then draw the melted liquid up into a syringe. Bonnie, my dear sweet-tough girlfriend, helped him. It looked like she'd done it often enough to know the operation. I'd seen pictorial magazine articles on a junkie's life, but this was real.

Bonnie helped her Manhattan pal tie up his arm with a rubber tourniquet, which he held tight in his teeth before he plunged the needle into a vein. He drew back the stopper just enough to suck in some of his blood to the mix and then rammed it home. A look of utter relief spread across his face as he pulled the tourniquet loose

and flopped back on a gray mattress. Although it sickened me, I gave
no outward sign.

One slogan above the mattress caught my eye. *Fuck art! True art
is fucking!*

There had to be more than egg creams to make New York worth
my while.

Bowels of the Bowery

Bonnie shook herself awake. "Jeez, it's sure taking those motherfuckers a long time to see you." We both chuckled over that profane endearment.

She'd fallen asleep on my lap right after the junkie zonked out. He still lay there, mumbling to phantom dreams, so we knew he wasn't dead.

"It doesn't look like they'll meet with you tonight, Ron. Eventually, though, they *will* accept you." She yawned and stretched. "But it'll be *un-cool* for you to stay here tonight." Taking my hand, she led me out. "I'll show you to my favorite place in Greenwich Village."

That turned out to be the corner of Second Avenue and St. Marks Place. A parade of flamboyant characters stalked the streets, a mix of whites and blacks with a heavy sprinkling of Puerto Ricans. All costumed in an eclectic assortment of loud, garish outfits. The peacock finery of flowing capes, bizarre bonnets, and wide-brimmed hats set at rakish angles dazzled me. Most of them *had* to be gay men, or transvestites, or embodiments of a complex range of undetermined sexuality. They all seemed obsessed with themselves, their every move artificial, overacted and poised for effect, as if hoping some talent scout would discover them and broker their career on Broadway. None expressed any emotion beyond the cold indifference of the catwalk. Bonnie's interest in these living robotic mannequins surprised me.

"That's some real artistry," she sighed. "Too bad, though, Ron. It's not as *happening* as I'd hoped this afternoon."

"Not to me," I said. "It's way over the top."

Bonnie laughed. "Well, you're just a rube from Chicago. Believe me, *this* is quiet. Anyway, we'd better get going to tuck you in for the night." She gave me a quizzical look and asked: "Ever heard of the Bowery?"

"Oh, yeah, I watched the Bowery Boys. It's New York's skid row. Right?"

"Ha! That old comedy. Well, now you can see the real thing. It's only about a half-mile walk. Come on!"

It was getting dark as we crossed Houston, a busy Boulevard, the sidewalks crowded with pedestrians. A short haired, clean shaven guy in a tan trench coat approached us. He looked straight, not at all freaky. Ignoring me, he smiled widely at Bonnie and asked, "Wanna share a joint with me?" She didn't seem to know him. He looked like a narc to me, but Bonnie surprised me by accepting his offer with gusto. This was her scene, and I let her handle it. We stepped into an alley, and he lit up, passed it around until it became a stub in my hands. I tried to hand it back to the guy.

"It's a *roach*," he declared, making no move to take it.

"Eat it," Bonnie commanded.

My experience hadn't run that far. I knew a roach was the leftover butt of a joint, but did she mean literally to *eat* it? We always had smoked joints down to the nubs and put the residue back in the stash to be re-rolled into a new joint. Afraid of *weirding out* my hip girlfriend more than I already had, I offered it to her. "Do *you* want to eat it?"

Scrunching her face with exasperation, Bonnie took it. The

quarter inch of rolling paper wrapped around the speck of shredded marijuana was barely enough to hold between her thumb and forefinger. She inserted it deep into the back of her throat and gulped.

As a *hick* from Chicago, with nothing to add to the New York oriented conversation, I felt alienated. Getting high on pot always made me paranoid. It didn't help my confidence that Bonnie seemed to be flirting with the trench coat man. I had to stay alert. She could slip away and lose me if she wanted to.

Our trek ended at 227 Bowery, an awesome redbrick, fortress-like building that gave me the chills. Above red double doors, we read the name.

Bowery Mission,

It stood out in bold Old English script.

"Ya know, Bonnie, the first and only time I've been on a mission, I was a fifteen-year-old runaway in New Orleans. The priest turned me in to the cops right after I checked in."

"Don't worry, Ron. This place isn't Catholic. It's run by Mennonites and the Christian Herald Association."

"I doubt they're any better than the brown-robed monks I knew."

I followed Bonnie inside and joined the check in line.

"Another thing, Ron. Only men can stay here overnight."

"So, you're abandoning me here?"

"No, I'll come back for you in the morning."

I nodded in stoic acceptance of my fate. Whatever the fuck happened, I had to remain calm and keep it together. Somehow, things would work out for us. If there still was an *us*.

After checking in, we had about an hour before they'd troop us men off to the dormitory. Bonnie hung out, giving me more confidence in where I stood with her. We were both stoned, admiring the expansive main room beneath lofty ceilings. It was filled with aging tired men and a few women visitors, who seated themselves on rows of metal folding chairs. I'd expect to find these wretched of the

Bowery, but a few youthful faces stood out. I heard music and singing.

Puff, the magic dragon, lived by the sea. And frolicked in the autumn mist in a land called Honahlee...

A well-dressed couple in their mid-twenties sat apart. The chubby man strumming a guitar spotted us. He stopped playing and waved us over to sit with them. The woman asked, "Do you like *Puff the Magic Dragon?*" Bonnie said she did, and then the questions became more pointed. "Are you two married?"

"No way," Bonnie sounded indignant. "Are you?"

"This is my husband of two years." She pointed at her companion and then fired another question. "Have either of you been saved?"

Ah-ha, they were missionaries fishing for souls. "I'm a Buddhist," I interjected as a counterpoint to her Jesus cult.

"Oh, really? But you're American, weren't you raised as a good Christian?"

Her husband set down his guitar and jumped in. "You know, brother, I've tried all that goofy Eastern stuff. It sounds nice, but it comes from Lucifer, the devil himself, to deceive and lead us astray." He grabbed my elbow. His earnest eyes probed mine. "Let me tell you, brother, the gospel truth! All other religions are false. They lead straight to damnation!"

He might be making his bones like a zealous young minister. All my life, I'd heard this paranoid God versus Satan talk. Poking holes in his demented faith would lighten my mood.

"How can you be so positive that another person's faith is wrong?"

"Well, I ..."

I didn't give him long to answer. "Which books about other religions have you read? Huh? Which meditation practices did you try, and how far did you get?"

His stumbling evasive answers told me he understood little beyond the narrow-minded slanders of his dogmatic faith. By Bonnie's tripped out expression, I thought my exposing this *fire and brimstone* Christianity entertained her. But our minister had an even more unexpected arrow in his quiver. With a strange, otherworldly smirk on his face, he asked, "Do you believe in flying saucers?"

"What?" That new tactic took me off guard. "Not sure. Do you?"

"Oh, yes, they're *real* alright!" Right on cue, tears welled up in his eyes. Preachers like him trained to seduce and overwhelm their prey with strong emotion. "I had my own very personal experience with UFOs," he said. "One summer day, I'd gone out into the countryside of upstate New York. I wanted to meditate with nature." He looked hard at me to impress me with his sincerity. "Then I took some LSD. My ears started buzzing louder and louder. The world changed as an unholy fear overwhelmed me."

"You're just not used to the silence of the countryside," I told him. "The clamor of the city drowns it out."

"But wait, brother, there's more. A cigar shaped spacecraft came down from the sky and landed right before me in the meadow where I sat." He looked up at the ceiling as though seeing it again. "Creatures came out of the craft who looked almost like men. They radiated a halo of light, but I knew, a little voice told me, they came from Satan."

"Why Satan?" I asked. "Everything in the world isn't all good or all evil."

"They spoke to me, revealing themselves as the very angels who'd come down to earth to seduce the daughters of man. They wanted my eternal soul. It was just as the holy word of God says in Genesis. Oh, but YOU don't believe in the Bible!"

"Oh, come on, I think there are some interesting things in there, but too many contradictions, because the writers..." He cut me off. "They were inspired by God, HIS instruments, to pass HIS unchanging word to us!"

Bonnie watched him wide-eyed. I wondered if this was the first Bible thumper she'd come across. The sweat ran off his brow as he worked himself into an intense state.

"The Devil, my friends, is as real as you or me. Satan leads the unwary astray with a false message of love. Young man, protect your soul. He traps you into the sinful pleasures of the flesh. LSD is the forbidden fruit, the devil's sacrament." His facial expression appeared demonic as he raved. Meanwhile, his wife, with eyes closed, was nodding her head to the rhythm of his words as if entering a trance.

"Those demons in their flying saucers demanded that I open my heart to them, but the love of Jesus, who died for us sinners, saved me from entering that spaceship."

Suddenly opening her eyes, the minister's pretty sidekick interrupted. "Oh, before I forget, tomorrow is Sunday." Her sweet, perky voice contrasted with her husband's booming broadcast. "We're holding a televised church service aimed at England. There will be lots of food, and you'll get seen on television. Would you like to join us?"

Bonnie squeezed my hand, a signal that she'd be happy for the crazy adventure, even if it meant being surrounded by proselytizing gentiles. So, I spoke for both of us.

"Sure, we're in."

The lady smiled like a cat that'd caught a mouse. "Good, we'll bus everyone over after breakfast tomorrow. It will be held in a beautiful, huge cathedral."

The Minister added with a mournful voice, "Church attendance in Great Britain is at an all-time low. Satan and secularism are gaining ground in what had been a God fearing Christian nation. Our special live broadcast will beam our sermons and prayers over for their repentance and cleansing from sin. We'll fire up the holy spirit and save Christianity."

The PA system crackled to life. "It's time for all visitors to leave. All men who've signed in, please line up single file at the door."

Bonnie stood up. "Gotta go, Ron, but I'll be back early for this." I snatched a peck of a kiss, and she was gone, ostensibly to argue my case to the Motherfuckers.

After a communal shower, I dropped on a cot among the huddled masses and mulled over my situation. This wasn't how I expected my first day in New York to end. Bonnie had dumped me on a skid row mission like she had no further use for me. The thought began nagging me, even though I knew it wasn't her fault. What else could she have done when her tribe wouldn't accept me? Maybe it's where I belonged.

At fifteen, two years before, I'd run away to New Orleans and survived in a flophouse on skid row. There I was again, just one of these broken, dispirited men with no future. A shiver ran down my spine. No, I had to buck up and remain hopeful. It was only for one night. Bonnie's collective would take me in as soon as they had time to consider my case.

This night at the mission was just an episode in my crazy life. It shouldn't depress but educate me. Remembering my Buddhist faith, I tried to view those wasted lives around me with compassion. They weren't so different from me. We were the former members of the Proletarian working class, castoff and abandoned when we were no longer of use.

Bonnie insisted we had all been failed by society. Not the other way around. The capitalist system squeezed the value from our lives, leaving only a hollow existence that drove some of us to drink and drugs or simple emotional collapse. She and I, however, had plans. Though lumped into the unlovable Lumpenproletariat, we could see through the swindle.

These others, our lost comrades, could be saved, their lives renewed with *correct* political consciousness. If properly educated and organized, they could play a part in the Revolution. Thinking thus made my situation more bearable. Bonnie, my well-read anarchist, would *not* abandon me. We had ideals and a loving bond. It was difficult, but I had to keep reminding myself of that.

Turning the Tables

"Judy! Oh, God, Judy. I'm *soooo* sorry..."

That voice trailed off as it usually did. It was yet another cry in the endless dark night. A night punctuated by the sounds of sleep talking, sobbing men. The names invoked were mothers or long-gone lovers. The men's bodies lay in ranks, like graves, on long rows of cots on either side of me. My interrupted dreams mixed with pathetic reality. My habitual optimism waned. A chasm loomed beneath me, waiting to swallow me when I dropped. Without something to hold on to, I'd fall in and never climb out. I, too, could become just another wasted human life.

Fuck no! I shook myself free of the doldrums. For I was only a visitor, sightseeing in that land of the dead. This empty existence could never be *my* future. Not unless I too became addicted or brain damaged beyond repair. I had to keep talking to myself, reminding myself that I didn't belong here.

Maybe I didn't belong anywhere. Not in New York City for certain. Bonnie had needed me to bring her home safe. It wasn't her fault that her tribe wouldn't take me in. My usefulness to her was at an end. I'd become an embarrassment. She often reminded me I was

167

just a Rube from Chicago. She said it with a smile. Playful? Maybe. Or maybe she preferred a more urbane dude than I could ever be.

Had she dumped me here? I couldn't rule it out. Fickle lovers were nothing new to me. Goddamn it, I was a survivor! But I'd learned not to hold a grudge. At least I tried. Compassion was the key. True love had to be boundless, embracing all, far beyond the desire for a single someone, no matter how wonderful she seemed. Compassion required my seeing things from *her* perspective, her wants and needs, not mine alone. Even so, I had to be realistic about *my* situation. If she didn't show up, I'd have to fend for myself in this strange city.

It was Sunday morning, September 28, 1969. My belly growled; I'd had nothing since that wonderful egg cream the day before. Thanks to the hospitable Big Purple people in New Jersey, I'd stuffed my face before we got to this city. Feast and famine, I gotta eat when I have the chance. If Bonnie didn't show up, I'd go back to the Big Purple.

The doors opened, and we *down and outers* filed into the dining room for an institutional breakfast. Piles of instant scrambled eggs, toast, coffee, and juice sat on the table before us. Trustees, former bums reclaiming their lives in service to their fellows, waited on us. Starving, I asked for seconds and ate my fill.

"Hey, Ron!" To my relief, Bonnie bounced in. "I promised I'd come, didn't I?" Brimming with good cheer, she granted me a warm hug and a wet kiss, making everything better. High octane confidence shot through my veins. With Bonnie at my side, nothing could go wrong. The day seemed sunnier, bursting with joyful opportunity as we trooped outside for another wild adventure.

Lines of motor coaches pulled up in front, and we fell into line with an array of shabby derelicts. Bonnie and I seemed to be the only young, freaky hippies in the crowd of older men. They'd been rejoined by a few drawn and haggard women from the night before. An assortment of sober faced Bible toting Christians, dressed in their Sunday best, mingled in. Bonnie and I were the un-sheared and unrepentant sheep in their flock. The flying saucer couple from last evening found us.

"Jesus loves you, brother. Don't you know he's your lord and savior?"

In no mood for his conversation, I only smiled, shrugged, and shook my head at the appropriate times, while looking for my escape. Entering the bus, I managed to squeeze Bonnie and me onto the far side of a seat by the window, with no room for him to sit near us. He soon found other fish to fry, and we had some peace.

After a long drive, we ended up in several acre parking lot in front of a huge cathedral. There had to be over a thousand people stepping off scores of buses from other churches as well as ours. Ushers with walkie-talkies oversaw a massive operation to funnel us all inside.

The upper and lower balconies filled first with regular middle-class folk. They held our group of Bowery losers back to enter last. They wanted us to sit up front and center on the main floor, directly under the television cameras that were set up to pan all around us. We were the photogenic representation of errant youth, the rebellious prodigal children they needed to bully into salvation. Soaring ceilings and spectacular looming stained-glass windows astonished us.

"Wow," Bonnie whispered, squeezing my hand. "I love the way the glass diffuses the sunlight. So many colors, trippy!"

"Quite a sight," I agreed. "What do you think, Bonnie? Is it enough to awe us into becoming born again Christians?"

Although sarcastic, I was also assessing her reaction. We'd never discussed her religious upbringing, whether she'd been raised Orthodox, Reformed, or as an atheistic Jew. Curious as I was to know more of her background, I figured she'd tell me when she was ready. But she kept mum on the subject.

The cameras rolled. Martial hymns set the mood.

. . .

169

Onward Christian soldiers marching as to war
  with the cross of Jesus going on before...

The sermons began with shrill cries to repent. Extreme evangelism rolled over us on its way to the faraway heathens of England. If, that is, they bothered to tune in their *telly* sets or gather in the satellite linked churches. The wailing and praying the syrupy love songs to *Jeeesus* went on far too long. Bonnie and I were plodding through purgatory and becoming less Christian by the minute.

The reverse feed from England's churches gave us intermittent reports. We heard Britannic accented preachers rousing their somewhat smaller congregations to sing and pray in a stiffer upper lipped version of the rabid American style. The shrill sermonizer on our side of the Atlantic finally broke the congregation into small prayer groups, each under the pastoral care of a deacon. Ours was the smallest group of all.

Our deacon was a short, balding, middle-aged man. He took charge of our group, just Bonnie, me, and him. He wore a faint permanent smile, as if relishing a private joke.

"You two lovebirds look happy together." He sounded envious. Bonnie and I suppressed giggles as he started. "Let us bow our heads in prayer. We are all of us sinners, oh Lord, in need of repentance..." He spoke in a hushed voice. With our heads together, we were inaudible to the louder praying groups. It seemed he was only going through the motions. His heart wasn't in it. Then he deviated from the script.

"Is it true what they say about you hippies? I mean the free love stuff. Do you all make love to each other in your, ah, communes?" His interest in our lifestyle changed the tone of our relationship.

"Alright, I have a confession to make to you kids. I have real doubts, you see. I'm feeling disenchanted with this Holy Roller life." He sighed and glanced around the room, making sure no one else was listening. "It all seems so phony to me now. My marriage, too. It's degenerated into a no fun at all, sexless partnership."

"I get it," I tried to comfort him. "Your generation, my parents too, are going through the same kind of thing. It's cool to want more out of life. Don't you think, Bonnie?"

"Yes, you're not alone, man." She put an arm around his shoulder and, with a soothing voice, went on. "Our way of life *is* more authentic, more honest than this mainstream churchgoer shit." She winked at me and went on. "Maybe you should find another lover." Bonnie's forthright comment surprised even me. "If you open up your marriage, it could, like, inspire both you *and* your wife to find happiness."

"Yeah," I added. "Let *her* try out another dude, man. Maybe she needs inspiration. You know? A wild turn-on. But don't get jealous. Let her go. If she comes back to you, she'll be way hornier."

In a surprising turnaround, we'd become marriage counselors. Bonnie and I flashed knowing smiles at each other. Answering his sad questions about getting into a swinging lifestyle gave me a hell of a rush. Bonnie's jittery excitement told me she felt the same. We'd won a round in the culture war. This was our cause celeb, to turn on the straights, to be the pied pipers who danced them away into a culture of life.

Bonnie didn't recommend joining the Motherfuckers, of course. They hadn't even accepted *me* yet. But we were evangelists for the whole hippie-freak way of life, confident that bursting out of the rigid Puritan tradition, opening to love in all its manifestations, was the answer. It was our revolutionary duty to steer this troubled man away from the culture of death into the life affirming counterculture.

We spun exaggerated tales of our short yet fulfilling relationship and brief encounters, like the flirtatious fling we'd had with the biker and his chick. Full of ourselves, despite our youth, we'd become experts on love and sex. Then, our spiritual chaperone gave us some history.

"Let me tell you, kids." He glanced around again to see the coast was still clear. "The best sex I ever had was in Germany after the war. Cigarettes were valuable currency on the black market. You could get a Frau, that's a woman, for a pack of *Lucky Strike*, sometimes even for just half a candy bar. I was in absolute heaven!"

"How did you treat those poor women?" Bonnie asked, frowning. "My parents met in a DP Camp after the war. It's not just about you, you know. Did you speak any German or try to get to know any of them?"

From my reading, I knew *DP* stood for Displaced Persons Camps, set up for the refugees dislocated by the war. That told me Bonnie's family had been there. They survived the holocaust.

"Well, I learned just enough *Deutsch* to get by, and some of them could *sprechen Sie English* real good. The women, most of them, went wild. They really enjoyed sex. At least more than my wife ever did. A couple of my buddies even married their Fraus. I wish to God I had. My wife doesn't know about any of that! How could I tell her? She was the girl from back home who wrote me, waiting for me to come home alive. Everyone expected us to get married, so we did. We don't talk about sex, and I'm too embarrassed to ask her to-you know-try things."

This man from our parents' generation may have been more sexually experienced at our age than either of us. Still, *we* were the free love hippie Freaks, representing freedom he'd surrendered for membership in his staid, conservative society. Bonnie and I congratulated ourselves on chipping away at the established culture's false morality. As our pretend prayer time ended, we gave him a hug and wished him luck in finding his way back to *real* life.

"Join a commune," I advised with utmost sincerity. "If your wife won't come, dump her. You both need to free yourselves."

Bonnie smiled at me, her green eyes twinkling with approval. That's all it took to boost my spirits. Between Jesus freaking ministers who believed UFOs were agents of Satan and churchmen who wanted to join the wild hippies and get laid, life was motherfucking crazy. We Freak had to be ready for anything. I was confident we were on the right course to blow the minds of straight people and transform our culture with positive, humane values. In the meantime, we had to deal with oppression, subversion, and infiltration by the police state. Those pigs wanted to turn the clock back to conservative 1950s; politically conscious groups like the Motherfuckers had to be careful who they let in. Bonnie was on my side. It should be only a matter of time before her tribe let me in.

Hello Darkness My Old Friend

Another long bus ride took us back to the mission, but something was missing.

"Hey, Bonnie, I thought they promised us food?"

She laughed. "With Christians, as with Stalinists, the ends justify the means. We'd probably have to sit through another long sermon to get it." She tugged my wrist. "Let's scram."

We started back to her East Village haunts. After our memorable day together, it felt like I was floating, euphoric. Then we ran into her friends, one after another. They bounced their tiresome litany of Manhattan's allure off each other. She didn't even bother to introduce me; I stood there like the invisible man. No doubt about it, Bonnie was distancing herself from me around her friends. I had no other friends, nowhere else to go.

Still no word from her collective. The motherfuckers disenchanted me as a group more concerned about the tough image they were creating for themselves than anything substantial. An aimless hour passed, watching the self-absorbed, artificial human peacocks stroll up and down St. Marks. That only reinforced my alienation. Serious faced, she turned to me.

"Come on, Ron, I've got another place for you to crash tonight."

She hadn't said *we*. It was for me alone. My spirits took a nosedive. It would be another night without her by my side. She led me into a tenement building, up long flights of stairs, and through a trapdoor to the sunny rooftop.

"Here you go, Ron." She waved her hand, indicating the endless horizon of brick and tarpaper roofs. "You can crash up here for a few days. It's pretty secure. Lots of people leave their stuff here, and some of them might also be sleeping up here." She sounded upbeat, as if this was a happy substitute for our being together. Then her voice flattened into a businesslike monotone as she filled me in on the rules.

"The doors are locked at seven o'clock every evening until six the next morning. If you're not back here on time, you'll have to wait until morning to get in."

Her impersonal voice told me I was an outsider looking in. What a let-down. Only a few hours ago, we'd appeared to be happy lovebirds, acting as New Age marriage counselors for the sexually frustrated deacon at the church. That heady experience seemed to have evaporated already, making me feel lost and in a similar situation to the deacon. Although we were born into different generations, we men confronted similar issues by getting along with our womenfolk.

I plunked my duffel bag beside several other backpacks stacked in a shady corner of the roof. Relieved to have it off my shoulder, I arched my back and stretched, then reached out to this woman I needed to win back. She shrugged me off.

"No time for that now, Ron."

"No time? Damn it, Bonnie, I feel like a dog on a leash. You take me out on walks and then dump me off in a kennel!"

She laughed and patted my head. "There, there, good doggie!"

"Woof," I barked, trying to play along.

"Don't look so glum, Ron," she grimaced. "I don't make love to dogs."

"Yeah, but why such a long wait? Why couldn't we just *get down* and *rap* with whoever runs your collective? You know I'm no fucking pig!"

"It's only, ah, maybe another day or two. They'll have time to meet with you by then. And if *I* have time, I'll see you here tomorrow."

She seemed in a hurry and left me with a peck on the cheek like I was a small boy. I kept a brave face as I watched her go. But I had to wonder, even if her collective accepted me, would we be together again?

Rather than mope on the rooftop, waiting to meet whoever else might be crashing there, I explored. It was a sweltering late afternoon, so I changed my jeans for shorts. It would turn chilly later, so I carried my long coat, just in case. That turned out to be a smart move. I rambled into the West Village, seeking some semblance of humanity.

"Hello there!" A smiling dark-haired guy walking his ribbon bedecked, blond Afghan hound greeted me. "Are you new around here?"

"Why, yes, I am." I wondered if being an out-of-towner was etched on my face. We fell into small talk, and then he asked, "Do you like poetry?"

"It's not my usual thing, but I once read something by St. Francis that I liked."

"I know just the one you mean. Hey, come up for a beer, and I'll show you my books."

He was the friendliest guy I'd met so far in this city. Having someone to chum around with made all the difference. I followed him upstairs to a small, tidy apartment. Entering through the kitchen, we passed into the bedroom. The bed, a nightstand, a bookcase, and stereo being the only furniture.

"Sit on the bed; make yourself comfortable while I feed my dog. Oh, go ahead, check out the books!" He recommended some titles, which I thumbed through out of courtesy. The flowery words seemed to hold no ring of truth, leaving me uninspired. He swung around the corner from the kitchen and plopped a cold can of beer in my hand, then put on a smooth jazz record. "Just another minute," he said and went back into the kitchen.

Cordial hospitality is something you take for granted until you're too long a stranger. I leaned back against the wall and sipped the cold Budweiser, grateful to be off the street. Then I noticed a peculiar sickening odor. It was like a musty combination of stale shit, unwashed asshole, and something chemical I didn't recognize covered up by cheap perfume or incense. The wafting odor of cooked food coming up through the open window from neighboring apartments didn't help.

Maybe the chemicals came from the beauty and perm treatments he'd lavished on his extra thin Afghan hound. Her long, womanly hair was done up with multi-colored ribbons. There's no accounting for what people do to their poor animals. After eating, she put her head on my lap, staring at me with gloomy eyes. There was something unhealthy about that animal.

A crazy thought flashed through my mind. He's fucking that dog! But no, he couldn't be. I tried to be an appreciative guest and suppressed the idea.

"Okay, I'm finished!" He placed another cold can in my other hand. I gulped down the first and popped the tab on the second as he plopped down, way too close, beside me on the bed.

"Did you find the St. Francis poem?" He reached across me to grab another book, laid it on my lap and pointed to the famous passage about loving all God's creatures. Seeing my lack of enthusiasm, he turned to another page. "Let me read you something I *know* you'll like."

Bright star, would I were steadfast as thou art-
Not in lone slender hung aloft the night
And watching, with eternal lids apart...

"That one's by John Keats. Ever heard of him?"

I shrugged my shoulders. "Sounds familiar, but I don't know a thing about him."

"Listen to this shorty he wrote."
Beauty is truth, truth beauty-
that is all ye know on earth, and
all ye need to know.

Um-hm, I mumbled. "Sounds cool, but I'm not sure if we all agree on what beauty is." I suppressed a chuckle. "Back in grade school, I'd loved the *Charge of the Light Brigade.* Later, I ran across Allen Ginsberg's *Kadesh* and *Howl.* Those poems resonated, man, exciting me deep inside. But most of the stuff I hear is too vague and flowery, flaccid. They irritate rather than excite me."

Midway through my second beer, he took it from my hand. I was about to protest when he grabbed my shoulder and pulled me back onto the bed, snuggling his wet mouth against my ear.

Shit! I should have expected this, but I hadn't wanted to believe that the only friend I'd made in New York was after my ass. Although disappointed, I didn't want to hurt his feelings.

"Wait a minute!" I broke free of his grip and sat up. "I gotta take a piss, man."

"It's right by the door," he called from the bed as I lurched into the kitchen. "Hurry back."

Passing the washroom, I went straight out the door, bolted down the steps and out into the bright sunlight. Fresh air! Woozy from the beer on an empty stomach, I hyperventilated to regain my equilibrium.

Maybe I should have stayed and explained to myself that the very idea of fucking a man convulsed me in nausea. Maybe we could still yak about it on an intellectual level, laugh, and be friends, whatever. But after he stuck his tongue in my ear, shit, that wasn't my thing. I didn't want to have to fight him off. Now, if we'd had a woman between us, well, that would be different.

Although my belly growled, I balked at blowing my last few dollars on a meal. As I continued my perambulations, a guy ahead of me put his hot dog on the hood of a car and boarded a bus. It was still hot, and half a dog was better than none. Someone laid aside a soda, another one a partially eaten sandwich, and then a guy dropped a huge slice of pizza in a trash barrel after only one bite. Well wrapped, it landed clean. My scavenging was as germ free as I could make it. But wandering afar without a watch, I lost track of time and had to reorient myself in the maze of streets to get back. Too late, I found my rooftop sanctuary locked. I'd have to pull an all-nighter on the street.

Cheer the fuck up! I told myself. It'd be an adventure exploring the city's night scape. A bunch of teenagers hung out in front of a grocery store, and I joined them, *shucking and jiving*. They came and went. All of them had places to be, and I didn't. It got colder. Good thing I'd brought my long coat. It covered my bare legs when I brought my knees up to my chin.

A bespectacled twenty-something man walked up to where I sat on the stoop with a couple of the remaining boys. "Any of you fellows want a free bottle of wine?"

"Why not?" I said. The other guys backed off, and I followed him inside. Sure, he was probably gay. I resigned myself to that. Who else would be asking young guys out for free wine? But I was in an expansive, tolerant mood, open to share conversation and companionship with anyone who gave me some consideration. And broke as I was, sure as hell could use the free wine to help me get through the night.

"I'm a psychology student," he said, shaking my hand. "I want to ask you some questions and monitor the effects of alcohol on your answers. Okay?"

That sounded familiar. Like the guy back in Hyde Park, this man was probably gay, trying a line that he thought didn't sound too obvious. Whether straight or gay, a horny guy can't just walk up and ask someone to fuck unless they're in some kind of bordello or something.

He led me to the cooler. "Do you prefer white or red?" I chose white, and he grabbed two bottles. "Let's go somewhere quiet to talk." We slid into the front seat of his car. "I'll drive you back here later."

He drove farther than I felt comfortable, but I didn't want to betray my alarm. I had to be ready for anything. The situation reminded me of the guy claiming to be a psychologist back in Hyde Park. I'd thought he had a sexual interest in me too, but he bought me dinner and never tried anything. Most people I ran across were decent enough. I was used to taking risks and was unwilling to be paranoid. But I was realistic and knew the risks. People could be underhanded. I'd watch him out of the corner of my eye. If he proved to be a son-of-a-bitch and tried something, I'd jump out of the car. In that case, I'd have to find my way back to familiar territory. Not something I looked forward to, but that's why life is an adventure. I'd take on whatever it sends me.

He parked in an empty back street parking lot overlooking a trash-strewn factory yard and handed me the first bottle. Sweet and refreshing, I chug-a-lugged it down in no time. He started reading from a clipboard and checked my answers, asking me about my origins, lifestyle, likes and dislikes, then some word association exercises.

"Just answer with the first thought that comes into your head."

My high school shrink had put me through all that nonsense. It was a *white-black, good-bad*, sort of thing. He handed me the second bottle."We'd better begin the serious phase." His eyes narrowed, boring into me. "Can you feel the effects of the wine yet?"

"Not yet." With more than a full bottle of wine in my gut, I didn't feel at all drunk, which surprised me as much as him. He probed my sexual history.

"Have you ever masturbated?" I gulped and admitted it.

"Ever screwed a woman?" That was easier to admit.

"How old were you that first time?"

"Earlier this year, I'd just turned seventeen." My youth embarrassed me, and I took another long swig, almost emptying the second bottle.

"Did you like it?"

"Sure, I LOVED it."

"Did you ever get oral sex? You know, a blow job?"

"No." That honest answer made me blush, self-conscious about my lack of experience.

"Would you like to get a blow job now? From a man?" His hand inched closer to my thigh on the seat.

"No, man, sorry." The wine I'd gulped relaxed me, but my brain remained crystal clear in taut survival mode. He dropped the pretense of testing and propositioned me outright.

"Look, man, nothing personal. I'm just *not* into guys." I got out of the car. "Thanks for the wine, though. Hope you got something you can use in your study."

"Wait." He sounded concerned. "How will you get back?"

"I'll find a way, but I don't want to put you out or fuck you for it."

"Don't worry, kid. I'll take you back; I'm a man of my word."

I released the door handle. He turned on the ignition and backed out of the lot. Being gay and looking for action didn't make him evil. We could be friends. On the drive back, we chatted about *my* problem with sex.

"Let's face it, kid; being such a strict heterosexual, well, it limits your options. Women are only half of the human race."

"So? Do you want to fuck all humans, babies too? I mean, really?"

"Don't be ridiculous."

It was ridiculous. I chuckled some more, remembering Bonnie saying that she didn't fuck dogs. And then there was that Afghan hound made up to look like a hussy. Maybe the poetic guy really was fucking his dog. Maybe if I was in prison for a long enough stint, I'd lust after men or even dogs. I broached the subject with this psychologist if that's really what he was.

"What about bestiality, huh? A dog will hump your leg, but do you want to hump a dog?"

He snorted. "I'm human. Making love is about connecting with another human being."

I burst out laughing again. Our whole conversation was hilarious

"So, you're not attracted to dogs? See what I mean? I'm attracted to women. Guys don't do that for me; they just don't turn me on. But, yes, I feel a human connection with them." I erupted into more laughter. "You too, man. That doesn't mean I want to fuck you. Get it?"

"Okay, kid." He sounded resigned. "You made your point. Here's where I picked you up." He pulled to the curb. "It has been a real pleasure conversing with you, kid, even if you did turn down my generous offer." He squealed a girlish giggle. "Maybe you'd like to reconsider. After all, we did make a nice connection. Don't you agree?"

"No thanks, dude. I'm not judging you, man. I just know what I like."

Standing up from the car, the wine hit me all at once. Whoa! I was tipsy and almost fell over, but damn, it felt great to be back on familiar turf. The boys were gone, and the little store was closed, but the night was still young and barely begun.

Drunk on wine, the glare of streetlights and flashing neon signs made the landscape around Washington Square a surreal wonderland worth exploring. But even if I had money to spend, the nightclubs wouldn't let me in. I was underage and could only watch the action like an alien voyeur at a human zoo.

A car pulled to the curb beside me, and a well-dressed young couple got out. The frizzy blond bombshell backed her tall, dark-haired man against the car, pulled his neck to her level, and kissed him like a ravenous beast. The crowd gathering on the sidewalk hooted.

Oo-la-la! One laughing guy hugged his own girlfriend and shouted, "Save it for later, man, we're late."

The kissing couple could be mirror images of Bonnie and me in our finer moments if only we could afford those expensive threads. Street Freaks like us wore cheap garb. If we'd join the mainstream, like our dear parents wanted, we'd have all the security and comfort this identical couple flaunted.

Breaking away from her lips, the dude grabbed his gal around the waist and steered her into a nightclub. The rest of the laughing, backslapping, jeering fellow revelers followed, escaping the night's chill inside. They'd gone where I, at seventeen, could not follow, to be sealed away from me in a parallel dimension.

The streets fell silent. Where was *my* society? For all, I knew Bonnie could be living it up with her citified *real* friends in one of those establishments. My feelings about her swirled around in circles, from hot to cold. She loves me. She loves me not. Should I stay, wait for her one more loveless day in New York, or get the fuck out?

From time to time, the streets came alive again as the crowd spilled out to stroll to other nightspots. A dour longhair in an incongruous patched and dirty three-piece suit walked among the revelers of the night. His head down, he kicked at debris in the gutters, stooping to pick up the un-smoked butts of cigarettes and the occasional cigar that he would wipe off and place with utmost care in his vest pocket. Now and then, he would light one and inhale, savoring each puff, his face transported, delirious with pleasure. Thin and haggard, although still in his mid-twenties, he seemed to be in the same predicament as me. I hailed him.

"Hey, man, what's happening?" Ignoring me, he focused on the prizes in the gutter. Imagining him as a kindred spirit, I shadowed him, trying to open a conversation, some rapport with him. Suddenly, he turned on me with bared fangs.

"Leave me the fuck alone, man! I got nothing to say to you." All he wanted was to wander the gutters unnoticed by the *swells* who tossed away the substance of his pleasure. His grubbing vocation seemed a waste for such a young man. There had to have been other goals at one time in his existence. There had to be someone, a community, other creatures, whether human or animal, that he cared about. Deep in my bones, I knew his truth. We were all just shadows passing through each other's lives, important only for what passing pleasure we could take from each other.

I, too, continued my scavenging. Seeing a well-dressed man exit a phone booth, I jumped in to check the coin return. Seventy-five cents! A bigger haul than I usually got. On to the next phone booth–

empty—but then I found a full dollar's worth of encouragement in another. So, from booth to booth, I roamed, rechecking them with occasional luck. More change turned up, sparkling under the lamplight on the street. My jangling pockets gave me fresh optimism and financial security.

If guardian spirits were real, I wasn't completely alone. An invisible Lady Luck watched over me in lieu of my dear Bonnie. Then doubts assailed me. This whole experience felt more like a hallucination than real life. Maybe I was still back in Chicago, tripping on acid and imagining all this. I kept checking my pockets, wondering if all that loose change would suddenly disappear. Maybe I'd awake from this strange dream as broken and alone as ever.

Alone! Despite all the friends, lovers, and manipulative con artists who'd passed through my life, I only ever had myself for company. Hallucination or not, this scrounging for coins wasn't the life I craved. Bonnie didn't seem eager to get me into her collective. Maybe I was fooling myself that we had anything in common.

At two o'clock, bars began closing. People poured back onto the streets, heading home. A couple of rugged, square-jawed, thirty-something men in flannel working men's duds approached me.

"Hey, man. Aren't you freezing in those shorts?"

"You bet! That's why I keep jumping up and down for warmth."

"Come stay with us until morning."

Under normal circumstances, I'd accept without hesitation, but all I'd been running into were gay men who wanted me to *put out*. These guys didn't look gay, but I needed to make my sexual orientation clear. I didn't want to give them the idea that I would be their date. Chicks had my complete sympathy. They had to deal with the demands of pushy guys who expected something in return for their hospitality or favors.

"Just so you know, man, I'm not gay. Okay?"

The guys laughed and elbowed each other. "We're just a couple of regular guys offering our warm apartment to you, man. No big deal. Come along if you want, or stay there and shiver."

Their posh building nearby appeared ritzier than the others I'd seen, but like all apartments in New York, rich or poor, it was tiny. I plunked down on the shag carpeting, dead beat, while they continued drinking and talking at the kitchen table. Finally, they each crept off to raised loft beds in open door rooms on either side of me.

"Hey, man," one of them whispered to me from his bed. "I don't bite. Come on up here. Get comfortable."

"No, thanks, I'm fine where I am."

"Don't be silly. I won't try anything, honest."

He kept insisting. Finally, I went up and drifted straight into la-la land. Something jarred me awake. My bedfellow was inching his hand up my thigh.

"Look, man," I sat up, pissed-off. "I told you I wasn't up for that shit. Dig?"

"Sorry. I didn't mean it. Uh, unless you want me to, that is."

I had to take a piss, anyway. Piled next to the door of the bathroom, I discovered three waist high stacks of pornographic magazines. Finishing in the bathroom, I glanced through them.

Wow! It was hardcore stuff. Nothing in the pile was as innocuous as Playboy magazine. Every full-color image featured the most explicit and raunchiest depictions of sex I'd seen in years. Women with huge tits, eyes smiling at the camera, sucked cocks, while other men fucked them from behind. Showing actual genitals performing sex acts was still illegal, not available over the counter. The only explicit porn I'd seen before dated from World War Two.

A friend's dad, an amateur photographer, had a five-inch stack of prints depicting similar activity stashed in his desk. He'd probably taken some of them himself in wild bordello orgies in the European Theater. Those were all black and white, but these new ones were in vivid color. Red-hot skin tones warmed my heart and crotch. Entranced, I perused several pages before I noticed something important in a full-frontal shot.

These narrow-hipped chicks had dicks! Turning page after page and digging deeper into the stack, I discovered that not a single picture featured natural born females. With cocks standing proud and erect, all these *women* were silicone enhanced lady-boys. That deflated my ardor. No way could I get it up for a chick with a dick.

When I didn't rejoin my host in bed, he got up and let me back out into the cold. The cigarette butt hunting derelict was still there, all alone on the lifeless street. He didn't even bother lifting his head to acknowledge my wasted greeting. As if under a witch's enchantment, he continued going back over the same gutters, again and again, seeking fresh deposits of cast-off smokes. He seemed to be the mere shadow of a real person. If I stuck around this town long enough, I'd end up just like him.

Pulling myself together, I made the difficult decision. The Motherfuckers didn't seem to want me, and I wasn't sure that I wanted them. Bonnie remained dear to my heart, but she was a New Yorker through and through and wouldn't leave. She was just stringing along, unsure what to do with a hick like me. I couldn't imagine what to do there and decided I'd better split while I could.

Part Four
Poles Realign

Break on Through to the Other Side

Streaks of red lit up the sky before sunrise. I found the roof unlocked, no one around, and my duffel bag–thank God–undisturbed. The day would be warm soon, so I didn't bother changing into long pants. Hefting my gear, I clomped back down the long staircase. Taking stock of my pockets, I discovered only two dollars in coins remained beside the five-dollar bill stashed in my watch pocket for a dire emergency. Some three or four dollars of my giant haul of change was missing. Maybe it slipped from my pockets lying down for my brief rest at the last house. That limited my breakfast choices.

It was Monday, September twenty-nine, my third day in New York, but I'd had my fill of it. A coffeehouse on First Avenue opened early. To judge by the rad posters in the window, it was a focal point of the counterculture. Maybe I could snag a ride or get directions to the highway.

A couple of swell looking chicks about my age sat at a table on the far side of the otherwise empty joint. The sight of them perked me up. Even though they seemed far beyond my reach, I smiled a cheerful *hello* at them. After picking up a much-needed coffee and

189

yogurt at the counter, I grabbed a seat at a table across from them. The brunette smiled back at me and whispered something to her platinum blond companion, who made eye contact and waved me over. Blown away by the offer, I approached.

"Hi, I'm Ron. Mind if I join you?"

"Please do!" The blond extended her hand, palm down. I kissed the back of her hand, European style, as I often did, and got a laugh out of them both as I pulled up a chair.

"I'm Karen Blake," the brunette said, extending her hand, which I favored in the same way. "We're sisters from DC."

Smitten by the brunette's come-hither smile, I missed catching the blonde's name.

"I'm from Chicago, and today I'm heading back that way."

They sat up straight when they heard that. "I'm sick of this dumb city," Karen said. "New Yorkers are too creepy."

Mustering my dwindling reserves of charm, I shared my recent adventures. Our warm conversation re-energized me, dissolving the effects of my miserable night. Within minutes, we'd become friends. Then I noticed a bright red poster on the wall beside us that sent a thrill up my spine.

"Listen to this." The chicks gave me their rapt attention as I read.

"Bring the war home!

"It has been almost a year since the Democratic convention, when thousands of young people tore up Pig City for five days. The action was in response to the crisis this system is facing because of the war, the demand by black people for liberation, and the ever-growing realization that this system just can't make it. This fall, people are coming back to Chicago: more powerful, better organized, and more together than we were last August. SDS is calling for a National Action in Chicago on October 8th-11th. We are going to bring those we left behind last year."

"Wow," I panted, breathless. "It's like they're talking to me. I missed the Democratic convention. Now here's my chance to make up for it."

SDS, the Students for a Democratic Society, had been organizing college campuses since 1960, advocating for the Civil Rights movement and then, as the Vietnam War escalated, the anti-war movement with demonstrations and campus takeovers

"SDS is becoming more militant," the blonde said. "They've been splitting up into factions. The Weathermen faction is calling for armed revolution."

"Weathermen?" I asked. "That's a weird name for a revolutionary group. Never heard of them."

"Really?" Karen sounded surprised. "They've been all over the news."

My coffee had cooled, but my brain was still fried. I chugged down the black medicine and took a deep breath. I'd need stimulation to keep my head on straight.

"I've been living on the street, out of touch with the news lately. I came out here to join the Motherfuckers, but they don't seem open to outsiders, wouldn't let me in."

"Ah, the crazy motherfuckers," the blonde said. "They're just a bunch of egotistic power trippers. Those chumps tried to take over the Fillmore East last year. Bill Graham set that place up from scratch, put his own money into it. After all, he did to get a big name, west coast bands to play out here. They called him a greedy capitalist. The Filmore East wouldn't even happen without him, and he did a lot to keep ticket prices affordable. The motherfuckers demanded free concerts. Even hippie bands need to make some money. They don't want to play for free.

"They brought in winos, bikers and Bowery bums, calling it a Free Exchange of goods and energy. Like hell it was. When the MC5 came, Bill Graham gave away free tickets for their concert. They're supposed to be a Revolutionary band, in sympathy with the Motherfuckers, but the crowd of deadbeats were out of control and trashed their equipment. The band just said forget this and took off. Fucking bums, that what I think of the Motherfuckers. Despite all that poor Graham tried to do for them, they trashed the place, and he was the one the cops came down on. They said he'd lose his license, and the Filmore would be closed.

All that validated my decision not to wait around for the Motherfuckers to welcome me into their collective. Much later, I read more about it in the *Rolling Stone*. Bill Graham helped start the music scene out in California when he opened the Fillmore West. Then he created the Fillmore East and brought Rock and Roll bands to New York. It was like a cross-pollination of our rising hip culture on both coasts. Bill Graham was on our side, not someone to alienate with barbarian overkill. We needed to confront the real enemy, the military industrial complex which ran our political culture. The action in Chicago seemed tailor made for me.

"What do you think about the Weathermen?" I asked.

The blond frowned. "The Weathermen are too violent. How can they bring peace by fighting the cops? Whatever happened to peace and love, nonviolent protest?"

That set me off on a tangent. "Peace? What about justice? They kill nonviolent leaders like Martin Luther King. Peaceful protestors have only gotten their faces smashed while they bomb Vietnam into the Stone Age!"

Karen squinted at me. Maybe I'd gone too far. I didn't want to blow this scene with them. Her words came slow and measured, like thick honey from a jar.

"You've got some goddamn balls, Ron." Unsure how to take that, I started to reply. She cut me off with a wave of her hand. "I dig that." The dreamy tone of her voice bucked up my confidence.

Her sexy bedroom eyes held mine. Her lips widened in a crooked smile, like a Cheshire cat that communicated volumes without a word. My head spun and lightheadedness overcame me. I was stoned without the aid of booze or drugs. She and I could go places together. I had to say something, or the moment would pass. They could slip away from me like a summer dream. With effort, I regained control of my voice.

Ah-hem. I cleared my throat and popped the question.

"Wanna come with me to Chicago?"

Karen grabbed her sister's hand. They locked eyes for a moment. "I'd love to, Ron. I want to see this country, and I hate the pigs too, but-"

Her sister broke in. "There's something we have to tell you, Ron." She leaned over and whispered something in Karen's ear, then back to me. "It's this guy we're with. See?"

Karen reached across the table to grab my hand. "It's Caesar. We'll have to break it to him somehow."

Caesar? As an anti-imperialist, maybe I'd have to pull an Ides of March on him.

Render onto Caesar

C *aesar*? That word only referred to a Roman emperor in my vocabulary. Was that how they addressed their lord and master? The Blonde spoke up. "He's Puerto Rican, you see. He's been great to us and everything, but, well, those guys can get jealous. So, we're not sure how he'll take losing Karen from our, ah, family."

Then I realized Caesar was his first name, not his title. I'd discover it was as common a name as Jesus in the Hispanic community.

Her sister nudged Karen toward me. "Maybe you should just go ahead and take off with Ron! I'll work things out with Caesar." Turning to me, she sucked in some air and ran down their situation.

"Caesar started out as *my* boyfriend. See? When Karen," she paused and shot a glance at her. "When Karen left home and joined us, well, it gets a little crowded in these New York apartments..."

Without being explicit, she implied Caesar had *slept* with them both. One guy with two women! He was living the dream of every man I knew. The thought crossed my mind that I could make it a groovy foursome. The group marriage I'd joined back in Taos could work here. But I'd have to be careful. I'd seen how relationships could

194

be mishandled to end in disaster. Polygamy is built deep into our male psyche, but women prefer exclusivity.

Maybe her sister was trying to get Karen out of the picture and keep Caesar for herself. I wanted to meet this Caesar, but it could be dicey. What if he was possessive, protecting his harem with a switchblade? He might even be a pimp, considering these fine ladies his merchandise.

Karen aimed another flirtatious smile at me. My heart beat a fast drumroll as I felt her hand clasp mine on the table. Only an hour ago, I'd felt abandoned on the heartless streets. Karen's interest changed my situation into a fantasy come true. The universe looked harmonious again; waves of calming vibrations coursed through my body.

Bonnie's face popped into my mind, along with a twinge of guilt that ran through me before I reminded myself that *she* had dumped *me*. Or had she? I got too many mixed messages from that sweet little motherfucker. Damn it all! She'd left me flat broke on the roof, and I had to fend for myself.

Karen kept hold of my hand as we stood up. They led me to Caesar's apartment, near the building where I'd left my bag overnight. We had a little time before he came home from his night shift, so they let me inside the small but well-furnished apartment. Feminine touches, like frilly curtains, sweet smelling flowering plants and doilies on all the counters, made it a cozy place for their lord of the manor.

"Karen," I said. "Let's grab your stuff and split before he gets here."

The ladies again exchanged looks. Karen's sister turned to me, rolling her eyes.

"I'd better talk to him, Ron." She faced Karen. "Alone, first." Then back to me. "Don't worry; I know how to manage him. Follow me."

She led me up the staircase and opened the trapdoor to the roof. "You better wait here." She had a nervous edge to her voice. Karen's face was expressionless, but she gave me a quick nod before following her sister back inside. They closed the trapdoor behind them.

A sudden silence engulfed me as I wondered what I was getting myself into. My imagination went wild. Could I trust these chicks? Maybe it was all an elaborate setup, like the wild stories I'd read in men's magazines. Latin lovers could fly into a jealous rage with little provocation. Would an enraged Caesar butcher me with a switchblade?

No, that was a crazy idea. These ladies wouldn't betray me. They'd keep me a secret. Maybe they'd make me their *kept* man, a gigolo hidden up on the rooftop for their enjoyment. While their official master, Caesar, remained unaware of me. He'd sleep with them, singly or in turns in his comfy bed, while I satisfied myself and them with quickies while he was at work.

The morning sun climbed over the horizon. Watching the orange glow cover the tenements calmed my jangled nerves. I tried to doze. Whatever mysterious fate held in store for me, I needed to stay calm to be ready for it.

Finally, the trap door reopened. Through bleary eyes, I watched a tall, slim Latino guy, the same lanky build as me, pop out of the hatch and walk straight across the tarred roof towards me. His long black hair tied into a ponytail hung over his right shoulder, almost to his belt.

Shit! The girls had given me up to their jealous lover. But something didn't fit. He was smiling and holding a tray with two coffee cups.

"Here, man, you must need this by now." He squatted, holding the tray before where I sat, offering a cup with dignified grace. I accepted his unexpected hospitality with a murmur of thanks.

"Cream or sugar?"

Still cautious, I tried a little of each. When he did, too, it reassured me it wasn't drugged or poisoned. This was turning out so differently than I'd anticipated.

"Look at this, will you?" Caesar waved his hand at the view

196

across the rooftops of the Village. "This is the best view in the Village."

We shared a moment of relaxed silence, sipping coffee together like old friends. Even so, I kept a slice of my mind on alert, just in case. Then, in a soothing conversational tone, Caesar asked: "So, you and Karen are going to Chicago, huh?"

Should I admit that? I needed to know what the girls had told him to keep our stories straight. Over his shoulder, I saw them peering out of the hatch. They seemed to nod that it was okay, so I answered.

"Yeah, Chicago's where I'm from, and I can't seem to make a go of it here."

"That'll be great, man," he said, a big grin on his face. "Karen's a terrific chick, and you seem pretty cool. I just want to be sure she's in safe hands. I went to Chicago once. It's a mellow town."

Caesar and I became instant buddies, the comradeship of men bonding over women. Some of the more radical women I'd run across would call it sexist. But we were dividing up the turf in an equitable way, with righteous consideration for all concerned. We needed no wordy explanations between us. We had trust based on a firm handshake, an assumption of integrity that transcended guile. It was a patriarchal pact, sure, but sunny patriarchy that conformed to what the women of this tribe wanted. After all, he was giving up Karen to keep her sister happy. That seemed matriarchal to me.

We rose and joined the girls downstairs at the kitchen table for another cup of coffee and a sweet roll. Karen had disappeared into the only bedroom to get her things together. Then, all smiles and twinkling eyes, she reappeared, transformed from a city girl into a rustic beauty.

"My god," her sister enthused. "You're absolutely lovely, Karen!"

Caesar and I smiled our appreciation for her. How lucky I was to have that tough, decisive girl on this journey. Only hours before, we'd been strangers. She stood before us, demure in a bright red flannel shirt and denim jeans, her long black hair tucked under a blue bandana. She looked like a pioneer bride ready to journey with her betrothed to a new homestead on the wild frontier. That was Chicago, all right.

I hefted the single strap of my duffel bag onto my shoulder.

"Let me help you," I offered to carry Karen's huge mountaineer style backpack too, but she was no wilting violet. Even though she packed more gear than I and needed my help to hoist her heavier pack onto her back, she insisted on lugging it herself.

Her sister began crying as she hugged her. "Have fun, Karen! Write to me how it goes."

Caesar wrapped his arms around them both and waved me over into a group hug. They followed us out the door to the landing. I, too, shed a tear. On this, my last day in the city, I'd met genuine human beings, people who made me sorry to be leaving. They stood at the top of the stairs, watching us clomp down, through the door and out of their lives, perhaps forever.

Maybe this place could have become home to me, but Karen and I had a mission. The Revolution beckoned our eager young hearts as much as our desire for each other. We'd charge into the fray and bring America's immoral war home to the heartland of America.

We forged through the crowded sidewalk until we reached the corner of Second Avenue and St. Marks Place. The gay peacocks were already strutting their stuff. A voice rang out.

"Hey, Ron!"

"Huh? Who could that be?" Turning around, I saw Bonnie standing on a raised porch twenty feet behind us. She bore a quizzical expression on her face as if surprised to see me and curious who I was with. With an abrupt flick of her wrist, she waved me over.

"Just a minute," I told Karen, who'd turned to see who'd called.

My heart thumped loud in my ears as I strode back to Bonnie. The golden Star of David nestling at her bosom shone brightly in the sun. Her frizzy hair was alight with the same solar radiance, making her as beautiful as I'd ever seen her. I began wracking my frazzled brain for what to tell this woman I still cared about. Did she care about me? Should whatever we had together mattered anymore?

"What's up?" she asked, glib and upbeat. Standing a head above me on the steps, her lidded eyes focused over my shoulder.

"That's Karen," I said, keeping my voice flat and nonchalant. "She's going back to Chicago with me."

I'd never been in such a situation and didn't know what I was supposed to say or how she would take it. The best approach was to introduce these ladies to each other. There was no reason to fight over the exclusive ownership of each other. We should all get along, one big loving family. I waved Karen closer, but she ignored me. I waved again with more emphasis. She approached within four feet and froze to hold her ground behind me. I turned sideways.

"Karen, this is Bonnie. Did I tell you about her?"

As Bonnie continued to study Karen with narrowed eyes, she pursed her lips. It looked like a flash of jealousy crossed her face, which aroused a mix of sympathy and perverse satisfaction in me. I didn't want to upset her, and yet I did. Yes, damn it; I wanted her to get a taste of her own medicine. That didn't mean I didn't care about her.

Like the meat in a sandwich, I stood between the two women I cared about, and it looked like I'd have to choose between them. I'd have to put one in my past and charge into the future with the other one. To choose between them felt like saving only one arm when I needed two, but I couldn't think of a way to keep them both in my eternal present.

"Too bad you're leaving, Ron." Bonnie's matter of fact voice betrayed no emotion. "The collective is almost ready to meet you. Just a few more days if you stick around."

Even if it was true, it would be a few more days of scavenging food from the trash, camping on rooftops, which I could handle, even enjoy with her beside me, but I knew she wouldn't be.

Bonnie glanced around, nervous. She looked unsure about her feelings or what to say to me. We'd only met six days before, almost to the hour. Brief as it was, she and I had shared an intense adventure. Our LSD trip led me to imagine we'd been lovers in a past life. Perhaps we were soul mates, but circumstances had changed. Neither of us was to blame. We rode the ebb and flow of life's tide. It was pulling us in contrary directions. However, we *had* a cosmic connection. Whether in this life or another, we'd meet again.

A thoughtful look crossed Bonnie's face. She reached into her large shopping bag of a purse, tore a scrap from a brown paper bag and wrote on it.

"This is my parent's address. They'll know how to reach me. Look me up if you're ever back in New York." I put it in my wallet with the address of the Big Purple.

Neither she nor I knew what to say for a moment. My head spun as if I'd been drinking. She opened her arms, and we embraced in a farewell hug. I felt her heartbeat with mine. Looking down into her upturned face, her green eyes softened, her lips looked inviting. I almost kissed them, but feeling Karen's eyes boring into my back, I only brushed my lips against her hot cheek. Pulling back, I saw a tear forming in Bonnie's eye. My tear ducts felt dry as I turned to rejoin Karen.

After a few steps away, I glanced back to see Bonnie still watching us. Before I could wave, she vanished, swallowed up in the milling crowd. A lump arose in my throat as the whole implication hit me. So much had happened too fast. It was impossible to process all at once. Karen, my new lady, walking beside me, deserved my full attention. I reeled her in for our first kiss.

Her eyes popped wide. "Wow, Ron, what's that for?"

"Do I need a reason?"

She smiled and shook her head. "No, but for a moment, I thought I'd lost you back there."

"Come here." Another hug and a kiss put a smile on her face.

As we trudged along, I couldn't shut off my tired brain running on adrenaline. Love, as we knew it, was a war zone. Women had evolved to compete with each other for mates, prestige, and resources.

There was no escaping the battle of the sexes because evolution and the whole human condition was my condition, too.

Fate, or destiny, works out our lives in strange synchronistic ways. Opportunity must be seized or forever lost. What if I didn't step into that coffee shop at the exact moment to meet Karen? The whirl of small choices confronts each of us every moment of our lives. The most trivial events can open amazing horizons of opportunities with no clue as to how they will turn out.

Karen had entered my life like a renewing spring breeze. Yet my joy remained diluted with sadness. This love, too, could pass as so many others had. *All meetings end in separation.* The Buddha's words gave me hard comfort. That truth helped me appreciate what I had for as long as it lasted, knowing that every cherished thing will be lost someday in death. Seeing the big picture alleviated my grief to focus on Karen, my new responsibility.

Although we'd forged an instant bond, Karen and I were still strangers. We were embarking on a great adventure that promised conflict and danger as much as building our new love-life together. Rollercoaster emotions rampaged through me. I felt as if I was dying and being reborn. In my sleep deprived, adrenaline fueled state, my grief mixed with overwhelming love. Faces flashed before me. All my recent companions, friends, and lovers who I'd barely gotten to know before they vanished crowed in on me. Countless smiling, frowning, ugly and beautiful faces right down to Bonnie and then Karen, trudging beside me. They'd all impacted my life, enriching my experience to reach that amazing present moment. Somehow, I had to hang onto this new girl; otherwise, I'd wander the world forever alone, a permanent stranger.

With that thought, a tear sprang forth that ran down my cheek. Maybe tears were the juice of life, the power I needed to harness.

We Look for America

Karen and I set off for Chicago in search of the Revolution and our personal destiny. We'd find it there, at the end of a journey that would be far longer and more grueling than was my journey with Bonnie to New York. On the way, we'd discover the real America.

After my long sleepless night on the street, my brain was foggy, but at least I was no longer alone. Together with my new lady, we set off to escape the city. Strange for both of us. Too bad, I'd neglected to ask Bonnie about routes out of the city.

"How do we get to Interstate 80?" I asked several times, only to get brushed off with typical Manhattan sarcasm in reply. In desperation, I turned to a cop.

"How do we get to the interstate?"

"Which one?" He was a short Italian looking guy, who resembled a friend back home, and gave us a warm smile.

"Interstate 80 or whatever goes west."

"You've got to go north, up to the Washington Bridge." There was not a trace of sarcasm in his voice. "Cross over that, and you'll find

Interstate 80." Then he told us which subway train to catch, and we thanked him profusely.

How ironic that a cop helped us without copping an attitude. In New York, the cops seemed to be genuine human beings, so unlike those I knew in Chicago. I never liked calling all cops pigs, even though some were every bit our enemy. They were working men, some with good hearts that I hoped we could persuade to the rebel cause.

That short interaction put me in high spirits, and I felt warm emotion gush out to all around me, to those I had long left behind me and those like Bonnie, who I was leaving then. Reeling in Karen, I gave her another kiss that made her gasp in surprise.

"It's only me and you now," I said and kissed her again, longer, with more tongue.

"You're a crazy guy, Ron." She used the same words as Bonnie. "I love that about you."

Cramming ourselves into the crowded subway with light hearts drunk on love, I started singing Simon and Garfunkel songs that popped into my head, even though I didn't remember all the lyrics. *The Boxer*, with its mix of elation and pathos, seemed tailor made to our urban experience.

Karen jumped in with, "And we all go to look for America..."

I added, "I said the man in the gabardine coat was a spy..."

While I had no idea what gabardine was, the image of the trench coated man who shared a joint with Bonnie and me popped into my head.

"I really love Simon and Garfunkel," Karen said. "They're prophets of the ordinary people."

"Sure are," I concurred, thinking of *The Sounds of Silence*. "The words of the prophets are written on the subway walls, tenement halls..."

Running out of the remembered lyrics, we hummed along,

uncaring what the somber faced people around us thought. We acted crazy-goofy, which was relevant somehow to our coming together in spontaneous destiny. Our lives were unfolding exactly as they ought.

Climbing out of the subway, our luck held. We snagged a ride with a gregarious fellow. Yakking with him about the deep political and social issues of the time, we missed our drop-off at the Washington Bridge.

"Oh, what the hell," he said. "We're almost to Yonkers. There's another west-bound highway farther up rather than backtracking."

"Okay," I told him. "We've plenty of time to get to Chicago." I smiled at Karen snuggled beside me in the back seat. "Don't we, hon?" She clutched my arm, resting her head against my shoulder. Everything was right in our world. My exhaustion and depression had long since vanished into boundless confidence and joy. Life had turned into an amazing adventure for both of us.

Northbound on Highway 9, a two-lane road on the east side of the Hudson River. Eventually we'd have to head west, across the river. Without a map, I couldn't be sure which turn to take and had to rely on the ideas of whoever picked us up.

Leaving the urban sprawl, rolling hills filled the horizon. Each hillock ablaze in different fall color. One rusty orange, the next brown, then red, or yellow, creating a magnificent patchwork. On our left, the broad sweep of the deep blue Hudson River awed us, well worth going out of our way to admire.

Waiting for the next ride, Karen opened her backpack. "There's something I'd better show you, Ron." Her face betrayed anxiety, and I wondered what the fuss could be. "I told you I was nineteen, and my name was Karen Blake, but that's just my alias. I'm a runaway, fifteen years old, and my real name is Karen Mucci."

Impressed by her revelation, I hugged her tight. "Your secret's safe with me. Let Karen Blake be your *nom de guerre*. Get it? Your alias or cover. Call it a war name." Mature for fifteen, she seemed the kind of girl I'd always wanted, level-headed, with looks as well as brains.

"Age is just a number, you know, Karen. I ran away at fifteen, too. We've a lot in common."

Her still serious face relaxed. "There's more to show you, Ron." She pulled a little black book from a pouch in her pack and she handed it to me. "This is my passport."

The few American passports I'd seen were long and green. Hers was black or dark blue. "It's a diplomatic passport," she explained. Maybe that accounted for the difference in color. The embossed seal, stamped over Karen's photo by the American embassy, looked genuine. It gave her real name, Karen Mucci, then her place of birth as Seoul, Korea.

I wondered if Mucci was a Korean name. Even with her long black hair, she didn't look Korean. "My father is Italian," she answered my unspoken question. This intriguing girl had no end of surprises. It appeared her father was in the diplomatic corps, maybe even the CIA. Karen only shrugged when I asked her. "Some things even I don't know," was all she said.

Her family must have some social prominence. No doubt they would look for her. The police too. Maybe I was risking a charge of statutory rape, or contributing to the delinquency of a minor, even though I too was under eighteen. I hated to have her throw away her documents, but if we were stopped, the cops mustn't see them.

"Bury them deep under your clothes," I told her. "They might come in handy later."

Young rebels against the status quo we knew the risks, but unless they had a driver's license, women didn't need legal identification. Only men over eighteen needed a draft card, and I wasn't there yet. Sticking to her alias, we would tell everyone she was seventeen like me.

Our lips met in a lingering kiss that sealed the bargain between us. We lovers with everything in common who had the rest of our lives before us were embarking on an unpredictable adventure that could unite us forever in life or an early death.

Under Thor's Hammer

It began drizzling by late afternoon. Another cheerful man took us a few more miles through the countryside. Pulling over, he said, "Sorry, kids, I've taken a little past my turn off. I can't bring you home with me. My wife would throw a fit if she knew I'd picked up hitchhikers."

Pointing ahead, he added, "I know it's starting to rain. We're due for a doozy of a thunderstorm, but there's a barn not far up ahead where you two could wait it out overnight."

Kaboom! An earsplitting thunderclap exploded as soon as we stepped out of the car, inspiring us to run for it.

"Good Luck!" the driver called out before making a U-turn and speeding back.

Immediately, the rain began coming down in sheets. We hollered, *let it rain!* Laughing like maniacs, we became soaked to the skin in the minute it took to run for the big red barn that sat fifty feet back from the road. We gloried in being wild and free.

The deserted barn's great door stood half open, hanging on a rolling rail. The aroma of sweet-smelling hay invited us in.

We found it a dry, comforting refuge.

206

"At least we got a nice rain rinse," I told her. "It's been a couple of days since I've had a shower."

Karen chuckled, her smile beaming brightly. "What a romantic getaway this is. We're out of the damn city at last."

"This is the perfect place for us to hole up for the night!" I agreed as I hoisted her, followed by her pack and mine, up into the dry warmth of the hayloft.

"We'd better get out of these wet things," I told her. Taking the first step, I began pulling off my shirt and pants. "We can hang them over this wooden beam to dry."

"It's too cold," she said.

"Don't worry, baby, I'll warm you up! If you leave those wet clothes on, you'll be worse off."

Unbuttoning her flannel shirt with a shy, self-conscious grin, she hesitated. Already naked before her, I assisted. Hidden under her bulky clothing, I revealed her breasts. They were voluptuous, much larger than I'd imagined when hidden from view. They were worthy objects of my veneration, begging me to kiss and fondle them. Doing so elicited moans of pleasure from my dear lady. Then I raised my eyes to meet hers.

"Wow, Karen, you are an absolute goddess!" I pressed her chest against mine and rubbed her shoulders to warm them. All I needed was her beside me. Her smile up at me was a good sign that she felt the same. Both of us were looking forward to our first night in each other's arms. My hungry eyes devoured her until the black night closed in.

"We'd better get under the covers," I said as I stood back with reluctance.

We opened our sleeping bags and put them together, as best we could, to make our shared bed. Mine, being a mummy bag, didn't open at the foot, so we put that one on the bottom where we had room for both pairs of our legs and draped her bag over us.

Outside, the sky turned black as the rain beat down in torrents, a deluge that drummed a deafening roar on the barn's tin roof.

Snuggling together in the fading light, we shivered from the chill, but more so from the thrill of each other's bare flesh against ours. Through the cracks in the sliding door and walls, we watched the dramatic spectacle. Lightning flashed, and thunder roared while we warmed each other, snug and safe on our mattress of sweet-smelling hay.

Using my hands, I explored her superb body. She had a little baby fat around her middle, but that only aroused me more. We kissed and fondled awhile before I allowed myself the pleasure of entering her with slow deliberation.

To the majestic symphony of Thor's hammer convulsing the earth, I rammed into Karen with ever greater force as she gasped and clawed my back. Flashes of lightning granted me brief glimpses of her naked body; her face contorted with the passion of pain transfigured into greatest pleasure. Thus, the consummation of our lusty love was in tune with nature's explosive drama. We were one with the natural universe in all its cataclysmic drama until, at last, our storm broke in a terrific release.

Exhausted, in calm repose while listening to the continued fury without, we melted into each other's body to slumber at last.

Silence reigned in the faint light of dawn. I half rose to gaze again at Karen's body beneath me. A surge of warm emotion shot through me, which aroused my steed, hot against her belly. She opened her eyes and smiled up at me, shy yet compliant with my groping desire.

That's all the inspiration I needed to buck her again. Eager, she wrapped her legs around me, her heels pummeling my ass in time to my thrusts, to pull me ever deeper into her. That second occasion of our coupling was even better than the first. I felt completely at home in this barn with this young and lovely lass, in my long dreamed of Eden. We both belonged in that rustic place. It would be home in the natural order of things, but we were still homeless and far from Chicago.

Woodstock Idyll

Tuesday, September 30. We rose, refreshed and ready for adventure in the primeval landscape. Among the oaks and maples clothed in multi-colored glory, we found apple orchards. We gorged ourselves on that tart fruit, all the breakfast we'd find. I filled my duffel bag to overflowing before a man pulled over. I ran up to his window.

"Where are you going?" I asked. He was over thirty, with a neatly trimmed beard and the gray medium-length locks of a hippie tied back into a ponytail.

"I'm Josh, heading back to Woodstock. Ever heard of it?"

I hadn't, but Karen had. As we tossed our gear in the rear and climbed into the cab of his pickup, she asked. "Isn't Woodstock where that big rock concert was supposed to be held a few weeks ago?"

Josh laughed. "They advertised it as the *Woodstock Festival of Peace and Music*. Some called it an Age of Aquarius' love-in. It ended up being a pretty big deal."

"Sounds like we missed it," I said.

"Me too," Josh said. "Maybe I'm too old for all that noise and jostling crowd stuff, anyway." He stroked his beard in thought for a

209

moment and added. "The concert got moved about forty-three miles away from Woodstock to the big Max Yasgur farm over in Bethel."

As we chatted, basking in the warm pleasure of his company, the enchanting fall colors of the natural woodland slipped by. Then we crossed over the majestic deep blue of the Hudson River and climbed into the Catskill Mountains.

"You kids will love the Woodstock area," Josh said. "We have an artistic community that really digs this rural setting. They blend well with the local farmers, who are glad to have some celebrities to hobnob with."

Karen sat up straight. "Celebrities? Like who?"

"Joan Baez and Bob Dylan are two you've probably heard of. We're coming up on their spread soon. We might get lucky and see them out on a day like this."

In a few minutes, he slowed to a crawl and pointed across us to our right. "See that? That pasture is where Joan Baez keeps her horses. He drove on a little farther. "And just over there is where Bob Dylan stables his horse. Those who can afford it come out here to unwind from the big city." He mentioned other names and pointed to other barns and pastures, but I wasn't familiar with many of the rich and famous.

"It's still daylight," Josh said, "but if you kids aren't in a hurry to get where you're going, you can stay for dinner, and I'll put you up for the night."

Karen and I nodded our assent, glad to accept his generous offer.

His cozy, dark brown wood paneled home had all the gas and electric conveniences. He took us on a tour, pointing out his modern bathroom and washer and dryer.

"You can take a shower and do your laundry. Make yourselves at home while I do a few chores and prepare dinner."

After our nice hot shower, we popped our clothes in the washer and relaxed out on the wide veranda. Sitting on the wooden backed porch swing overlooking horses romping in the luscious green pastures, Karen nuzzled against my chest.

I ran my fingers through her long black hair. "Would you be happy living out here like this?" She looked up at me with a contented smile. "Sure would. You told me about those communes out west. Think we could join one?"

For a would-be country boy like me, Karen seemed the perfect mate.

"How about we head out there right after Chicago? My parents are holding my money. I don't really want to subject you to them. My dad is impossible, but we'll pick up my cash and be gone."

The idyllic scene and scent of sweet alfalfa hay lulled us into a sense of security. We had time enough to do all the things we dreamed of. Our host soon joined us. There was plenty of room for all three of us on the swing.

"So, you kids are headed to Chicago, huh?"

"We're going to the big SDS demonstration to bring the war home," I said.

He shook his head. "I'd probably be doing the same thing if I was your age." He stretched and looked up at the sky. "I marched for civil rights in Birmingham. That was years ago. I've gotten older." He grinned widely at us. "But no wiser!"

Karen and I cracked up at that.

"It's all up to you younger people now." He fixed me with a stare. "Bring the war home, you say? Well, somebody's got to do it. Just be careful out there." He seemed lost in thought for a moment. "I bought this little place and, well, I guess I'm settled down into this quiet rural life." He slapped my knee. "Come on, let's make dinner. Does your old lady know how to cook?"

Karen laughed. "I'm not that old! But can I cook? You bet. I can boil, bake and fry with the best of them."

She even set the table. I helped Karen cut up a few vegetables and plucked a freshly killed chicken that Josh brought in. In no time, we had a feast. Josh popped the cork off a bottle of chilled red wine, and we sat down. Karen and I hadn't had anything except a few

Ronald J Schulz

apples that morning, which had only made us hungrier, so there were no leftovers.

Our bellies full, we discussed the politics of the Left with Josh. Although he wasn't a firebrand anymore, he sympathized with our commitment to the ongoing struggle. Being an avid reader, he had a good grasp of history.

"Nothing ever happens," he said, "until someone with guts puts his life on the line to force the issue. We'd still be under a British monarch if those wild, delinquent Sons of Liberty hadn't started smashing things up in Boston. You kids are the next wave. You're young and footloose. It's your turn to fight on against injustice."

I could only agree. Even so, I *grooved* on the domestic peace and tranquility of the moment. It was something I'd rarely tasted and realized I'd missed. Josh got up to put a stack of albums on his turntable, saying, "Let's hear some nice music."

Karen and I plunked down on the shag carpeted floor, and Josh sat above us on the sofa. The living room's picture window presented a relaxing view of his back pasture. As the darkness closed in and twinkling starlight took over. We let the music carry us away.

Goodbye to my Juan, goodbye, Rosalita,
Adios mis amigos, Jesus y Maria;
You won't have your names when you ride the big airplane,
All they will call you will be "deportees."

I'd heard the lyrics before. *Deportees*, by Woody Guthrie, subtitled *Plane Wreck at Los Gatos*, never failed to grab my heart. It personified our unfeeling society, which devalued humans as chattel, disposable workers. That's how I'd felt slaving away at my warehouse job, under a screaming, merciless boss, trying to make enough dough to get back on the road again. But that night, my black-haired Karen nestled against me like my very own Rosalita. The song punched my

212

heart harder and brought silent tears to my eyes as I identified Karen with the song's theme. Our future was uncertain, and we could lose each other at any moment.

The crops are all in, and the peaches are rott'ning,
　　The oranges piled in their creosote dumps;
　　They're flying 'em back to the Mexican border
　　To pay all their money to wade back again

The money I made only lasted so long, and there I was, flat broke and on the road again. But at least I had love. My brain froze when I tried to imagine our future. The battle in Chicago lay before us. After that was the possibility of joining some radical collective. Although it hadn't worked out for me in New York, Chicago was my home turf. If that didn't work out, we could head out west.

Drop City would welcome us. We'd find our niche on the land and get back to our natural agrarian roots. The more I thought about it, the more I considered that to be a better choice than staying in the city. Snug in our sleeping bags right there in the living room, we enjoyed a restful night.

State Troopers

I kissed her forehead, and Karen blinked awake.

"Good morning, sweetheart."

She stretched and smiled up at me. Waking up beside this beautiful gal, fully rested and fed for once, filled me with the sweet bliss of total satisfaction. I was the luckiest guy on earth and needed to keep reminding myself of that. I knew all too well how fast good things could fall apart. It was Wednesday. October First. Chicago was seven days away.

After an early morning breakfast of eggs and toast, Josh wished us luck as he dropped us along the highway on his way to work.

"You need to follow this road to Interstate 81," he told us. "Go south through Scranton. There, you can hook up with Interstate 80, which will take you straight on to Chicago."

It sounded easy, but the rides weren't going our way. By midafternoon, we were desperate enough to accept a ride that took us away from the freeway. The grizzled driver in work jeans insisted.

"Whizzing along the freeway is boring, man! This way, you two can have a scenic tour through the Mountains. You'll love it, I promise."

"Don't worry," I told Karen. "We have plenty of time to get to Chicago by October eight."

We hopped in the back of his pickup truck, ready for the back road adventure. Soon we were winding along secondary roads deep into the countryside. He dropped us near a freeway somewhere in Pennsylvania, where night descended on us. It was too dark to see where we were, and the traffic dried up. We crawled under the cover of some bushes close to the on-ramp to keep the dew off us. Snuggling together in our cozy sleeping bags was still our greatest thrill.

The hazy mist of morning faded, revealing a billboard advertising free coleslaw at the motel restaurant below the sign. Breakfast! I shook Karen awake.

"Look, honey!" She blinked at it, but didn't seem impressed.

"Okay," I told her. "I never liked coleslaw before, but it's food, and we're broke." I laughed aloud, hoping to cheer her up. "Hobos on the road like us have to be flexible. Come on, let's try it."

Being the only customers at that early hour, the older lady eyed us with suspicion mixed with a touch of sympathy as we came in.

"Go ahead, she said. "We have plenty more of that in the back."

We thanked her and filled our plates with free coleslaw from the buffet table, and took a seat. The waitress approached us.

"Real food has to be ordered from the kitchen. Want a menu?"

"No, thanks," I told her.

Her face softened. "The hot water is free too." She sighed. "I'll fetch you kids a couple of tea bags."

"Thanks," Karen called after her. "We appreciate it."

Famished, we each gobbled down a large plateful and went back for more. For some dietary diversity, I experimented making ersatz tomato soup from packets of catsup and hot water. *Ew!* Karen turned up her nose at that.

"Well," I told her. "It's enough to satisfy our hunger for the moment. Fortune may soon smile upon us, my dear." High hopes were all we had.

As it was illegal to walk on the Interstate, we stood on the ramp.

Traffic was sparse. One ride brought us only another two exits farther. We had nothing more for a couple of hours.

Karen asked, "Where are we?"

"Without a map, I can only guess at our location." I needed to inject some humor into our situation. "We were somewhere between the Atlantic Ocean and the Great Lakes, lost deep in the wilds of Pennsylvania." She managed a chuckle, and I gave her a hug for the effort.

Finally, two cars pulled over, but the sight of them filled me with dread.

Two Pennsylvania State troopers wearing Smokey Bear hats parked and approached us with nasty frowns. Their eyes were invisible, shaded behind dark sunglasses, like in the movies. Only one spoke.

"How old are you kids?"

"I'm seventeen," I said. Karen insisted she was eighteen, to their apparent disbelief.

"You got any money on you?"

"No," I told him. "That's why we're hitchhiking."

Hands on his hips, the trooper rocked back and forth on his heels, eyeing me with a withering gaze. "You kids are in violation of the vagrancy laws of Pennsylvania."

He paused for dramatic effect, then, with a laconic, menacing voice, he drawled on, sounding more like a southern redneck sheriff than a northern lawman.

"I am sick and tired of all you goddamn hippie hitchhikers! You are imposing on the graces of the great State of Pennsylvania. Here in Pennsylvania, we have chain-gangs for vagrants like you. We can make you work for your keep."

That surprised me. I thought chain-gangs only existed in the Jim Crow south. Could he be joking? The other trooper, arms crossed, with a faint smile on his face, seemed less menacing. I hoped he would intercede, but I said nothing to aggravate things further. Silently, we waited for the sentence to be pronounced on us.

"You had better get out of this State on the double quick. The next time I see you, I'll run you in for loitering and give you a real taste of our hospitality. A few weeks of hard labor in the hot sun wearing ankle bracelets should cure you of your shiftless ways."

"Me too?" Karen asked, sticking her chin out as if doubting him. Too late. I squeezed her hand in warning, but she went on. "Do you put girls in a chain gang?"

"Don't you test me, young lady. We have chains in your size too, and then you'll get sent back to your parents where you belong."

Spitting into the culvert at our feet, the trooper turned on his heels with military precision, waved his companion back to their cars, and they drove off. But as I watched him fade into the horizon, his words still rang in my head.

I had no way of knowing whether the chain-gang threat was real. Even in the hitchhikers' hell of Colorado, the State troopers never mentioned chain-gangs. While a week or two spent on a chain gang could be a dramatic Hollywood experience, something I could brag about when it was over, I'd lose Karen for sure. We couldn't chance aggravating them, but their arrogant contempt for us made me more determined to face the pigs in Chicago. We needed to topple these smug upholders of inhumane laws.

As if in answer to our prayers, a white station wagon pulled over. Running up, I saw it was driven by a hippie couple. The bearded, long-haired man smiled a toothy grin at us. "Need a lift?"

"Sure do, man," I told him as Karen and I hustled into the back seat. "We've just gotten hassled by the State Police. They threatened us with the chain gang if they ever saw us again. Can you believe that?"

"I wouldn't put anything past those fuckers," said the woman, dressed in a flowing dress of all the loud clashing colors of the rainbow, a true hippie outfit. "We've had our problems with them. Tell 'em, Dave."

"Sure have. I'm Dave, and this is Cynthia, by the way. We've just

217

the thing to settle your nerves." Winking a broad smile at Karen and me, he added. "Do you smoke weed?"

We introduced ourselves, shook hands all around, and then Cynthia began rolling a joint as Dave drove up to the next exit.

Surprised to see him take the exit, I exclaimed, "Is this as far as you're going?"

"No, man. Don't worry. We do this run across Pennsylvania a couple of times a week. Going back and forth, we've gotten to know where all the speed traps and pig hangouts are. So, we'll take the back road scenic route; bypass them without all the hassle."

We passed the joint up to Dave. He took one toke. "That's enough, I'm driving. You can have the rest."

Cynthia giggled and rolled another one as we swapped our life stories. I leaned back and enjoyed the scenery as we rolled through forests, fields, and tiny towns.

"We're anarchists," bragged Cynthia. "We're into sabotaging the system any way we can."

"Cool," Karen said. "We're going to the battle in Chicago. Ever hear about it?"

They hadn't but insisted that any blow against the status quo of our corporate culture was a blow for human dignity.

As we entered the next town, he said, "Watch this, you guys. Pay attention to the traffic light." It was red but several blocks away. He kept a steady cruising speed.

"We've got it worked out what speed to maintain to let us roll through every green light in every town without stopping."

Sure enough, just as I thought he'd better hit the brakes, the light turned green, and we sailed on through. This became a thrill for us to watch as we breezed through each village on the way without him touching the brake. Not even once.

Sparking a lively conversation, Dave expounded their anarchist philosophy.

"Stealing from the system is actually liberating what belongs to us, anyway. It's not really stealing, not like you're taking it *from* the people, but *for* the people. But who are the people if not us?" He half turned to look back at us, dead serious. "Dig it?"

We nodded in agreement.

"After all, the capitalist system was built on genocide and slavery, ravaging Mother Earth's resources to profit only the rich fucks who don't give a shit about the rest of us."

Abbie Hoffman and the Yippees touted this same line. Abie even published a book entitled *Steal This Book*. While I agreed in principle. Stealing from corporate conglomerates that were out to rape the earth was one thing, but I was torn about the effect of stealing on a personal level.

We stopped for gas at a general store. "I bet you're hungry," Dave said, knowing I didn't have any money. "Grab a few things for you and your woman." He didn't mean to buy them. "Here's where we put our beliefs into daily practice."

Karen went to the toilet. The young, early twenties guy running the store couldn't be in two places at once. While Dave paid for the gas and made a point of distracting him, Cynthia slipped a few small cherry pies, rolls, and a package of cold cuts under her billowing dress. She winked at me as if to signal that the coast was clear.

My conscience tortured me. I'd done my share of shoplifting as a kid but never felt guilt-free about it. The young clerk could get into trouble for the missing items or be accused of stealing them himself. Karen and I hadn't eaten since the coleslaw and needed something. I slipped a package of mini white powdered sugar donuts under my long coat and walked back to the car.

"Is that all you got?" Our driver sounded incredulous. "You could have cleaned the place out for as long as you were in there!"

"Yeah, guess I'm not cut out for shoplifting."

"No, you just need more confidence and practice. To teach you a lesson, we're not going to share our haul. You'll learn!"

The donuts were a poor substitute for breakfast. I swallowed my share, along with my guilt at not being enough of a revolutionary warrior. I needed to steal, if only to support my lady, Karen.

Pennsylvania was a big state, and we were still in it. With only the short distance rides we'd gotten, it seemed to go on forever. By late evening, Dave dropped us at a rest stop somewhere along I-70, south of Pittsburgh. Interstate 80 was still far to our north, but it was dark. There was almost no traffic, and we were played out.

It was another night camped in the bushes, curled up with Karen in our sleeping bags. We listened to owls hooting, scampering rodents, with the occasional whoosh of a car on the road a few feet away. My happiness became muted by my concern for Karen. She was too silent. Our bellies growled, but we had each other.

My cajoling couldn't get a laugh or grin out of her. If I'd learned anything from my parent's dysfunctional relationship, it was to beware of a silent woman. Her apathy could be a calm, false front, hiding her secret rage before her dammed up emotions burst forth in an explosion of recrimination. Against me!

She had plenty of justification. This journey had become a grueling challenge. I was used to privation, but she, from what I could learn about her, was not.

The Taverns of West Virginia

At dawn, we saddled up and stood at the on ramp. The highway was still deserted. Off in the distance, I watched the approach of the first oncoming car. As it came near, I recognized it.

"Shit! It's another State Trooper."

Grabbing Karen's arm, I pulled her down the incline into a low spot between the winding cloverleaf and the raised freeway, hoping he hadn't spotted us. The earlier patrolman's chain gang warning reverberated in my ears.

Maybe we'd soon discover if the threat of a chain gang was only a cruel joke or awful reality. The thought of them taking Karen away from me stabbed physical pain into my chest. What if I never saw her again? To keep panic at bay, I gulped deep, steady breaths and hugged Karen tight. It might be our last moment together.

She felt so warm and comforting in my arms. My chin and nose rested on Karen's head. The musky-sweet smell of her hair thrilled me. An intense wave of love rushed through me, heightened by our present danger. While I told myself I was comforting her, in truth, I was as much comforting myself. Karen peeked around me and then squeezed my shoulder, staring at something behind me.

"Turn around, Ron."

My worst fears materialized. A Pennsylvania State Trooper stood with one foot on the guardrail, leaning on his knee, looking down at us. Like the other Patrolmen, he wore the wide brimmed Smokey Bear hat. His eyes, hidden behind dark sunglasses, made him appear cold, robotic, a malevolent entity. Trapped, I turned to face him.

"Have you kids had anything to eat today?" His kind tone surprised me. He sounded so unlike the last snarling trooper, but my guard was up. Was it a trick to lull us into complacency? Frozen in my confusion, I nodded in the affirmative before I found my voice.

"Yes, we've eaten." It was a lie, but I didn't want our hunger used against us. Maybe he'd use it as evidence that we were the poor vagrants, without visible means of support. Indeed, we were what we appeared to be.

"Okay, you kids, be careful now." He backed off to his patrol car, leaving us alone and free.

In an instant, I wished I'd admitted we were hungry. His kind voice indicated he'd feed us. He wasn't a *Blue Meanie* but a rare, kind officer of the true law. His example kept me from hating all police.

A ride came at last. The unkempt black-haired driver seemed to be almost as young as I was, maybe eighteen, with a heavy accent that I'd heard before. Appalachian migrants had moved into my neighborhood when I was a kid and attended grade-school with me.

"I'm Eugene," he said, extending his hand through the window. "I've been working my ass off in a factory. Now I'm come'n back home for a spell in West Virginia."

"We're on our way to Chicago," I told him.

"Well, If'n you don't mind tagging along with me, I'll put you-all up at my place overnight. Gotta get back to Ohio in the morning, so I'll take you all the way to Toledo."

"Sure," I told him. "We'll keep you company."

I sat up in front to keep our voluble driver entertained so Karen could stretch out and snooze in the back seat.

"Let me tell you," he said. "I'm so gosh darn glad to be getten' back home. I'm gonna take you folks on a tour of every bar in West Virginia!"

"Is West Virginia that small? How many bars is that?"

He laughed and slapped my shoulder. "We'll see. So long as we have ourselves a good 'ole time."

The thought of his drinking and driving made me a little leery, and Karen looked skeptical too, but I figured he wouldn't get so plastered that he'd have a wreck. His undented car looked in prime condition, a good sign, and he claimed to have done this bar tour every time he came back home.

Eugene drove along two-lane roads that wound through an ever-hillier countryside, telling me he worked out of state, hated his job, and came roaring back to cut loose on long weekends.

"The state line is just ahead." He elbowed me in the ribs. "I'll buy us a drink at the first tavern."

The first roadside tavern was a ramshackle affair on the edge of a gully. Despite Eugene's insistence that they would ask for IDs, Karen insisted that she'd stay out in the car. Being underage, she didn't want to chance any hassles. Although only seventeen myself, I was used to bluffing my way into the right kind of bars. The bartender didn't even give me a second look. Having heard so much about rednecks hating hippies, I felt self-conscious of my shoulder length hair, but four middle-aged customers slumped over the bar paid me no attention.

Eugene had a nodding acquaintance with the bartender; I didn't doubt that he knew every bar in his state. He ordered both of us a shot of whiskey and then another, two stiff drinks that we sloshed down fast. I kept an eye on him, hoping he wouldn't overdo it. My empty stomach metabolized the booze as fast as I drank it. I'd only eaten a couple apples from my horde and already felt drunk, but of course, as a man among men, I hid it as best I could. It wouldn't do to be a wimp.

Eugene looked into my eyes and asked, "Are you ready for more?"

"Suuuure, you're the driver. You okay?"

"Course I am. Let's scat to the next place."

I was glad I wasn't driving and hoped Eugene knew what he was doing. Karen and I had put our lives in his hands. The next bar and the next after that were much the same, rundown, clapboard establishments with a darkened interior. There were few customers that early in the day. We downed only one shot apiece after the first stop, then we drove on to hit two more places before turning onto a paved rural road flanked by farmsteads, barns, and cows out in the pasture.

"We're taking a shortcut I know to another local watering hole," he said.

Eugene seemed to be driving alright, handling his booze better than I was. We drove by three men chatting at a mailbox, who gave us a friendly wave as we passed. Fifty feet on, we came to a rural intersection with a stop sign, but the car seemed to slide too far to the right. Suddenly, we were on the right shoulder with the stop sign lined up directly in front of me in the passenger seat.

Wham! We hit it, and the sign flopped down, but Eugene didn't slow down or stop. Drifting even farther to the right, we hopped the shallow drainage ditch to confront a line of fence posts. *Pop-pop-pop-pop*, one, two, three, four. They snapped down in front of my eyes like dominos. I heard a loud *bang* and a thud underneath the car, and we came to a dead stop.

"Goddamn shit!" Eugene fumed, gunning the engine but going nowhere. His red face blanched as he turned to me, wide-eyed in shock. "What the fuck just happened?"

"You hit the stop sign," I told him.

"The fuck I did. What stop sign?"

Eugene lurched out of his seat and stumbled around the car, kicking and swearing at the tires of his useless vehicle as if that helped. The car sat diagonally across the culvert, nose down into the plowed field, like a beached whale. A fence post wrapped in barbed wire was jammed up against the undercarriage, the tangled stream of barbed wire splayed out behind it, connected to all the other posts he'd knocked down back to the stop sign, which stared its dire warning up at the sky. The car didn't look drivable to me.

The men we'd passed walked over. One of them was likely the owner of the field we were stuck in. It amazed me that they didn't seem angry.

"Hello, friend," one of the affable neighbors greeted us. "Looks like you're in a bit of trouble there, son."

"Naw," Eugene said, his voice beginning to slur. "Don' cha worry 'bout me. I'm a get outta here."

"All wrapped up in wire, you ain't going nowhere."

The others agreed with his sober assessment. The right front wheel sat on its side at a ninety-degree angle.

"Your axle's broken," was the solemn verdict.

Our drunken friend waved them away, as angry at their proffered help as at the hopeless situation he was in. "I don' need your *goddamned* help!" He shouted as he kept stumbling around, insane, trying to lift the front end up and kick the wheel straight with his puny strength. Eugene intended to get away from there, whether or not Karen and I came with him.

"Get back there and push," he ordered me and revved the engine. It roared, but the only effect was to bounce up a little on the fencepost, like a high jumper testing his pole. He tried backing off the post, but his tires only dug deeper into the ground. He was going nowhere.

One of the men, offended by his harsh language and attempts to leave the scene, slipped away to the farmhouse. He came back, whispering to the rest of us that the Sheriff would arrive soon.

"We may as well cooperate and smooth things over," I told Eugene in a useless attempt to calm him down. He pushed me away, unable to accept that his car was dead. No amount of revving and pushing would make it drivable.

It took a while for the trooper from the Sheriff's department to arrive. Like the farmers, he, too, surprised me by his composure. They must have had plenty of experience dealing with drunks, using tact and friendly persuasion.

"Settle down, son," the thirtyish cop said. "You don't want to get in more trouble than you already are. Right now, you'll have to pay for damages. If they agree, I might wave the fine. Ever been in trouble before?"

He followed Eugene, who continued circling the vehicle. "You don't want to add *leaving the scene of an accident* or other offenses. Do you?

Eugene didn't answer. He finally slumped, dejected but uncuffed, in the back of the patrol car, leaving the door open and his feet on the ground. Karen and I grabbed our gear out of the car and stood with the growing crowd of curious neighbors.

They didn't pay attention to us. Eugene was the driver. We passengers were mere spectators, watching our erstwhile friend in trouble but unable to help. I wondered how this affected us. We were stranded in the countryside, far from the highway. A farmer approached me.

"We called for a tow truck. Looks like him coming now."

The red tow truck navigated around to hook up to the car's front end. Lifting it up, then it took considerable time to unravel and cut off the barbed wire that was looped around the undercarriage before they could haul it away.

The owner of the land got busy estimating the damage to his fence to be charged to Eugene. The stop sign needed its metal post straightened or replaced, but it was county property. A couple of laughing neighbors began trying to bend it backup straight.

The sheriff finally turned to us. "Are you kids with the driver?"

"Just recent acquaintances," I told him. "He picked us up in Pennsylvania, said we could stay the night at his place."

"Not much chance of him going home tonight," the sheriff sounded doleful. "You're passengers with no responsibility for this mess." He sighed as he surveyed the damage.

"Eugene's mother will bail him out. This sort of thing happens too often. Too many of these country boys have to work far from home. Fools that they are, they can't wait and get drunk on their way back."

Waving his hand over the wreckage, the sheriff said, "We got plenty of witnesses here. You're free to go."

I was relieved. This cop was much friendlier than I expected from my recent experience in Pennsylvania. We were still vagrants, after all. Hoisting our packs, Karen and I legged it away from there before we became implicated somehow.

Our erstwhile companion still sat in the rear of the patrol car, looking glum. Our brief acquaintance had been quite an adventure. It taught me how variable people are in different parts of the country. West Virginia folks kept their cool when dealing with drunks and accidents better than where I came from.

We trudged quite a distance along the empty road before a car came.

Someone called out, "What the hell are you folks doing way out here?"

A brief outline of our story got him to offer us a ride out of his way to the main road. We found ourselves in a semi-rural residential area as the sun dropped over the horizon. A wooded lot sat between well-kept middle-class houses. Vegetable gardens all around tantalized our famished souls.

"We'd better bivouac here for the night," I told Karen. "There's no traffic anyway, and I'll find us some food."

When it grew dark, I ventured forth, picking a bagful of ripe tomatoes and summer squash. Seeing how overripe some veggies were saved my conscience. Unless we ate them, they'd rot on the vine. Karen and I had nothing except apples and whiskey all day. The juicy tomatoes and raw squash tasted amazing, healthy fare that refreshed us. With our bellies filled, we lay back in each other's arms, content to smell the fragrant wildflowers while listening to the wind whisper in the trees.

The Doldrums of Ohio

Early the next morning, a middle-aged woman picked us up. "I'm on my way to Wheeling. Where are you off to?"

We told her we were on our way to Chicago and explained how we had gotten off course with a drunken driver.

"I'm a social worker," she said, shaking her head. "In my work with these hill people, I often hear stories like that. Alcohol is so much a part of the culture here, even with some of the religious folks, like Pentecostals. Some men think they're tough guys and can hold their liquor, but alcoholism takes a toll. We have homemade stills brewing up White Lightning in parts of the backcountry."

As we chatted, she drove along the winding Ohio River. "I have a little time before I have to get to work. I'll go to the river and drop you on the Ohio side."

"We'd sure appreciate that," said a happy Karen.

She took us out of her way. The road wound through Wheeling and up over a bridge. She deposited us by a freeway ramp in Ohio.

"Stay on Interstate 70 to Cambridge, then take I-77 north to 80."

After two or more hours standing at the same spot, our rides were not forthcoming. In desperation, we accepted a ride from an old farmer and his wife.

"We'll take you halfway to Uhrichsville," the wife assured us. "Farmers around here are friendly. You won't have any trouble getting picked up. We enjoy this scenic route and bet you will, too."

We veered north on US 250, a secondary road through wonderful open spaces. They dropped us along the two-lane road in the middle of nowhere. Although traffic was brisk, no one stopped, so we preceded by foot, turning to thumb passing cars or just holding out our left arm, thumb up, as we continued.

Onward for miles through rural farmland, we drove northwest toward New Philadelphia, Ohio. Cars whizzed by, but none even slowed down. Stolid Karen proved her mettle, trudging beside me like a donkey under her towering backpack. Our chips were down, yet she never complained. Too bad I had to subject her to such hardship. She was the perfect woman for me, a boon companion on this mad cross-country adventure. How lucky that I'd found her, but I needed to take better care of her. We were starving.

Then I spotted something on the side of the road. Two bottles of beer! Karen drank half of hers and claimed she'd had enough. I finished the rest. Then, a little farther on, I spotted a bonanza. A whole six-pack of bottles lay unopened, still in their cardboard carrying case, on the side of the road. What luck!

I drank a couple more to fill me up, stashing the rest in my duffel, wondering why someone would toss out so many. Maybe the cops were chasing them, and they got rid of the evidence of drinking and driving. It was our good luck to find them, but despite the euphoria it brought me, we, especially Karen, needed solid food.

"Come on, honey, beer has nutrition, you know. Another beer, and you'll feel better."

She finally relented and shared another bottle with me, which got her smiling, but I drank far more than she did. More beer kept appearing along the desolate highway. My duffel bag was soon full, plenty for later.

229

Ronald J Schulz

But I feared Karen would lose heart if she didn't get something more substantial than beer. Her silence worried me. I knew how easy it was to lose a girl's affection when things didn't go well. Coming from a family of five feuding sisters and a bitching alcoholic mother, it was up to me to fix the situation. Refreshed and more than a little buzzed, I attempted to cheer her up.

Manna from heaven appeared in answer to my prayers. A hamburger still wrapped looked like it hadn't been there long. Opening the wrapper, I gave it a long and careful smell test. It was cold, but otherwise okay.

"What do you think?" I held it out to Karen's nose. "Should we?"

She didn't make a face and nodded affirmatively. "They put lots of preservatives in them, but I'm all right. You eat it."

I took a nibble. "It tastes good to me. Have a bite. Come on, we need food."

Karen, unused to surviving by any means necessary, refused. Then I spotted another bag. Two untouched burgers with fries, then another, all edible! I soon lost track of how many I found.

They sure tossed away a lot of beer and fast food in Ohio. After eating my fill of the freshest, I tossed the rest to the birds, who circled us like vultures. That assured me that the food had to be fresh, or the crows would have torn them open by then. Sharing our good fortune with our flying friends convinced me we were producing great karma. If we perished out there, we give them our bodies too, just like the bodhisattvas of old.

Still no rides. Karen and I may as well have been fenceposts along the road for all the drivers speeding by cared. We trudged on into the dark night. Neither of us cared to stop for sleep. If we ever got away from there, we'd remember this long journey.

A car full of teenagers slowed down to look us over. Thirty feet ahead, they pulled onto the shoulder and waited. We finally had a ride! Elated, we ran up to them. As soon as I reached the driver's window,

Whoosh! He floored it, his tires flinging gravel back at Karen, who was still running to catch up, her heavy pack jouncing up and down on her back. Through the rear window, I saw three teen faces laughing at their cruel joke, enraging me.

"Goddamn those sons of bitches!" I screamed at the sky as if calling down retribution from on high. "Don't those arrogant bastards feel compassion for fellow travelers? They're no different from us, but they can't see it."

Karen, steadying herself with a hand on my shoulder, caught her breath beside me. "No, Ron, they're nothing like us." She gulped a few more breaths of air. "We have a vision for the future of America. Those middle-class kids are stupid mamma's boys. They never had an original thought or cared about anyone except themselves. They never went hungry, never felt the urge to explore beyond their pathetic narrow world."

"Wow, Karen, you said it." I swung the strap of my duffle to the other shoulder. Pulling her close, I gave her a hug and kissed her forehead.

"I should be more compassionate to those fuck ups, lost souls. You and I are special. We were Pilgrims, wandering the open road.

Inspired, I continued to expound my usual sermon on our culture's faults. "Those guys think they're tough. What do they fear of picking us up?" My contempt won over my compassion. "They're hooked on the American car culture of isolation. Buttoned up in their flying coffins, chugging from point A to B, with no heed to their fellow beings, they feel no camaraderie with others on the road."

My anger, I realized, was unjustified. As a hitchhiker, I depended on them for rides. No one *owed* us a ride, but it was such a small courtesy to share the journey with someone. Sharing not just a ride, but ideas, jokes and good vibes.

My patience was exhausted. We had a mission waiting for us in Chicago. We had to get there before October eight. I picked up a long stick that became my staff. I imagined myself an angry Hebrew prophet, leading *my people* from the American desert to a Promised Land, or at least new grazing territory.

The next car came barreling down the road. I stepped out in front of it and raised my staff out before me. The car swerved around me and vanished over the horizon. Another, coming from the other direction, swung around in a wide U-turn and came back our way. I raised my staff as before, and they pulled over beside us. It worked!

"Hey," the dark-haired man called. "Where're you guys headed?" The woman beside him smiled to hide her uncertainty about us. My righteous anger dissipated into a happy smile. "Chicago."

"We're not going that far, man, but we can get you up close to Cleveland."

"I'm Chuck, by the way." He stretched his hand out the open window, and we shook. Karen and I squeezed into the backseat before he'd turn into a mirage and drive off without us.

"I'm Ron, and this is Karen."

"We passed you guys earlier and saw you raise your staff. Crazy man! I told my girlfriend—Charlene, by the way. Say *hi*, Charlene."

"Hi."

"I told her I just had to give those crazy guys a ride and swung back around for you."

"Well, thanks, we really appreciate it. Been there all day long."

Chuck warmed up to us, telling us he worked in a factory and was a hell raising party animal, just cruising around with his girl. He dressed like a greaser in a muscle shirt, his medium length black hair slicked straight back. He was no hippie, yet he was our kind of people.

Charlene turned around and started making small talk with Karen, wondering how she was holding up and how far we'd come.

"We've been hitching from New York by way of West Virginia," she told them.

"Wow! Aren't you scared or anything?"

"Shit, I don't know, sometimes, I guess."

Karen told them about our latest adventure with the hill billie while I offered them each a bottle of beer from my scavenged horde.

"This shit feels too warm," Chuck complained. "Charlene, get 'em a cold one from the cooler. You guys hungry?"

They fed us a few snacks that rejuvenated my wilted Karen. Sometime after midnight, they dropped us at an I-80 ramp near Cleveland.

"Hey, man, could you give me a ride?" A disheveled, exhausted looking guy, pack on his back, came running up to the car.

"We're just turning around, south to New Philadelphia," Chuck muttered as he shifted into drive and sped off. Charlene gave us a quick wave before they disappeared.

"Shit!" The new guy swore at the receding vehicle. "Motherfucker! I have been here all goddamn day!"

I stuck out my hand, "I'm Ron..."

"I don't give a fuck who you are. With the girl, you ought to get picked up soon. Don't crowd me, man."

He moved upstream from us, so whoever came would see him first. I sympathized with him. Ohio was a hitchhiker's hell. It began to rain. The ramp wound under an overpass that Karen and I stood under for shelter. The other guy pulled his plastic hood over his head but remained where he was, desperate to not miss the chance of a ride.

Traffic was sparse that late. An hour later, a car finally pulled over and stopped between us. The driver motioned to Karen and me, but the other guy he'd passed sprinted after him and jumped in. I approached to ask if they had any more room when the driver gunned it, and they disappeared into the gloom. Our fellow hitchhiker didn't even wave *so long* at us, which struck me as rude. We ought to see ourselves as comrades on the road.

The ramp was all ours, but that was the last vehicle for hours. The rain alternated with light drizzle between torrents. With no traffic, Karen and I curled up under the overpass, wrapping our sleeping bags around us to warm our chilled bodies.

Cuddled in my arms, Karen said little. At least she didn't pull away from me like my mother would from my dad when she was moody. We caught snatches of deep sleep, from which I had to rouse myself whenever I heard a car approaching. Then I left Karen's side and ran down the embankment to stick out my thumb, all to no avail. It was dead out there.

A part of me wanted to give up. What if we didn't make it back to Chicago in time and missed the Weatherman's action? Would it be selfish to forget about the Revolution? I could ignore the drumbeat of my conscience to just relax and build a life together with Karen, *my* woman. Maybe it would be better for the world if we raised a few kids, a new generation of free beings who wouldn't succumb to this deadly culture.

But no, without fighting the system, the problems would snowball into the next generation. Every day more bombs fell on the people of Southeast Asia, and there I was, lolling around in the comfort that my class and skin color gave me.

Comfort? That was a relative thing. I cuddled with my girl in the postmodern concrete jungle of Ohio, not far from the once wild Maumee River. A century ago, Mad Anthony Wayne had whipped the desperate woodland tribes into submission, right there in the Battle of Fallen Timbers. History would keep repeating if we didn't rise up and stop it.

Should I care? Yes, I had to believe in something more than just my safety.

Traffic increased in the faint light of early morning. Most were big tractor-trailer trucks. They waved and honked good luck as they raced by. I'd never ridden in one. Companies had rules against drivers picking up riders. Since the rum-running days of Al Capone, trucks often get hijacked.

Our bellies growled as noon approached. Our situation looked hopeless.

"Looks like we'll have to walk out of here," I told Karen as I tried to figure out which way to go to escape this twisting maze of ramps.

Then an eighteen-wheeler pulled over, and I had to pinch myself to be sure I wasn't dreaming. We grabbed our gear and ran up before the mirage vanished.

"I can only take you up to the Toledo exit," he said.

"Anywhere has to be better than being stuck here," I told him.

I boosted Karen up into the cab and climbed in behind her. Popping it into gear, we took off. We had to shout over the loud engine noise was so, but the driver was cheerful.

The Toledo ramp he dropped us at took traffic going both east and west. The only ones who stopped were going back the way we'd come. It was another day of getting nowhere. By late evening, we gave in and took a ride back to Cleveland to escape. The trucker swore that the ramp he was taking us to would be a better location to snare a ride.

"Jeez! This looks familiar," Karen said as we jumped down from the cab.

"All these ramps look the same," I told her with smug confidence. But after glancing around, I saw our footprints at the edge of the pavement and realized she was right. We were back where we started, in the twilight zone.

Another wasted day passed. Karen huddled in her sleeping bag while I stood a few feet away, thumbing without results long into another night. As another dawn lightened the horizon, a big dump truck pulled up.

"Thank god," I yelled up to the driver. "We've been trying to get out of this place for two days!"

"This is a terrible spot," he agreed. "You ought to wait at an oasis on the Interstate. There, you could meet, talk, and negotiate with people. No commercial trucker is likely to pick you up at one of these ramps in the industrial area."

He dropped us at the oasis that straddled the highway midway between Cleveland and Toledo. Drivers going both directions stopped to eat and gas up. Karen and I filled up on their cheapest breakfast special. Food at last! Karen bounced back into the livelier girl she'd been when I met her.

"Hi," I asked people leaving the restaurant who looked cheerful. "We're going to Chicago and need a ride. Do you have room?"

Unsure if the cops passing through would hassle us for begging rides, I tried to keep a low profile. Karen refreshed and prettied herself up in the restroom. Standing beside me, she sweetened the deal with bored and lonely drivers.

A four-door sedan pulled up in front of us at the entrance. Out of the back seat popped a white man with a five o'clock shadow and short, curly black hair. Everyone else I could see in the car was black. He dressed like a pirate, with one earring and flashy colored beads around his neck. I said nothing as he walked past us, shoeless in black silk stockings. The car waited at the curb with his door wide open. He returned, eating a fish sandwich.

"Are you going to Chicago?" I asked.

"Yes, brother, but sorry. As you can see, our car is full." Exuding sympathy, he handed his sandwich to me. "Here, man, take my sandwich. You and your lady need it far more than I do."

He shined a benign smile at us. "I'm a musician playing with B.B. King. Good luck to you." He had to arouse some sleeping forms to slide back into his seat. With a wave, the good-hearted fellow was gone.

Karen didn't turn her nose up at the sandwich. I still had one of my salvaged burgers, and we washed it down with a beer. I still had at least six bottles.

An hour later, under the hot midday sun, a ragtag group of bleach-blond hippies, barefoot in red and blue tie-dyed shirts, passed us on their way to a school bus, painted in whirling psychedelic designs.

"Here are some of our people," I told Karen, confident our luck had changed. One of them had a gold earring peeping through his long hair. Before I opened my mouth, he answered my unspoken question.

"We're going east to New York, man."

"Shucks, we're headed west to Chicago."

While his companions boarded the bus, he stayed behind a moment. "We're the Children of God," he proclaimed, fixing me with icy blue eyes.

"Cool, man." I assumed it was a generic statement, as we were all supposed to be children of God. "I follow a Buddhist path myself." My words set him off.

"It's only by faith in Jesus Christ that you can be saved, man." With fire in his eyes, he harangued me with a spittle-flecked sermon. "You need to abandon Satan's false prophets! Wash yourself in the blood of the lamb, the blood of the sacrificed Son of God, and you will be saved from the fires of hell."

With that, he got on his bus, which spared us from enduring more of his tirade. Thus, I learned of the Children of God, a tribe of wandering Jesus freaks.

Late in the day, we got a break. A trucker, in his mid-thirties, climbed down from the cab of his tractor-trailer and called out to us.

"Hey, you kids, want a ride?"

"Sure, we're going to Chicago?"

"I'm going to Blue Island, close by there. Just going to take a piss and fill my thermos with coffee. If you're still here when I get back, I'll take you."

Coming back, he shot us a conspiratorial wink and whispered, "I'm not supposed to pick up passengers, see? So, wait for me over there while I fire up my rig." He pointed toward the exit ramp to the expressway as he hurried on to his truck.

We did as he said. The climb up into the cab was difficult for Karen. I had to push her up before tossing her the backpacks and then hoisted myself up. The spacious cab fit us beside the driver, sitting in comfort on padded leather seats. With grinding gears, we took off, relieved to be on our way. The truck was so loud we had to shout.

"If you're sleepy, you can climb in back," he yelled, pulling open the curtain behind us. It covered a crawl space made into a cozy bed chamber with a mattress and blanket. Karen took him up on it and crawled in, leaving the curtain ajar. Opening the curtain wider, the driver turned and peeked at her with a lewd grin, then came back to me.

"She's a damn fine good-looking girl," he said before turning his attention back to the road. After a moment, he nudged me and smirked. "She's got a nice figure. I suppose you know!"

Embarrassed by his blunt assessment, I nodded in agreement but didn't answer. We barreled along the highway in silence for a while. The driver didn't talk about himself, whether he was single or married, happy or not, but I could feel the wheels turning in his mind. Finally, he spoke up.

"I tell you what," he took a deep breath and continued. "It's been a long haul; I'm gosh-darn tired, but have a little more time before I have to deliver this load." He pulled the curtain open to peek at Karen again. She looked fast asleep. He riveted me with his eyes. "What is she to you, anyway?"

The question flummoxed me. Karen and I hadn't defined our relationship with labels, like boyfriend and girlfriend. From our first meeting to our lovemaking amidst thunderclaps in the barn, to the sudden fear of losing her as I hugged her tight when confronted by the Pennsylvania Patrolman, my feelings had intensified. I tried to deny the instinct of possessiveness growing within me. I ascribed that to an evil male chauvinism. I didn't *own* her, but yes, she meant everything to me.

The trucker winked, still leering."You're a lucky dog, you rascal. Is she any good in bed? She's so fine. Be a sport. Cut me in!" He winked and nudged me again. "Maybe we could, you know, stop at a motel or something. I'll pick up some beer, and we'll have us a little party? Would she be game?"

Game? Would I be a *sport?* In principle, I agreed with sharing love among comrades. This guy was our benefactor who'd saved us from the doldrums of Ohio. It seemed fair enough. We owed him for the ride, but I didn't think she'd go for this guy, not willingly. I didn't own her and wouldn't force her, but felt obligated to try.

"I'll ask her about that."

Karen sat up; her blank face stared at me. Maybe she'd heard everything we said. Could I ask this sexual favor of her? She was my woman, my partner, risking herself with me on this desperate journey. Unsure how to put it, I brazened it out.

"Do you wanna party? You know, spend some time with this guy?"

She made no reply; her expression was unchanged, and I was in no mind to push her.

"She said no, doesn't want to," I told the driver, my duty to him done.

He sighed, exasperated, as he focused on the road, grinding his gears with exceptional noise. It was hard to tell if the racket indicated his anger or was a natural part of driving that big rig. Karen climbed back in front to sit between us guys. With a sweet voice, she chatted with our driver. Lonely and horny as was, she may have felt sorry for him or understood we needed to keep him on our side. Night came upon us, and he looked exhausted. He pulled off the highway to park on the shoulder between a couple of motels.

"I'll just get some sleep here in the back," he said. "Then we'll go on, but it'd be a hell of a lot more comfortable in a nice motel bed." Addressing Karen directly, he tried again. "You are sure you don't want to party at a motel? It'd be a lot more comfortable than cramped in this cab."

"Ah, I don't know." Karen looked at me for support, her eyes pleading as she gripped my hand. My duty was clear. Whatever idealistic presumptions I had about sharing love, the honorable thing was to protect her.

The driver emitted another loud sigh of disappointment before climbing into the back to snooze. Karen snuggled against me in the front seat. I drifted in and out of sleep, my radar attuned to each sound that could indicate an unwelcome, potentially hostile advance from our benefactor.

Part Five
Coming Full Circle

Sweet Home Chicago

Our driver climbed back up into his seat with the faint pre-dawn light. Wordless, he fired up the engine, put it in gear, and we rolled back onto the Interstate. It was Wednesday, October eight, the day we were supposed to be in Chicago. Despite our long circuitous journey, Karen and I would arrive in time. With the radio turned on full blast, we caught the top local news story.

The Weathermen faction of SDS has claimed responsibility for blowing up an iconic statue in Chicago's Haymarket Square. On the evening of October six after eleven o'clock, an explosion rocked the Haymarket Square neighborhood, shattering over one hundred windows. Parts of the statue's legs landed on the Kennedy expressway. The statue commemorated the seven policemen who lost their lives in the labor riots that rocked Chicago back in 1886...

Karen, half awake in my arms, looked up at me. I grinned back at her.

"The Weathermen are setting the stage." We were closing in on our date with destiny.

The Haymarket statue is of a policeman in old-fashioned garb, with a helmet like a Keystone cop, standing upon a high pedestal. It had a stormy past, commemorating seven policemen killed while disrupting a peaceful worker's demonstration back in 1886. At least some may have been shot by their own side. Several Labor leaders, charged as agitators, were hanged. Years later, a more progressive administration exonerated them of all blame and placed a pro-workers monument where they were buried in Waldheim Cemetery.

By blowing up the statue, the Weathermen were connecting their struggle to the labor movement, setting the mood for their upcoming *Siege of Chicago*. The City got ready for it. Days off for Chicago's ten thousand-man police force had been canceled from October eight through the eleventh. Detectives had to report for duty in uniform. Large reserve police forces were stationed at strategic locations around locations where demonstrations were expected. They would be ready to respond like minute men to any trouble. I didn't discuss the news with Karen or our driver, but I knew we were in for some heavy action.

Compared to Ohio and Pennsylvania, Indiana was a narrow state and slipped by fast. Gary, with its acrid, polluted stench, popped up. Then East Chicago, soon we found ourselves in the south suburbs of Chicago. Our driver pulled off the toll road and meandered through an industrial area to pull into the loading bay of a warehouse. The guys on the loading dock helped us back in, after which they called out.

"We're going to lunch. See you in an hour."

"What!" our exasperated driver yelled back. "I can't wait around here that long, gotta get going!" He told us he wasn't an hourly worker on the clock like they were, but got paid by the trip for on-time deliveries.

"Hey, man, we're already late for our break. If we don't take it now, we lose it. You can wait until we get back or unload the damn thing yourself. Bye!"

Karen and I looked at each other. We needed to show our appreciation for the lift that rescued us from the doldrums of Ohio.

244

"We will help you unload," I told our truck driving man. That calmed him down.

He swung open the back of the truck. The sides had a series of moveable arms that connected in the middle to hold the sides under a roofless top. We unlatched and rotated them to either side as we worked our way through the cargo, which constituted of valves and machine parts, individually wrapped in burlap bags tied with twine.

Our driver tossed us each a pair of leather work gloves and climbed onto the seat of a crane. Karen stood waiting on the loading dock while he lowered the cable to me on the truck. After I hooked a package to it, he raised it onto the dock for Karen to unhook. A couple of times, he climbed down to help her with some of the more unstable and heavy pieces. It was hard work on an empty stomach. Just as we unloaded the last piece, the employee came back, signed his receipt, and our driver hopped back in his truck.

Giving us a high wave like a salute, he called to us as rolled out. "You kids are on your own now. Good luck!"

He was still upset that he didn't get to screw Karen, but we'd more than paid for the ride by unloading his truck. I'd never been to Blue Island and only knew that we were within the greater Chicago area. It was afternoon on the eighth of October. We'd arrived right on time despite so many detours.

Out in the bright sunshine on the street, I asked a little old lady. "Which way to Chicago?" She directed us to a northbound street, and we stuck out our thumbs. A middle-aged man soon picked us up.

"I'm not going far, but I can drop you kids off at the next CTA train station."

After our experience in Ohio, it amazed me how much easier rides came for us. His cordial conversation put us at ease, but as he let us out, he said, "I give you kids a ride because I never believed all those stories. How bad people say you hippies are."

That struck me as hilarious. Without cracking a smile, I said, "Oh no. We're not bad people. I haven't killed anyone all day long!"

He didn't laugh, and I realized my sense of humor went too far.

Did he imagine I could be a dangerous killer? As he drove off, I called after him, "Just kidding, man!" Straights could be too literal. Joking around, I may have fed into the prejudicial rumors against hippies. But I'd been on the road for endless days, too worn out to beware of every word that slipped out of my mouth.

I still had enough change for train fare because I'd not spent anything on this trip. We rode all the way north to Alice's Restaurant Revisited on Wrightwood. After my unbelievable odyssey through the wilds of the East, it was good to be back.

While I fished my five-dollar bill out of its hideaway to spend a couple dollars of it on a cheap meal, we met a serious short-haired guy who gave us the scoop.

"I'm one of the organizers," he said, sitting at a table scattered with pamphlets and cards. "People are coming in from all over the country. We're assembling at volunteer churches scattered around the city."

Churches? I hadn't expected that.

"Sure, man. This demonstration is not only a hard-core Weatherman thing. RYM II, PL, they'll all be running their own shows at the same time. The liberal, anti-war churches have agreed to shelter people coming in from out of town."

When his long-haired partner came back with coffee, he patiently explained the political landscape to us. SDS had split into rival factions. RYM, the Revolutionary Youth Movement, backed Black Nationalism.

Bob Dylan sang: *You don't need a weatherman to know which way the wind blows* on his Subterranean Homesick Blues album. Inspired by this, the most radical members of RYM created the Weatherman Manifesto. It attacked "white skin privilege" and supported women's Liberation, and advocated immediate armed struggle in support of the People's Liberation Wars around the world, especially in Vietnam.

Others agreed but advocated patience. They believed in a more traditional Marxist approach to build a revolutionary vanguard party before going to war. RYM I then became the Weathermen. After heated debate, the others broke away to become RYM II, Revolutionary Youth Movement II. Because of these ideological differences, Weathermen called RYM II "running dogs." I heard this slur bandied about often with the Weather people but didn't grasp the full meaning of it.

PL was Progressive Labor, which sought to forge a broad common front with students and straight working people. The goal was to get students to blend into the working class to organize them on a common front for class war.

"Those fucking PL guys want us hippies to cut our hair. Fuck that! I'll keep my hair and hippie identity, thank you."

His short-haired partner took a sip of coffee and chimed in. "Hair just gets in my way, man. It makes us an obvious target for the pigs to hassle. I'm sick of being stopped and frisked for dope."

Turning back to us, he added, "Stay in your affinity group."

"What are infinity groups?" I asked.

"No man, that's AFFINITY groups."

"Huh?"

"People you know and trust. We gotta be careful about undercover pigs trying to infiltrate. Dig it? Be careful talking to anyone you don't know, even me. Who did you come with?"

I pointed to Karen. "She is all the people I have. We just came in from New York, but I'm originally from Chicago."

He showed us a list of churches. Garret and McCormick Theological Seminaries were both up in Evanston. The University Disciple Church was down in Hyde Park. Finally, there was St. Luke's.

"You'd better go to St. Luke's. It's the closest, at 1500 west Belmont. Midwestern people are gathering there."

"Good, we're beat after all our hard miles."

"Well, looks like you have to hit the ground running. We're assembling for speeches in Lincoln Park tonight. You don't have too much time left."

With a no-nonsense look, he added, "Get rid of anything incriminating, such as dope. You're bound to be hassled by the pigs on the way over. Even the coordinators at the church might frisk you because they don't want trouble. Getting busted, locked up for a stupid joint while you are needed in the streets, would be a real waste."

As we walked away, I told Karen, "I suppose that gives new meaning to the song *Get me to the church on time!*"

"Very funny." She rolled her eyes and then grabbed my sleeve. "Wait a minute." She set down her backpack and reached in to grab something from a hidden pocket. With a worried look on her face, she showed it to me in her cupped hands, shielding it from any bystander's view.

It was a pretty blue hashish pipe that looked so innocuous. They were sold openly in all the head shops, but if there were any residue inside the bowl, it could be enough for both of us to be charged with possession. Sure enough, there was black residue.

"Lucky the Pennsylvania cops didn't frisk us," I told her. "We'd better get rid of it, like the guy said."

"Yeah, too bad. It's kind of special. Caesar gave it to me."

After she said that, I hated to throw the thing away. Caesar was good people. Straight couples had rings to express their love. We needed mementos too, however corny, artifacts from our life's journey together. We'd come across the country and expected to have many more miles to go when this Weatherman Action thing was over.

"Look at this." Karen stooped to pick up a driver's license. "Maybe you could use this as fake ID if the cops get you." She laughed. The guy who lost it was in his early twenties and heavier than rail-thin me.

At the last intersection, before we crossed the street to the church, I reached up over the stoplight and placed the pipe above the control box behind the *walk* sign. Hopefully, no one would find it for a few days. We could fetch it afterwards before moving on.

The light changed to green. "Ready for the church, Karen?" She smiled, blushed, and shook her head.

I wondered what she was thinking. Marriage? Although I didn't believe in *straight* marriage, maybe there was something to pledging our love for each other. A crazy idea, but maybe someday. Who knew?

I took her hand in mine, and we marched across the street and straight into the church. Inside, there was a table set up. An SDS official sat behind it and handed me a pen and an index card for each of us.

"Sign in here. So we can bail you out if you get busted."

Karen listed Blake instead of Mucci as her last name. There was no sense in taking any chances, but I had nothing to hide and put my real name and parent's phone number down.

"Empty your pockets too."

"Why?"

"To make sure you've got no dope, nothing they can bust you for."

I gave him the ID we'd found. "Maybe someone on the run who really needs an alias could use it."

We added our backpacks to several others piled up along the wall in the basement. Only eleven people ended up at St. Luke's Church. Most of them were gone by the time we'd arrived. With only a couple of hours before the action was to begin, we took a quick rinse in the restroom. Then a voice called out.

"Are you guys ready? We have a car."

After swinging by to

Pick up stragglers at the other churches. We returned to Alice's Restaurant. Juiced up on excitement, we immediately joined the jam-packed carload.

The Bonfire

"**L**et's go!" I led Karen down to Lincoln Park, where it was all to go down. What exactly that was, I could only guess, but the talk of instigating People's War, just like in Viet Nam, hinted at the prospect of a street battle.

Where Lincoln joined Wells, we kept left, passing a little hole in the wall café where sat a hulking road hippie with long blond hair halfway to his waist and a lean dog on a leash that was but a common string. Other than his dog, he sat alone, the only customer.

"Come join us," I called.

He gave me a wary smile and raised two fingers in the "V" peace sign. It had meant "Victory" to an earlier generation fighting fascism. "I'm for peace and love, man. I don't want anything to do with those violent radicals in the park."

I raised my fist. "This is our peace sign, man. It means struggle. There's no peace without standing up to the war machine."

Turning to Karen, I said, "These peaceniks don't get it, but they're still our brothers and sisters have a role to play in the Revolution."

From the door of the café, I could already hear the racket in

Lincoln Park. Indistinct warbling and screeching voices came over the public address system. As we got closer, a woman's strident words came in loud and clear. It went something like this.

Brothers and sisters! All our lives, we've been told that love is the answer! Well, I'm telling you we must learn to hate! We must hate the PIG to fight him. Our hate is a revolutionary love for our oppressed brothers and sisters...

Her words both chilled and thrilled me. The crowd roared back, "Right on, sister! Fucking A!" Someone mentioned the speaker's name, Bernardine Dohrn.

Darkness fell as we entered the park. Everything appeared eerie in the dancing firelight of a roaring bonfire. Some guys were tearing apart park benches.

"For the bonfire," they explained. My conscience rebelled. The parks belong to the people, but swallowing my qualms, I joined in, remembering that you cannot make an omelet without breaking a few eggs. We had to tear up some of the good aspects of this culture to create the fuel to destroy the old and start over.

It was hard work wrenching off a slat bolted tight to the concrete supports, but once off, we used it to pry the rest of the wood slats free.

People threw meat on the bonfire. "We're roasting pig meat," someone shouted. It was like a symbolic voodoo offering to stoke up our killer instincts.

I caught glimpses of Bernadine on stage in the bonfire's glow. It gave her a sleek, sexy look. I'd become smitten with the rock star image of Bernadine, illuminated in the dancing flames. *Man,* I thought, that wildcat was my kind of woman, forgetting for the moment that I was with a hell of a chick already. She'd been at my side throughout the rigors of our long journey. That's the kind of chick I hoped *my* Karen would turn into, a real fireball!

A five-foot, skinny woman in a helmet shrieked from the ranks. "We women are battle-ready! We're goddamn fearless Amazons who don't need to hide behind our men in this fight."

Shouts of *Right on sister* erupted around us. Karen clutched my hand tighter. She was *my* woman now. No matter what these hard-core women said, I wanted to keep her out of harm's way as much as I could. It remained to be seen whether they, or any of us, were ready for combat.

The cadre of hard-core Weathermen and Weatherwomen stood at attention in their tight packed affinity groups. I kept hearing that over and over. "Stay in your own affinity group."

"We don't have one," I yelled. They won't let me join if they don't know me.

"Just form up behind us," a woman in a football helmet said. "We're going to take off soon."

A cheer broke out: "Here comes our own Riot Squad!" A one hundred strong phalanx of lean and mean dudes marched in wearing an assortment of football, army, and motorcycle helmets. In tight formation, they faced away from the speakers before the bonfire, as if bodyguards. They looked as angry and tough as the Greasers I'd gone to Fenton High with. This vanguard was well prepared. Most had clubs or sturdy sticks, and I even saw a few hiding tire chains under denim jackets. Some carried vintage gas masks to protect themselves from tear gas. Yellow stars on red and blue Vietcong flags fluttered above them, along with a banner featuring Che Guevara's iconic face.

The cops had us surrounded, but didn't interfere. I suppose they figured they had us contained in the park. Rounding us up would be easy once they'd listed enough charges against us to make it worth their while.

I overheard random comments. "We expected more people. We're less than a thousand."

"Some didn't make it, but we'll have enough for tonight. There will be more tomorrow."

It wasn't a huge crowd. Not everyone on the left or on the fringe of mainstream society was ready to take a stand. We'd to push the slackers off their fence, show the zoned out white peaceniks how selfish it was, sit on your ass and cry "Peace, peace" while the *man* came down hard on the rest of the world. We'd show them the way forward.

The various chants and slogans were becoming familiar to me. I would hear them again and again in the ensuing days and years to come.

The Second Battle of Chicago, by Tom Thomas, 1969, excerpted in WEATHERMAN by Harold Jacobs by Ramparts Press in 1970, page 201, bears quoting here:

Three defendants in the Conspiracy Trail were in the park–Tom Hayden, Abbie Hoffman, and John Froines. Hayden told the rally, "People have been saying the Conspiracy Eight are against this demonstration. That is not true. While there are some differences among the 'Eight,' we are all united in the need to intensify the struggle to end the war.

We are glad to see people back in Lincoln Park. We are glad to see the militancy of Chicago increased," Hayden added.

At 10:15, a member of the Weather Bureau (the national office of Weatherman/SDS) announced himself under the pseudonym of Marion Delgado and told the crowd they were going to march on the Drake Hotel, "where the rich people live." "Judge Hoffman (who is presiding in the Conspiracy Trail) is up at the Drake, and Marion Delgado don't like him, and the Weatherman don't like him, so let's go get him."

The hard-core groups stood in ranks at ramrod attention before the bonfire, as if awaiting a signal. When the last speaker began a chant, about 10:25, I was caught off guard by the sudden roar that ripped from a hundred throats.

Che! Che! Viva Che! Like an invocation to the patron deity of People's war, the chorus of shouting continued as the People's Army sprang to life.

HO! HO! HO CHI MINH! NLF is going to win! HO! HO! HO CHI MINH! Dare to struggle–dare to win!

Then someone shouted *Marion Delgado.* "The only direction is insurrection, and the only solution is revolution!"

Ronald J Schulz

The crowd that reporters later claimed numbered about two hundred and fifty, charged west at a fast trot. Caught off guard, Karen and I ran to catch up. One girl ran smack into a tree in the darkness, an early casualty. Karen and I surged with the others, out of Lincoln Park to Clark Street. The North Federal Savings and Loan was the first large building we targeted with a rock that smashed the large plate-glass windows. A legion of shouting voices combined with the crescendo of dozens of windows smashed at once. Dinging alarms went off, adding to the mayhem. It had a chilling effect until I reminded myself that we were only destroying corporate property, whereas the pigs took human life.

By the time Karen and I reached them, only one bank's plate-glass window remained unbroken. What luck, a large piece of concrete lay on the street; it must have bounced off from someone's earlier shot. With all my might, I heaved it, shattering the glass.

"Wow," Karen smiled at me, elated at our small victory. We'd joined the new American Revolution. But there was no time to gloat. Our phalanx moved forward, the pigs were coming after us from behind, and we had to keep ahead of them. Someone shouted.

"Turn left at the next street–pass it on!"

It was Goethe Street. It seemed the heroes of the past were joining us. A drama on the sidewalk cut my musing short. A well-dressed man stood before a ritzy, upscale apartment building. The windows on the door were smashed, and the wood panels splintered.

"You bastards are all cowards!" Spittle flew from the mouth as he hurled invective against the rioters. "Come on and fight me one to one! Somebody fight me, goddamn it!"

Well padded, club wielding rioters ran by. No one stopped. My mind flashed to ancient combats, to the Iliad and the Old Testament. Individual champions like David and Goliath, Achilles, and Hector, fought each other while the armies of both sides paused to watch.

I shouted to the flitting figures running by, "Does somebody want to fight this guy?" Not me, of course. I had to look out for Karen.

But we were the new barbarians at the gates, not Bronze Age

254

Champions seeking personal glory. It wasn't personal at all; he was just an angry collateral victim of the struggle. There were bigger issues at stake than *honorable* glory or valiant death.

Our orgy of destruction was to be aimed at corporate property. It shocked me to see some of my comrades attacking poor, beat up Volkswagens parked on the street.

"Those are people's cars," I shouted. "Leave them alone. We should stick to trashing the Cadillacs of the rich war profiteers."

But there was no time to manage the unleashed passion of this untrained army of wild youth.

We took a right on State Street. The head of our column ran smack into a police line forming at State and Division. The leading affinity group charged straight through them, only to be cut off as the pigs reformed their ranks.

From my position farther back, I could see that those following veered off. Shouldn't we break through to our trapped comrades? But I grab Karen's hand and follow the shouted commands of our new vanguard. Twisting through back streets and alleys, we ran until we found ourselves on Lake Shore Drive.

Another police line closed in, firing tear gas.

"Everyone, break up into your affinity groups!"

Then another voice shouts, "Walk, don't scatter, stay together!"

Are we still under Weather Command or agent provocateurs misdirecting us?

Still holding Karen's hand to keep her *cool* amidst the mayhem, I was unsure whether she was scared or excited. Her face was blank, but I thought I read fear in her eyes. Maybe I should have left her back at the church.

All this changing direction disoriented me. We raced into a parking garage and out the other side. Then we smacked into the same, or maybe another police line. Back we ran into the same or another parking garage, where a line of police, standing to either side, clubs at the ready, seemed to have us cornered.

Karen and I had no weapons. We had no choice but to pass

through the gauntlet single file, within an arm's length of our enemies, unsure if they would club us down and arrest us. These policemen were too few and unprepared; they wore soft hats rather than the white riot helmets of the main force. They must have been dragooned into service at the last minute. Jabbing their clubs to indicate the direction for us to go, they channeled us along, and we filed out of this trap. It felt like running through a haunted Halloween house full of menacing spooks and goblins or herded like cattle into a pen. I breathed a sigh of relief when we made it through unscathed.

At Menomonee Street, I heard shrieks from behind and turned to see an unmarked car plowing right through our group, bumping people out of the way. From all the windows, the uniformed torsos of cops in white riot helmets leaned out, clubbing the youths wheeling out of their way as I described in the opening of this book.

They're bulldozing us; run for it.

Policemen spilled out of the car, forming a thin blue line facing us. I let go of Karen's hand, and she ran back with the others, leaving me to stand with a few scattered stalwarts. It was only a suicidal, haughty male pride that caused me to face the revolver of one of these blue meanies. My racing brain covered much territory in the seconds it took before they fired two volleys. Although they hit none of us, they made their point. We could be no match for them.

In that moment, wondering if I would soon plunge headlong into death, my love for Karen became paramount. The future we'd joked about: joining communes out west, enjoying nature, building a loving, open-minded, non-judgmental community that would be so unlike the families we'd come from, all that would vanish as if it never was. My brief existence would have no meaning, leave no legacy, no child who could continue into the bold new dawn. I had to survive for Karen and a stake in our future.

We were no longer an attacking phalanx but scattered individuals and small groups wandering through the dark streets. Some, from out of town, appeared lost. Although I couldn't find

Karen, I had faith some comrade would take her in tow. We'd reunite back at the church.

I found a pretty blond girl, all alone, with tears streaming down her face.

"Are you lost? Need help?"

Sobbing, she shook her head no, but I took her hand, anyway. She didn't pull away, and we ran together for several blocks before she stopped and faced me.

We all had to watch out for each other, as I hoped someone would do for Karen. Whether she admitted it or not, the girl needed someone beside her.

"Thanks, I'll be alright now." She squeezed my hand and released it. "This is my neighborhood."

Up ahead, I saw a subway station. With no money for the fare, I jumped the turnstile and caught the northbound train. An overjoyed Karen embraced me.

"Man, that was a hell of a night," she said. A shiver of excitement ran through her, and she looked up at me with a smile. "Guess what, Ron."

"Hmm?"

"Tomorrow I'm going to the Women's Action. Men aren't supposed to join us, so you gotta wait here." She exhaled a long sigh. "I'm beat."

"Me too."

We wanted nothing more than to unroll our sleeping bags and catch up on some much-needed sleep. Before we could do so, one of the organizers came up.

"Grab your gear. St. Luke's don't want us here anymore. The evening's events scared 'em. Damn liberals don't understand the need for People's War."

They drove us to McCormick Theological Seminary in Hyde Park. Where we flopped into happy unconsciousness for a few hours.

The statistics came later. Sixty rioters arrested; fifteen reported injured, as were eight cops. That evening, the Governor of Illinois

Ronald J Schulz

mobilized twenty-five hundred National Guard troops to defend Chicago. Our force of less than five hundred Weathermen had punched above their weight. Whether any of this would contribute to a wider uprising of white youth against the Establishment remained to be seen.

Panthers and RYM II

After a women's meeting designed to raise political consciousness, Karen left with the *Women's Militia*. She returned much earlier than expected.

"It was a flop," she said, dropping beside me on the floor.

"What happened?" She told me that the Women's Militia, also grandiosely referred to as the Women's Liberation Army, intended to attack the Armed Forces Induction Center in the downtown Loop. Bernadine Dohrn met about one hundred women gathered at the statue of General Logan in Grant Park. This statue had been featured in an iconic scene of protest during the Democratic Convention the year before.

Bernadine exhorted the women. "You're people living behind enemy lines. We will fight behind enemy lines."

Most were helmeted and padded, two carried Vietcong flags, and several had long clubs. "Pigs, pigs," they shouted, charging into the police, injuring several cops, but surrounded and outnumbered, most of the women dropped their weapons and gave up. Twelve, including Bernadine, were arrested. The rest escaped into the subways.

That was only the start of our day. Rumors flew, and plans

changed by the minute. There was talk of liberating students in the high schools, but the pigs were wise to it and cordoned them off.

"Listen up, guys," a rail thin young man in spectacles who looked like he belonged in a college classroom called us into a huddle. "We're going to the Federal Building, where the Conspiracy Trail is going down. The Panthers and Young Lords are speaking. The damn Running Dogs will be there too. Let's go and support the Conspiracy Eight!"

Chorused shouts of *Right on* and *fucking A* fired us up. The Conspiracy Eight were the defendants blamed for causing the riots at the Democratic Convention the year before. They were being railroaded by Judge Hoffman's biased court and had become martyrs to the Revolution.

Karen and I squeezed into the backseat of a car driven by a blond woman with a deep scar across her cheek. She dropped us at Jackson and Dearborn, the Federal Building Plaza. It was early afternoon as we joined the mixed crowd of all ages, colors, and political persuasions, surrounded by helmeted police who looked ready to jump us if ordered. Few demonstrators wore helmets; a street brawl wasn't expected. The atmosphere was electric, like a carnival. Freaky long-haired white guys in tie-dyed shirts and beret wearing Blacks in leather jackets hawked underground newspapers.

"*SEED, SEED*, buy the Chicago *SEED*, only thirty-five cents."

"Get a copy of the *Black Panther* right here, only a quarter."

A few silent black men incongruously dressed in suits and ties held up copies of *Muhammad Speaks*, the Black Muslim paper.

Banners read *Free Panthers Now. Free Bobby Seale. Free the Conspiracy Eight. Jail Judge Hoffman.* Listening to the snippets of conversation swirling around us, I realized most people there didn't support the Weathermen street battle. Many un-hip older men and women in denim work clothes were Union supporters. Some of them came on lunch break from nearby factory jobs. That encouraged me. I was sick of factionalism. We needed to support each other in standing up for social and political change.

Someone yelled, "Wow, did you see that?" I looked over to see a couple of plainclothes cops hustling a handcuffed longhair out of the crowd. "The pigs are picking off our leaders, man. They got files on us all."

On stage, a young white guy, who I later learned was Mike Klonsky of RYM II, introduced Fred Hampton. Fred was chairman of the Illinois chapter of the Black Panthers and beloved by the audience. Shouts of *Right On*, and *Solidarity*, came from the crowd, but the theme of his speech surprised me.

"We do not support people who are anarchistic, opportunistic, adventuristic, and Custeristic," Fred shouted. He condemned the Weathermen's action, likening their strategy to Custer's Last Stand, a suicide mission. He continued making his case. "We do not believe in so-called premature acts of revolution. We support the actions of RYM II and no other faction of SDS. We've got to spend our time now on revolutionary education..."

I studied the unsmiling face of one of the Weatherman leaders standing across from me for signs of what he was thinking. He leaned against a pillar, arms folded, scanning the crowd as if wary of undercover pigs, but I caught no overt reaction to the speech. Weathermen idealized the Panthers, but insisted our *white skin privilege,* which protected us from the pigs' heavy-handed response, prevented many of us from a full commitment to the revolutionary cause. We had to go all out to prove ourselves worthy of our place in the People's Revolution.

Fred Hampton continued. "No matter how many pigs there are, there are more people than there are pigs. We want power of people, by the people, for the people! Fuck this shit of the pigs, by the pigs, for the pigs!"

The crowd cheered, *Right on, brother!*

Hampton's speech impressed me. If the Panthers wouldn't back the Weathermen, why should I? He was right that we needed to organize and grow in numbers and strength, and the random smashing of property, especially that belonging to ordinary people, would alienate more than recruit, but I craved action. Maybe Weathermen would tone done their activity and mend fences with the other factions of SDS before it splintered beyond repair.

The scar faced girl we'd come with turned to us. "Come on, we're going to another rally in support of Unions. We arrived about three o'clock at Twenty-sixth, and California Avenue, the International Harvester Plant, and I recognized many of the same faces. The plant was across the street from Cook County Jail, where another rally was scheduled immediately afterward.

The plant was in a drab fenced-in compound with the high concrete walls of the jail on the other side. Here was visible proof, if any was needed, that a job in this dreary modern industrial world wasn't much different from jail.

Our gathering crowd brought feeling and color into this dreary landscape. Some carried banners and signs reading, "Death TO US IMPERIALISM" and "CHICAGO ARTISTS AGAINST GENOCIDE." As we passed through the encircling police lines, they mocked us.

"We're going to get you commie bastards, you long-haired freaks. Police power is real power."

Many of the plant workers were there. They had walked off the job that morning to be our side. Together we listened to speakers and shouted, "RIGHT ON!" at the appropriate moments. This exclamation was to become a standard applause to speeches in my life for years to come. Jake, a black worker, spoke from the stage.

"Eighty thousand people need work in Chicago, and they're tearing down this plant to build a jail. The union ain't doing a thing about it." The uneasy crowd murmured, "Black workers are being sold out by the fucking United Auto Workers."

An expansion to the jail would be built on the site. The auto plant would reopen in a lily-white suburban neighborhood. Most of the employees who were black would not be able to relocate there. Not in our system of de facto segregation. The Union had betrayed their membership. Capitalists ran an ugly scam, pitting white against black in the scramble for decent wages and opportunity. We all had to stand together, freak and straight, black and white, Men and Women. Brothers and Sisters, we were all in this together.

There was also a Vietnam connection in this. This plant sent tractors to clear the jungle and root out the Viet Cong. International Harvester had even bought the land on which to build a plant right in Vietnam, hoping to exploit the cheap labor there and undercut American workers. International Capitalism used everyone without compunction, making our own people more expendable even as they exploited the peoples of foreign lands.

Another worker named Slim added, "When this plant opened, it was established that white guys got skilled jobs and black workers got unskilled jobs—and the union didn't do nothing against it then, and it hasn't done nothing yet."

Jake spoke again, "You can die with the white man in Vietnam, but you can't work with him in this plant."

After more speeches, we broke into a rousing union song.

Solidarity forever, solidarity forever, solidarity forever, for the union makes us strong.

I remembered hearing verses we didn't sing. The lines in the original version, written by Ralph Chaplin for the IWW, Industrial Workers of the World, better known to us as the famous Wobblies, brought tears to my eyes.

When the union's inspiration through the worker's blood shall run, there can be no greater power anywhere beneath the sun...

I embraced Karen and kissed her, remembering our evening in Woodstock and the song by Woody Guthrie that also brought tears to my eyes. We were hippie proletariats, the rebellious young, dropouts and runaways running to a bright future that we had to create somehow. We had come a long, hard way to get where we were, and yet I knew it could all end in gunfire, police clubs and handcuffs.

Kay and the Covenant
Church Raid

After the demonstration, Karen and I mingled with all the warring factions as we shuffled between churches and other locations to attend formal and informal meetings, one after the other. Exhausted, those events blurred together with a dreamlike, psychedelic quality. Someone must have fed us something, but I cannot recall.

Friday morning, we found ourselves in Elmhurst with members of RYM II, watching a bookish guy argue for Stalinism with some Trotskyist stalwarts. He was fierce in his pedantic dogmatism, that had no place in the world of actual people and events.

"The revolution with never end," he insisted with supreme confidence.

"Why?" I asked.

"Because even when we seize state power, there will be counter-revolution, or the government we put in place will become oppressive, and we or our descendants will have to rise against it. The cycle of thesis and antithesis that will go on forever."

"So why bother, then?"

"Exactly. We'll work to organize quietly in the background

without charging into police lines. When the Weathermen are crushed, we'll still be here organizing students and the working class. Maybe then we'll even open up to women's issues and that gay stuff."

In his cautious way, he made sense, but there was no drama to create momentum, to shake up the smug, complacent people who ignored the horror of what we were doing in the Third World. People who smiled with pride as their sons went off to Vietnam because the news broadcasts showed them most of the dying were on the other side. They had little sympathy for the severe suppression of black civil rights, as long as they had their bigger share of the spoils. Those complacent white people needed to see their own lily-white sons rise against the racist status quo. Only that might move them to see through the lies and turn against the oppression.

We were not far from the West End neighborhood where I'd meditated. If ever there was a time to hop off the revolutionary bandwagon and enjoy some measure of cordial hospitality, this was it. But I wanted to see and participate in the whole Chicago Rage. I felt we were taking part in living history. This would be the spark that set off a whole cataclysm, people rising to force the establishment to back down, maybe deescalate the war, address the myriad social inequities that gave the lie to our system of liberty and equality.

All manner of radicals, from hardcore Stalinists and Maoists to Trotskyites, engaged in endless arguments with each other. Karen and I had little chance to put in a word or two. Their opinions and revolutionary theories were too dogmatic and unyielding, creating an avalanche of words.

We must mobilize the workers. No. The alienated youth. No. Ally with Black, Third World people. Attack our white skin privilege. But that could put off organizing white labor. What about women? We must support Feminism. We men must confront our Male Chauvinism and Sexism. We need to focus on the struggle against racism first; the proletariat would be alienated by women's issues. What about our gay, homosexual, and lesbian brothers and sisters? They must join the common struggle of their race, their class, or their gender. That smacks of individualism, adventurism, and maybe elitism. What about...

Who held the *correct* line in this fractional, factional Left? There were so many isms and so many conflicting theories swirling around, demanding our attention and trying to bring us to commit wholeheartedly to one or the other, excluding the rest. But I saw them all as parts to a whole. Back in Chicago, we were invited to join another meeting.

"You go," Karen said, "I'm exhausted." Although tired myself, I wanted to watch and maybe take part in the planning. At the Covenant Methodist Church, at 2525 Hartrey Avenue in Evanston, I'd gotten myself into a seven-hour long slog through endless, droning speeches and arguments while packed with two hundred others in a back room. Bleary-eyed, I couldn't follow much of the unfamiliar, overblown jargon.

Self criticism was a phrase I heard over and over. At first, I thought it a great thing that the leaders, referred to as the Weather Bureau, admitted mistakes. Their headlong charge through police lines had cut them off. The affinity group leaders hadn't shown enough initiative to smash on through. The expectation had been too high. Few of them had military training. To expect them to transform into assault troops would be too much.

A guy in his mid-twenties pulled me to the side, speaking in stage whispers that had to be audible to those nearby.

"Are you ready to join me in some direct action against the pigs?"

"Like what?"

"I need you to buy some gasoline. I'll give you the money. Then we'll make Molotov cocktails and blow up some of the pigs' buildings."

I'd heard warnings about undercover agents, provocateurs, who would try to set us up to get busted for serious charges. Even in a room full of tough talking radicals, dangerous for an undercover pig if found out, I couldn't trust anyone.

Weatherwomen railed against social evils. "Monogamy is the

enemy of our revolutionary unity. Fucking each other pulls us together and builds our sense of community. We need to bond with each member of our affinity group."

The concept attracted me. The memory of the group marriage in Taos, although it failed me, was still my ideal social structure. It remained to be seen if Karen and I could build such an affinity group.

They talked of attracting the *alienated youth culture*. My ears pricked up at that. They meant me as much as anyone sitting scattered on sofas or filling the carpeted floor in the packed room. The real problem with all these SDS guys was that they were so hidebound. They quoted Mao, Lenin, or even Stalin like so many seminarians at theology school. Some may have been just that.

One of the Weather leaders spoke against the use of terrorism.

"We must remember that the purpose of this action is to build a Red Army. ... Blowing up a few things or shooting a few pigs from rooftops may do more damage. We may get into that later, but not at this time."

A blond woman introduced herself as from the Iowa contingent. "It's hard to become as violent as our action requires. Although I know he's a pig, and I should hate him for it, I can't help but think of him as a person."

Another woman from Michigan agreed. "We don't like to hit people... but the pig, whether he's a person or not, is the only thing holding the Man up, and the pig must be smashed... Off the pig."

Several in attendance shouted the refrain, "Off the pig!" Offing, which I heard for the first time, was an indirect way of saying kill or eliminate.

The girl from Michigan added, "Offing a pig is more than just hate; it's love. Love for the revolution, love for the oppressed people."

"Should the Vietcong fight?" someone asked. "Do they have the right or even the choice whether to defend their homes?"

The girl from Iowa said, "Yes, but there should be an alternative for people living in America in 1969."

"That is exactly the white-skin privilege that we have been

talking about," shouted an East Asian man. He rose from the floor, incensed. Someone whispered that he was an exchange student from Vietnam. His eyes afire, he panned the room for our support.

"She can just sit there and say the Vietnamese should fight, but she doesn't have to. She is a nationalist chauvinist racist. The Vietcong would kill her. She shouldn't even be here. We should kick her out."

That was too extreme. I felt sympathy for the girl voicing her honest opinions. Kicking her and so many others out, instead of welcoming them, would continue isolating us from the base of support we needed. As other voices rose, shouting in hostility at the girl, calling her a pacifist and a defeatist, she looked on the verge of tears. I had to say something.

We are more intent on fighting each other than the real enemy," I said. "Let her stay, save our anger for the pigs tomorrow."

"Right on, brother," said a thin woman in a kerchief. She helped me feel that what I said mattered.

The conversation moved on to our need to develop a fighting spirit. A leader from New York stood up before us.

"You've got to go out there knowing you're going to win, knowing you're going to win even if you die."

The girl from Iowa moved next to me, whispering, "Thanks for sticking up for me." She stuck out her hand. "I'm Kay, by the way, a student at Grinnell College." I took her hand and whispered back a longer self introduction.

"I'm Ron, from the streets of Chicago and a vagabond wanderer across the whole country."

"Wow, that's far-out, man. You don't seem as mean and crazy as most of these other Weatherman guys."

Yeah, I'm new at this. I don't think all of us could become trained soldiers overnight. Maybe some don't have to. Even the Vietnamese. Like this guy. He's a student over here, not fighting in the jungle back home. But I think he's where he can do the best, help change our people's opinions to understand and support his cause."

Kay wasn't as pretty as Karen, but her honesty and vulnerability attracted me. I reminded myself that I didn't believe in monogamy. Maybe she could join our happy tribe in the making.

It was about three in the morning. I got up to stretch my legs and use the John near the entry. As I was passing the front door, I heard a commotion. A guy ran up the steps from the front door shouting.

"It's the Pigs!"

I looked down to see a white helmeted policeman banging at the locked glass door. It took several swings from his club to smash the glass and club at the ready. He stepped through. I was the only one there to face him. Should I try to make a break for it, or was this the moment to make a stand? Some of the others inside heeded the warning and managed to escape out windows on the other side of the building, but this cop came right at me. It was useless to run.

I grabbed one of the football helmets laid neatly in rows along the wall. Holding it before me, I crouched in a defensive posture to face the charging lawman.

He froze. His eyes were wide behind his face shield. His baton gripped tight in both hands, ready to swing at me. For one fantastic moment, I found myself again eyeball to eyeball with my enemy. He was young and trim, without the donut and beer fed paunch sported by so many of his middle-aged comrades. His more cautious comrades took that moment to clear the glass and splintered wood from the shattered door before making their careful way through it. Seeing that resistance was hopeless, I straightened up and dropped the helmet back along the wall. The first cop charged past me to the main room. Those following herded me in with the others.

"Up against the wall!" they shouted. "Keep your heads down and don't look at us."

Kay took her place beside me, and I put my raised hand over hers against the wall and whispered encouraging words. Whether or not it was sexist, we men had to take care of our women. I prayed Karen was safe at the other church.

The cops came down the line behind and frisked us with

deliberate roughness. Taking apart our wallets, they looked for hidden compartments, and some stole people's cash. In my case, they had a few coins, too little to bother with.

They marched us in small groups down into the basement, where they lined us up in rows in the middle of the room. Despite their repeated threats not to look at them, I checked them out with sideways glances and noticed a number of black cops for the first time. They were less hostile and aggressive in handling us than the white cops and went out of their way to treat us with gentle care. I attributed this to some sympathy for our cause. They appeared to be in a subordinate position to their white counterparts.

Despite the contempt and anger the white cops showed us, race was still a factor. As white prisoners, we benefited from *white skin privilege.* The black cops may have felt that treating us roughly could backfire on them. Several of us whispered encouragement. *We're on your side, man,* but you couldn't expect them suddenly to change sides.

There were approximately two hundred of us lined up for inspection. They singled out and arrested forty-three of us who they identified as leaders or as having participated in Wednesday's riot. Some had jumped out of windows and escaped when the cops first barged in, so the cops didn't get everyone they sought.

The rest of us kept our spirits up, playing childish games with our captors, such as the POWs on *Hogan's Heroes* did. Many of us had been high school boys, used to being in trouble. We considered our verbal jibes a form of psychological warfare.

"Oink-oink, piggy," I called after a white cop passed by. He turned in a flash, demanding, "Who said that!" Someone on the other side of him produced a loud belch, which turned into a piggish grunt.

The red-faced pig turned again. "Shut the fuck up. Do you fucking think this is funny? We could take all of you mother-fucking punks in."

They continued circling around us, eying us with malevolence while slapping their Billy clubs into their hands, "If any of you move from your ranks, you will be arrested to enjoy the hospitality of Cook County jail."

The voices of the *pigs* trailed off into silence, but it could be a trap. We remained in our ranks for cautious moments to be sure the coast was clear. Then a few ventured out and discovered the pigs had split with their prisoners and booty.

Kay and I seized each other in a tight hug; we'd bonded by the heady experience and didn't want to lose each other. The scar faced blond woman drove us back to the other church, and I led Kay to where Karen lay sleeping like a baby and shook her.

She sat up and rubbed her eyes. "What's happening, Ron?"

My mind raced over how to introduce these gals to each other without inflicting jealousy.

"Hey, Karen, this is Kay. She came in from Iowa, and the cops barged in on the meeting. It was a wild scene."

Kay kneeled down and gave her a hug. "Nice to meet you, Karen. The past few days have been something, huh? After this is over tomorrow, maybe you guys can come to Iowa with us. We can squeeze you in the car."

"It sounds like a good idea," I said. Karen's face remained blank. Whether or not she felt threatened by Kay joining us, I wasn't sure, but I'd smooth over the situation with careful diplomacy.

Kay, at eighteen, was a year older than me and three years older than Karen, making her a perfect balance to our triumvirate. Whether she or Karen would be up for a threesome in the spirit of radical sisterhood remained to be seen. The idea psyched me up, and I had to breathe deep and focus on my heart chakra to calm myself.

Kay became animated, chattering away about her effort to promote feminist programs in Grinnell college.

"Hugh Hefner sent photographers for a big Playboy photo shoot of the coeds of Grinnell. Did you hear about that?" Karen and I shook our heads. "No? Well, we got a group of college girls together to march up and down the street in front of their office. She paused, inhaled, and exploded. "In the nude!" She giggled like a mischievous schoolgirl. "That got plenty of public attention for our cause."

"I bet it did," I said. "But using nudity *against* Playboy probably increased their magazine sales."

"Oh, we're not man haters or against sex. A woman can be sexy *and* smart, you know. Straight media packages us as a commodity to be bought and sold."

Kay hesitated, glancing at Karen and then me. "Playboy's leering objectification of women is no different than the way the Miss America Pageant showcases us as helpless and brainless."

"Good," I told her, and gave Karen a sly wink. "I think our sexuality is a dynamic, natural expression of who we are. Why should we be ashamed of it?" I refrained from telling her I thought Playboy, by smashing society's puritanical attitude, helped break down the double standard and gave our sexual revolution a boost. I didn't want to say anything that could upset Kay this early in our acquaintance.

Kay giggled. "We're not against sex. No way! We support our brothers struggling against their sexism. Men and women are all in this together. See? But displaying us like pieces of meat misses who we are."

Kay shot me a sexy smirk, intriguing me. The magic that happens between men and women doesn't have to make logical sense.

Monogamy, as Bernardine Dohrn and other Weatherwomen proclaimed, was a problem in the movement. Hostile competitiveness that turned women against each other affected affinity group cohesion. The solution was sharing our sexual partners with a bold and generous revolutionary love. Thereby bonding our affinity group into a tight family and interdependent unit. One that could work and fight together for the better future we wanted.

All this time, Karen had been listening, mute, but interested. She finally spoke. "Shut up, you two, and let's get some sleep."

People who'd come from all over the country remained in their little groups for security's sake, leaving us plenty of room for ourselves. Rolling out our sleeping bags side by side, I was in the middle, with Kay on my left and Karen snuggled on my right side. Without bothering to undress, I realized instigating a *ménage trios* would have to wait. Exhausted, I gave each a brief smooch before drifting into a slumber that proved far too short. It was already tomorrow.

The Haymarket

A bearded man nudged me awake. "Grab your shit and go. They want us out of here already." We'd imposed ourselves on the church people long enough, and they were anxious to be rid of us.

It was October eleventh, the climax of the Weatherman's action. But with Karen still snuggled on my right shoulder, and Kay spooned against my back, I awoke satisfied, charged with optimism from my short rest.

"Good morning, sleepyheads," I whispered, kissing each of their foreheads in turn.

Karen groaned. "Ahh, I need more sleep."

"We all do," yawned Kay. "Don't worry, this will be over soon, and we'll get back to normal life."

As we trooped off to the church bathrooms to freshen up, I reflected on how my fortune had improved from an eternity of wandering the streets with John. I took it as a sign that I'd cleansed my karma enough for these divine manifestations of feminine shakti to pop into my life. Together we had the proper yin-yang balance to keep our batteries charged and dynamic. I hadn't asked if Kay had a lover among her Grinnell companions, but if she did, I was confident we'd roll him into our growing affinity group.

"You and Karen can drop your packs in my friend's car," Kay said as we saddled up to move out. "You're both coming back to Iowa with us, right?"

"Yes, of course, we are," I spoke for Karen too, although she hadn't said a word.

"Good." Kay's sunny smile told me she meant the invitation. "Maybe you'll join our student group in Grinnell. They ought to be parked somewhere around the Haymarket. Come on."

Although the day was cold and overcast, we were stepping out into a new era with a bright new future. From Iowa and points west, we'd join others to build our new community, an extended loving family.

"I see them. Over there, Ron." Kay propelled us to where her Iowa friends stood by their parked car. "This is Ron and Karen," she called out to them. They're coming back to Grinnell with us."

A tall, lanky guy shook my hand. "We're going to sit this Haymarket thing out," he said. "We've had enough of these Weatherman. The pigs already pulled us over and hassled us, searching for weapons."

Turning to me, Kay said, "Go ahead, drop all your gear into the trunk."

With considerable relief, I tossed in my duffle bag. *Klink.* The sound told me I'd cracked one of my remaining beer bottles from Ohio. Too careless of me, but my sleeping bag would need washing anyway when we got back. The rest of the beer, warm or cold, would taste good then.

I placed Karen's pack with more care on top of mine. She stood at my side, still silent with a grim determination on her face, and asked her.

Kay took her hand. "Is everything alright?" Karen nodded. "Do you want to wait with my friends at the car?" Karen hesitated and clutched my hand tighter. "No, I think I can hack this."

What a gal. My heart pounded, and tears came to my eyes for this tough girl who'd stood by me through thick and thin. No matter what else happened, we'd stick together. She and I would make babies who would grow up wild and free to carry this Golden Age on into the future.

A burly, short, dark haired guy in his late teens materialized without a word on Karen's other side. He wore a long black coat, and I'd noticed him hanging out with her when I came back from those long, boring meetings. I couldn't be sure what she thought of him, but he seemed smitten by her.

A ripping sensation tore through my heart. My love for Karen burned stronger than before, but I had to be faithful to my universal ideals and couldn't allow myself to be jealous. Monogamy was selfish. We had to be inclusive to build a more honest and loving society. We'd avoid the mistakes our parents made when they drifted into suburbia after World War Two, isolating themselves in pair bonds that cut them off from the social whole.

Caesar's open generosity had shown me the way. I should allow brothers as well as sisters into our blossoming affinity group. We'd become stronger if we all made love together, as the Weathermen advised.

"Come here, man," I called, but he gave me a wary look, so I reached over and pulled him over. Then I reached out to Kay on my other side.

"Welcome to our affinity group, man," I said, locking us all into a group hug that felt so right. Unknown pitfalls lay before us. If something happened to me, he would be there for Karen. No matter how well it starts, real life is never a happily ever after fairytale. Our group was like an insurance policy for mutual support.

Once again, the scar faced girl drove us to a rendezvous in some sort of large school building. Hundreds of us hunkered down on the floor against the walls of a long corridor.

Twenty-two-year-old Mark Rudd was one of the founders of Weatherman, and he addressed us with a long-winded pep talk. He dressed more like a straight laced college boy than a hipster. His short dark hair and clean cut handsome looks made him a Rock Star of the Movement, ever since he'd led the 1968 takeover of Columbia University.

Up and down the hall, he paced, stepping over our outstretched legs as he rattled on about whatever high-flown revolutionary issues of theory and practice came to mind. Struggling to keep my eyes open, I couldn't follow it. This revolution was too wordy, in my opinion. Over and over, whether from PL or RYM II and the Weathermen, I kept hearing such stultifying rhetoric repeated that seemed to have little to do with confronting the oppressors. They all insisted that we had to learn their version of Marxist theory by heart, or the struggle could be co-opted and sold out. Our sweat and blood spilled for nothing.

The jumble of words overwhelmed and lulled my exhausted mind to sleep. Dialectical materialism, social contradictions and their solutions, thesis and antithesis, the conflict of opposed ideas that combined after bloody conflict into the synthesis of a unified whole, until that too needed to be overthrown by the next contradiction that arose in some sort of inevitable cosmic rhythm. It seemed irrelevant when we were about to smash through police lines.

Maybe Mark Rudd was as haggard as the rest of us operating on raw nerves. He wrapped up his talk and preceded us to the Haymarket Square. When we got there, I later heard that he and four other leaders were jumped by fifteen undercover officers and hustled into a paddy wagon. Such are the fortunes of war. Other leaders would take his place, and the struggle would go on.

The Haymarket was hailed as the birthplace of the American Labor Movement, a site steeped in conflict and repression. Just being in that hallowed spot thrilled me. As if I'd taken my place in the ongoing history. My life trajectory was in accordance with some cosmic plan, and I had to rise to the occasion.

Besides the plainclothes agents posing as newsmen mingling with the crowd, Blue Meanies surrounded us. Uniformed officers outnumbered our four hundred strong group that day. Fred Hampton's speech suddenly bounced into my head. His choice of words still haunted me. *Custeristic*, he'd called the Weather strategy, but I felt confident, jazzed, to be in on the last action.

Our anticipation of the march from Haymarket Square to the downtown Loop overwhelmed our exhaustion. We hadn't eaten since the day before. Fasting so long gave me a spacy, lightheaded euphoria.

We joined the crowd milling around the empty pedestal. The missing cop statue had been blown off days ago. A young man in a blazing red football helmet began a speech.

"That's John Jacobs from the National Office," someone nearby whispered. More high-spirited Weather troops arrived, boosting our confidence. We linked arms; our little four-person affinity group formed up into a phalanx with the others.

Forward, we surged, marching south around the corner, and turned east on Randolph Street. Our outnumbered band of about three hundred was a bubble encircled by a tight cordon of well-armed police. It would be an unequal struggle at best.

Many of our comrades had melted away. Mindful of Fred Hampton's speech and the safety of my ladies, I considered pulling out too, but it was too late. My arrogant pride told me I had to see it through. Our voices chanting in unison gave us a sense of power.

When we reached the Chicago River, the bridge rang, vibrating with our tramping feet and full-throated chants.

Mao, Mao, Mao Tze Tung!

Che, Che, Viva Che!

Ho, Ho, Ho Chi Minh, NLF is gonna win

Ho, Ho Ho Chi Minh! Dare to struggle, dare to win!

At Lassalle, we turned south. One, two blocks farther on, we marched without incident.

"Break!" The shouted signal was followed by a roar as those in the lead charged to the left, erupting off the approved route, into and smashed through the police line. Our little affinity group, still linked

arm in arm, held together as we charged after them, forging east on Madison Street to the sound of thuds and smashing windows. Here and there, scattered cops attempted to subdue individual rioters. Exhilarated and feeling invincible, I wanted to join the fray.

We passed a guy on our left struggling with a cop. Dressed in a long green coat and an incongruous top hat stuffed with rags, he reminded me of a Charles Dickens character. As I watched, another cop ran up to assist his comrade. While the first cop held the green man by the arm, the other came in swinging his club. Here was my opportunity to do something meaningful.

"I'll help him and catch up with you," I shouted, breaking free of Karen on one side and Kay on the other. The momentum carried them ahead as I ran back to help.

The green man managed to pull his left arm free and was flailing the cop with it. I grabbed it and, with a couple of good yanks, wrenched him loose. He ran after our vanishing parade, but my exultation at that victory was short-lived as I ducked the cop's club that swung close past my ear. Before I could run off, the first cop grabbed my coat and pulled me into a bear hug against his chest.

My face pressed up against his shiny silver badge. It would make a great souvenir. Fastened only by a single thin pin, I pulled it off the black leather jacket while I attempted to duck out of the cop's embrace. Just as I wrenched myself free with the badge in my right hand, the second cop arrived. His club came down hard on the back of my head.

Crack! Then *wham-bam*, more blows rained down. I found myself on my knees with twinkling stars dancing before my eyes. So that's what the cartoons try to show, I thought as my ears rang, muffling all sound, turning everything into a slow motion dreamscape.

With another *crack-crack* against my forehead, I rolled into a ball on the pavement to protect my head. Trapped between them, I couldn't escape unless someone came to my rescue.

"Let go of it, you *fucking bastard*!" Through the stars in my head,

Ronald J Schulz

I realized that he must be talking about the badge. They'd never let me go as long as I clutched that symbol of their authority. One kneeled on my back, pinning me on the street, as another booted foot crunched my right hand into the tarmac. The badge cut into my fingers and palm, but even if I wanted to, I couldn't release it.

"Let go of it I said. You goddamn hippie scum!"

Attempting to twist free, I swung at them over my back, but with their full weight on me, I knew it was futile. One finger at a time, they pried the badge loose and snatched it up. Pulling my arms behind me, they slapped on handcuffs.

Laughing in sudden relief, the first cop buttoned his badge back on while his partner kept me pinned under his knees. Both cops were in their mid-twenties, no older than many of the Weathermen. Other cops ran up to help.

"What have you got here?"

"That son of a bitch tried to steal my goddamn badge. He let another punk get away. We'll make him sorry."

They pulled me to my feet and dragged me onto the hood of an unmarked car, and slammed my face into the hood. My left eye was blinded, covered in blood. My ears still rang. Although dazed, my throbbing head felt little pain. A disheveled band of cuffed and bloodied long hairs, my comrades, with bruised and sullen faces, joined me there.

If only I'd taken Fred Hampton's Advice

The din of battle grew distant. As a helpless, cuffed and defeated prisoner, I allowed a moment of calm to wash over me. It felt like being in the eye of a hurricane and wouldn't last, but time enough to take stock of my situation. I'd fucked up.

Idiot, I mumbled to myself. The pain started growing in my head, but it couldn't distract me from the bigger pain in my heart. Self-loathing jumped up from a hole within me, a hole of despair that I'd struggled against since childhood, forcing its demons back down with a desperate veneer of optimism. But I'd thrown away the best love I'd had in my life to help someone less deserving than my girlfriends. What would happen to them? Karen, especially, was my responsibility, and I'd failed to protect her.

Filled with shame, crazy thoughts of ending my stupid life. Like a defeated samurai, I should commit hari-kari and redeem myself with macho honor. It was too late to cry about it, but I knew letting myself fall into depression would be useless. I had to find a way out. Where there's life, there's hope.

Yes, I was an idiot, but Karen and Kay were tough, smart women. They had that new guy, too. Although I hadn't said two words to him and didn't even know his name, I had to believe he'd watch over Karen. At least until I got out of jail.

SDS lawyers should bail me out. Some of those arrested Wednesday had gotten out by Friday. Even if it took longer and I couldn't find Karen in Chicago, she'd probably be with Kay. I'd hitch to Grinnell, where I'd find my little affinity group, my tribe, my loving family. We'd be together again, start a commune, get back to mother nature. Our forever after would last for as long as the grass shall grow and the rivers shall flow.

My heroes inspired me. The Lakota warrior Crazy Horse, the Tibetan bodhisattva Milarepa and Rudi Vrba, who'd escaped the Auschwitz concentration camp and given me, as a fifteen-year-old runaway, the courage to escape my school nightmare at fifteen. David Stirling, the founder of the British SAS Commandos, had a motto that I'd made my own. As another bound prisoner was thrown onto the hood beside me, I whispered it.

"Who dares, wins!" We'd shake off our despair and live to fight another day.

About Ronald Schulz

RONALD SCHULZ was born in the nineteen-fifties in Chicago. He dropped out to explore the Sixties radical counterculture before hitchhiking across Europe and Africa on a roundabout Buddhist pilgrimage to Nepal. Now a semi-retired hobo, and a new author writing his honest history of those tumultuous times, he hopes to honor the memory of departed friends before he too vanishes from this planet. He has taken advanced writing classes at the University of Washington and Hugo House. Ronald is a father of two, grandfather of three, who believes in living life to the fullest, regardless of circumstances.

CPSIA information can be obtained
at www.ICGtesting.com
Printed in the USA
LVHW031341020722
722602LV00002B/7

9 781928 094838